A JOURNEY THROUGH MEDICINE

Also by N. M. Jacoby:
Paediatric Diagnosis and Treatment, Pitman
Medical.

A
JOURNEY
THROUGH
MEDICINE

N. M. Jacoby

The Book Guild Ltd
Sussex, England

To Leslie

The Book Guild Ltd
25 High Street
Lewes, Sussex

First Published 1991
© N. M. Jacoby 1991
Set in Baskerville
Typeset by APS
Petersfield

Printed in Great Britain by
Antony Rowe Ltd, Chippenham, Wiltshire

British Library Cataloguing in Publication Data
Jacoby, N.M. (Norman Maurice) 1911-
A journey through medicine
1. Medicine-Biographies
I. Title
610. 92

ISBN 0 86332 585 8

CONTENTS

PREFACE

In recent years the status of medical practice and the status of medical practitioners have undergone the most profound changes, not always in the same direction. Though the former has been continuously upward, it is unfortunate that the same cannot be said of the latter, and it is therefore perhaps appropriate that the relative positions of both should be recorded as they appeared to one practitioner in the period 1928 to 1976.

This book is neither an autobiography nor a catalogue of recollections, though both appear from time to time, and when they do the reason is solely to indicate the situation at that time so that it can be compared with the state of affairs in the present day. Occasionally they are a little light hearted, but mostly the implications are surprising, startling or even horrific, and they have been included for the purpose of revealing what the training, practice and ethics of medical practice were in those intervening years. It has not been the objective either to criticise or castigate the past; but solely to attempt to convey what affairs were like at the time, and how the profession viewed that particular situation.

Nowadays everybody is aware, since the media keep them so informed, that medicine has been advancing in its knowledge of disease, diagnosis and above all treatment, and these are facts about which there can be no argument, but what may be less obvious is that the advancement has not been at anything like an even pace. If Hippocrates and Greek medicine were taken as the starting point, the graph of medical progress would reveal a small and fairly constant upward slope, interspersed with occasional peaks, as for example with the discovery of smallpox vaccination; chloroform and ether anaesthesia; antiseptic surgery, and several others both earlier and later. This state of affairs continued until just before the Second

World War when the curve suddenly took off at a much more acute angle with the discovery of sulpha drugs and antibiotics, and ever since then, aided by ever more complex mechanisation and computerisation, the ascent has become steeper and steeper until it is now almost vertical. It is salutary to realise, though this is only possible with hindsight, that the sum total of advance made in the millenia up to 1931 was not really very great. In the field of diagnosis much had been achieved, but in therapeutics progress had been quite small, with the result that a good many of those who were admitted to hospital received remarkably little or no benefit from their stay, and some would have been better advised in the light of modern knowledge to have stayed away. Of course the profession had a treatment for every disease that it was possible to diagnose, and although they knew that some of them were not and could not be of any curative value, it is highly probable that they just did not recognise how much of the dietetic, physical and pharmacological regimes they fervently believed in were almost equally ineffective. In their defence it must be said that of course they were totally ignorant that some of their treatment was actually harmful, had they been so aware, such treatment would never have been carried out. Fortunately everyone, both lay and medical, believed that the treatment was beneficial; often the nastier or more painful it was the greater good it would do, and unquestionably most of the patients were comforted and assisted toward recovery, even though they would have managed it spontaneously, and some people actually had their lives saved.

These limitations produced a situation that had an enormous advantage over modern medicine in that it was *relatively-cheap to administer*. The nursing staff was largely vocational and as such woefully underpaid. The ancillary services were undemanding in wages and salaries, the administrative staff was minute, the senior medical staff in Voluntary hospitals was unpaid and as well as those who did receive salaries never did consider what hours they worked. Any one of them would probably have swooned had anybody mentioned overtime. Finally the equipment that was needed was infinitesimal in amount and miniscule in cost compared with the present time, and the only really expensive articles were those for radio-diagnosis and therapy. Laboratory services required little more than some glassware, a few microscopes and an incubator, whereas nowadays the cost of essential diagnostic and investigatory machinery runs into five, six or even more digits. In this particular respect there is an additional factor to be considered, and that is that no matter how expensive a machine may be, at the moment that it is bought and installed it is already obsolescent, because a newer model, more powerful, more speedy and much more expensive is already being developed to keep up with the advances, and it will have to be provided in the not too distant future.

Perhaps these facts help to make it clear that when the National Health Service was founded, it was quite possible to visualise the State providing comprehensive medical care from the cradle to the grave, provided it was based on the assumption that the cost would rise in an arithmetical progression, and for some years this proved to be the case. The difficulty that now arises is that there has been a change from an arithmetical to a geometrical progression, which in fact is much the same thing as the politicians proclaiming so vehemently that financially it is a bottomless pit. If medical science continues to progress at the present rate, and there is every reason to believe that it will, if not even faster, those who are concerned to provide a health service will have to bear these facts in mind, as also will those who have to provide the wherewithal with which to carry it out.

Matters such as these barely entered the reckoning in 1928, when for example it was the fashion for each of the London Teaching Hospitals to have an annual 'rag day' on which medical students went about in fancy dress collecting money. They may perhaps have raised a few thousand pounds, a sum that was quite significant in hospital finances, whereas nowadays even when translated into a comparable inflationary figure it would represent little more than petty cash. Such are the changes that have taken place in almost every respect. This book merely records some of the conditions of the past, even if it does nothing to solve the problems of the future.

PART ONE

POINT OF DEPARTURE

A journey, long or short, direct or devious, to the North, the South, the East or the West, and no matter for what purpose it is undertaken, has to start somewhere, unless, like the Irishman who was stopped by a passing motorist and asked for directions to get to Dublin, replied 'If I was you sir, I wouldn't start from here.' My own journey through medicine starts out from the unlikely situation of the matriculation class room at Parktown Boys High School, Johannesburg, in January 1928, because something that happened there changed the entire course of my future voyaging.

This was to be my final year at school, with the Transvaal Matriculation coming up in November, and after that, who knows? As we were settling down for the day's work, the headmaster, a very tall, austere, somewhat forbidding but well loved pedagogue came in and said to one of the boys, 'Ah Cowin, as you are taking the London matriculation in June before you go to Liverpool University to do architecture, you had better come and arrange for some extra Latin lessons with me after school.' There was certainly nothing very dramatic about that interlude, except for the fact that anybody taking the London rather than the Transvaal matriculation was completely unheard of, and so we all sat up with a bit of a jolt. Had I known what an effect it was to have on my future I should never have believed it, because what I was to do at the end of the year had not been decided, and only barely discussed. At various times my mother had suggested that I should be sent 'home', by which she meant England, to become a doctor, but as there had never been any medicals in the family before, (incidentally none, other than my own children, have since emerged) there wasn't any strong family tradition for the idea. I myself had no preconceived notions about my future beyond the fact that I was reluctant to enter the family business, but as we sat down to supper that evening, I related

13

what had happened at school, and asked my parents if they thought it a good idea that I too should enter for the London matriculation. My Mother jumped at the suggestion, and my Father reluctantly agreed, though neither of them could have had the remotest idea of what it would lead to, and I had even less.

As neither of my parents had any academic background, they were totally ignorant of how to proceed and the details were left to me, who was equally ill informed. Fortunately Douglas Cowin's parents and the headmaster had already set the wheels in motion for him, and all I had to do was to follow in his tracks. The syllabus for the London examination differed very little from the S African, except in the matter of organic chemistry, where the demands were wider than those catered for by the school. Unfortunately the senior chemistry master was a fairly advanced alcoholic, or as would now be euphemistically described, 'had a drink problem', more interested in the bottle than teaching, so we were given text books, allowed the run of the laboratory, and left to more or less fend for ourselves. The syllabus, now long forgotten, could not have been very comprehensive, because in spite of the limitations on our instruction, we both managed to pass the subsequent examination.

As far as my personal position was concerned, the decision having been made, from then on events swept me along on an inevitable tide, until six months later when we were required to present ourselves as candidates for the London matriculation examination. This did not take place in the familiar surroundings of the school, but in a room at the University of the Witwatersrand, and apart from us two boys there were some fifteen or so other people, all of whom bar one were, to my horror, adults who told us that they had taken and failed the examination several times before. It seemed that if such erudite and experienced men had failed so often, what hope could there be for me? I suppose that it was due to my immaturity that the idea of ignorant or even stupid adults had never entered my head, and I imagined that their failure could only have been due to the inordinate difficulty of the test to come. Somehow I managed to survive the week that the examination lasted, and then returned to normal school routine, but by this time it had become obvious that if I was to go overseas, some arrangements would have to be made for me to enter a British medical school at the start of the academic year in October.

In view of the fact that our family was completely devoid of doctors, or for that matter any other university graduates, my parents were about as ignorant of English medical schools as it was possible to be, and they had only ever heard of two such places, Guy's Hospital and Edinburgh University. Of course I later became apprised of the fact that Edinburgh is not in England, and that Scotland is a separate country, but it is a fact that must cause unending annoyance and pique to Scots and Gaels, that everyone in every country in the world thinks that the terms Great Britain, or United Kingdom are synonymous with England. It so happened in those days, that Guy's Hospital was very much the place that attracted S Africans, and as in addition I had relations in London, it was decided that to Guy's I should go. Getting admission to a medical school was not difficult, and to the best of my knowledge the only requirements were a basic qualification such as the matriculation or the School Certificate, and equally if not more important the ability to pay the fees. I think it would be fair to say that places were allocated on the principle that Guy's men's children had first priority, other doctors' children came next and any other vacancies were allocated on the basis of first come first served. Recently I have heard it said by a Bart's man, that at the medical annexe to Smithfield Market, the selection was done exclusively by the Medical School secretary, who judged applicants solely by their appearance. It will no doubt be considered a heinous crime and grossly reactionary to say that with almost sixty years experience behind me, it would seem that the modern demand for three high grade A level passes hasn't made all that difference to the end product.

As the time for my departure approached, the examination results had not been received, so that I finally had to leave S Africa not knowing whether when I got to London I would be a medical student, or would have to have another attempt at the matric. Thus at the age of 17, never previously having left home, I set out on my odyssey. I left school on Friday, Johannesburg on the following Wednesday, Capetown on Thursday and arrived in London fifteen days later, where I started at Guy's on the following Thursday. It must have been one of the most rapid metamorphoses from schoolboy to medical student, which no doubt accounted for the fact that I qualified rather young. It is just as well that one is not gifted to see the future, at least as far as ordinary mortals are concerned, because as the ship cast off from Capetown docks there was no doubt about what my future was to be. I should qualify as a doctor in England, and then return to Johannesburg to practise. How very differently it all turned out. In the nigh unto sixty years that have elapsed since then, I have spent exactly seventy days of them back in the land of my birth.

I left Capetown in very rough weather aboard the Union Castle mail steamer, in third class accommodation, and the cost of the passage was £19 as a student concession, which even in those days could not have been considered excessive. Our cabin was sited at the stern, just above the propellers which vibrated like a massage machine when they came out of the water as the ship pitched and rolled on its journey north. The cabin we occupied had walls which were the unadorned plates, rivets and beams of the hull; but this must have been infinitely superior to the 'steerage' in which my father had made the journey in the opposite direction some thirty-seven years earlier. He had slept in a communal dormitory, and had been lined up naked on deck and hosed down by the crew in lieu of a bath. Our fellow passengers were mainly school teachers on long leave, nuns, clergymen and failed emigrants. We shared a cabin with a Cornish tin miner who had worked many years in the Witwatersrand gold mines, and had contracted a disease called miner's phthisis and was returning to England to spend his remaining years in Cornwall. He was a rough diamond, but a kind and caring travelling companion, which was just as well in view of the fact that we were cooped up in a fairly confined space for nearly three weeks. At that time I knew nothing at all about disease and it was not until some years later that I discovered that silicosis, which is the technical name for miner's phthisis, could be and frequently was complicated by tuberculosis, so that had our companion been such a case in that confined space, we boys would have been in grave danger of ending our careers almost before they started. Fortunately we escaped such a fate. Geography had never been one of my strongest subjects at school, and anyway we studied Africa rather than Britain, so I had only the vaguest idea where Cornwall actually was, and by no stretch of the imagination could I have guessed that fifty years later I should have a son living in Penzance, and that on my visits there I must pass near the grave of that rugged man as he sleeps somewhere in the Redruth, Camborne area, and whose brief aquaintance left such an impression on my mind.

When we were approaching the equator, a telegram arrived to say that I had successfully defeated the examiners, and I celebrated by consigning my school books to the depths of the Atlantic, where perhaps they instruct the denizens of the deep in English, Afrikaans, Latin, chemistry and physics. It was not until some weeks later that I received the official pass list from the University, which revealed the fact that of all those who had sat the examination with us in Johannesburg, just about three had passed: Douglas Cowin, I and one other, and I still wonder how many of those who had failed once again continued their efforts, and how many succeeded in the end. Of course I shall never know, and it is a salutary thought that by now most if not all of them are dead.

Thus in October 1928 I found myself in London. My schooldays were over and done with and I was about to become a 1st. M.B., B.S. student of the University of London at Guy's Hospital. My journey through medicine was about to begin.

MEDICAL SCHOOL

Preclinical Students

Guy's Hospital Medical School, which no longer exists as a separate college since it has been merged with that of St. Thomas's Hospital on the north bank of the Thames, was just one of the many parts that went to make up the University of London, and in 1928 it provided a complete medical course from 1st. M.B.,B.S., to the final qualification. During my six student years there, nobody was ever obliged to have any contact with any other colleges or institutions that combined to form the largest university in the United Kingdom. In retrospect the splendid isolation of just one section of just one faculty was a great disadvantage, since it deprived its alumni of the contacts with and experience of other disciplines, which by definition is what a university should supply. At Guy's any idea of universality was non-existent, and we lived in a totally enclosed medical world, made even narrower by the fact that it was restricted to one hospital alone. It was a very long time before I became cognizant of the virtues and vices of those who had trained in other London medical schools, in other parts of the United Kingdom and in overseas countries. The insularity that then existed is fortunately now no more, and its disappearance will be mourned by few. The degree to which it was carried was extreme, and I doubt whether one could have found a non-Guy's trained nurse, or, bar one University appointed professor, an 'alien' doctor. Nowadays the position seems almost if not quite reversed.

The academic year opened with an intake of a class of about thirty 1st. M.B.,B.S. students, none of whom had, as is now the rule, the equivalent of three A Level passes in chemistry, physics and biology which would excuse them from their pre-medical year, and consequently the entire curriculum was geared to our needs. Each of us was interviewed by the Dean, Professor T B Johnstone, who for the first time in the hospital's history was not a Guy's man, but had been imported from Edinburgh. He was a dour, somewhat humourless Scot, and an anatomist of some eminence who edited *Gray's Anatomy*. Prior to his appointment, all previous Deans of the Medical School had been clinical consultants, a practice that was fortunately reverted to shortly after the end of the Second World War. My first contact with him was brief in the extreme, and consisted of just two questions 'Where are you living?' and 'Can you pay the fees?' Having satisfied him on both points, I was dispatched to the outer office to write a cheque (my first ever) for £34.13s.0d. to cover a year's tuition and a £5 subscription to the Clubs Union.

With these not exactly overwhelming preliminaries completed, our studies began, and I discovered that although the majority of the new entrants were my equals in immaturity and inexperience, there were also a not inconsiderable number of 'failures' from earlier years. Some of these were but of a year's standing, others twice that time, and a small number of perpetual students who had been around for as much as ten years. It turned out that very few of them ever qualified, though one who was a fellow countryman of mine managed it in the same year that I did, but it must have taken him quite fifteen years en route. Many years later when I became a member of the medical school staff and attended disciplinary committees I discovered that as long as the annual fees were paid, nobody was asked to leave. There were also a small number of what might have been called cards, one of whom finding that lush, as opposed to a student standard of living cost a lot of money, found that he could extract the extra cash from his doting father if he explained that he had to buy various pieces of apparatus necessary to his studies. Needless to say the more obscure the name of his requirements the more easily the money came to hand. Running short of terms, he told Papa that he had to buy a 'pair of fallopian tubes', which are in fact part of the internal female reproductive organs, and serve no other purpose. His father, not recognising the term, wrote to the Dean telling him that he desired his son to be fitted out with the 'best pair of fallopian tubes that London could supply.' We never saw that chap again as he made a rapid return to South Africa, where no doubt his talents allowed him to amass a fortune far in excess of that any of us ever achieved.

In a totally different category, one student of considerable intellect and ability, who incidentally qualified in the minimum time, had a penchant for the 'horses'. At one stage his parents sent him some £5 to buy a new suit, but his other interests made it impossible for him to return home for many weeks, due to the fact that his belief in a hot favourite proved unfounded, and it took time to find the wherewithal to purchase the clothing. The modern medical student has not only had to achieve three high grade A level passes to gain admission, but if unfortunate enough to fail a course examination, is unlikely to be allowed more than one further chance before being dismissed. Things have certainly changed. My first encounter with the lectures and lecturers proved a terrible shock to one whose only previous experience had been of school discipline. Although we were now addressed as 'Gentlemen' rather than boys, any evidence of the sort of behaviour expected of the former was entirely lacking, and things turned out to be a battle between the 'old hands' and the lecturers. The professors and the senior staff maintained a reasonable control through force of personality, but where the teaching was done by those who had started their careers in the medical school as 'Lab Boys' and worked their way up the ladder by a long and arduous apprenticeship, they were only too often no match for the enemy, so that every now and then they had to flee the field of battle, and lectures were abandoned. This stupid and inane behaviour is exemplified by an occurrence in one of the small basement lecture theatres, where the ringleaders shut all the doors and windows and everybody smoked pipes and cigarettes as hard as possible before the entry of the lecturer. The atmosphere we created would have made the legendary smoke filled committee rooms of presidential conventions seem like idyllic country air, but to us it was all jolly good fun, and of course in those days nobody had heard of the connection between cigarette smoking and cancer. It took only a very little time for those who wanted to learn to pick and choose which classes to attend, and it was the introduction to the openly confessed and much vaunted characteristic of Guy's Hospital that it was a great place in which to learn how to teach yourself. Like any other institution, standards varied from one department to another, and chemistry under Professor C S Gibson was no place for fun. He was a diminutive figure but a strict disciplinarian, and the rest of his staff followed suit. He was famed for the contribution he had made to the manufacture of mustard gas in the First World War, and for which he had been elected an F.R.S., the only one at Guy's for many years, but such was the bitchy nature of the staff that one wag told us that the method he had devised had injured far more British technicians than German military. We never discovered the truth.

The biology department was headed by T J Evans, a very Welsh Welshman with a Punch-like face. He exuded kindness, erudition and sincerity, and was said to be able to complete *The Times* crossword in four minutes flat. Of course none of us believed it then, but subsequent events during that distinguished journal's annual crossword competition have made such an achievement very slow. His influence extended down to the newest lab-boy, and without any suggestion of sanctions or punishment there was never any rowdiness, hooliganism or vandalism in that department. It was in the realm of physics that mayhem reigned supreme. In the first place, most medical students find it an unattractive subject, difficult to understand and to master. To add to this disadvantage, the staff was inadequate for the job, and though the professor was eminent enough, he was no great teacher. His deputy was a well meaning but ineffectual ex-laboratory technician, who knew his subject quite well, but we who were his subjects he understood not at all, and he never seemed to learn. I am afraid that we turned his lectures into a circus and the practical classes into a shambles, so that when the examinations came a good many of us paid the price.

At the end of the year those who had managed to satisfy the examiners, perhaps about 70% of those who started the previous year, went for a long and happy summer vacation, at the end of which we returned to enter the worlds of anatomy and physiology, subjects that at least seemed to have some connection with what we were aiming to achieve. Our boyish stupidity and infantile behaviour had gone like the effect of sunlight on morning dew, as we got down to the task of learning anatomy. This was one of the best run departments with its erudite administrator and excellent teacher Professor T B Johnstone, under whom the demonstrators were highly qualified people, waiting in the wings to be appointed surgical consultants or registrars, preferably on the Guy's staff. The syllabus was enormous, entirely academic and covered every detail of every area of the body. It would be true to say that none of us had the remotest idea of what out of all this material would or would not be germane to our future, and most of it, one regrets to say, turned out to be irrelevant.

The physiology department was under the direction of Professor Marcus Pembrey, a dear old man who had been an eminent physiologist, but a very eccentric and uninspiring teacher. Probably the only thing any of us remembered from his lectures was the constant reiteration ad nauseam of his favourite phrase, 'everything works together for good', when to so many of us it obviously did not. The result was that we had to learn the subject from our books and the demonstrators. These men, whose ranks I was destined to join some years later, also held part-time jobs as Medical Registrars in the special departments, and for those labours they were paid a salary of £150 per annum. Thus a second job enabled them to double their princely income which in modern terms would be the equivalent of about £3600. Most certainly we were not rich.

Apart from our studies, the medical school provided very little in the way of social amenities beyond a cafeteria with tables and chairs, and sets of draughts and dominoes. There was also a restaurant serving very good cheap meals, but these were quite beyond a freshman's means, as I seem to remember the charge for a three course lunch was one shilling and sixpence (7½p in new currency), and my allocation for that meal was only sixpence (2½p). As a result we tended to congregate in the basement cloakroom in the medical school building which was presided over by a long service ex-naval rating, affectionately known as 'Com'. He delighted to act as a sort of father confessor, guardian, guide and friend to all, and was happiest to be at the centre of a gathering. On one occasion he informed us that out of the new intake of thirty men, only two would gain their M.B.,B.S. degree in the minimum time, and only five would ever get the degree at all. Naturally he was laughed out of court, but as might be expected his estimate proved exact in the first case, and not all that far out in the second. The explanation for this apparently poor result is not as grim as it might seem, because all the new students entering the medical school were required to register as university undergraduates, and those who did not fall at the first fence went on to take the second M.B.,B.S. examination at the end of the pre-clinical course. However, beyond that point and towards the end of the clinical period it was possible to take the Conjoint Board finals, and qualify as M.R.C.S.,L.R.C.P. three months before one could even start to sit the third and Final M.B.,B.S. examination. In addition, the latter had to be taken either in all parts at once, or in two parts, but the second of these did not take place until nine months after the first, which was a whole year after they had already become registered medical practitioners. This meant that a young doctor, after qualifying and starting a clinical career, had to continue with academic studies for at least three months, and possibly a further year. One certainly needed a strong incentive for such diligence, and for most it did not exist since they were intending to go into General Practice, where at that time there was no advantage in possessing a further parallel qualification. A few did take the examination, but it was those heading for consultant status and an M.D. or M.S. who considered it essential. The British practice of multiple medical qualifications as opposed to the solitary M.D. in most other countries is something that foreigners find difficult to understand.

As might be expected in any new group of students, several fell by the wayside almost as soon as the term began. One unfortunate man sat staring down his microscope from two until five in the afternoon when the demonstrator, after admiring his diligence, suggested that he might like to go home. He rose from the bench and made a violent assault on the unfortunate demonstrator, and had to be forcibly removed to a hospital for mental disorders. Our numbers were further reduced by the loss of those who decided that a career in medicine was not really for them, and of course the two M.B.,B.S. examinations took their toll. The result was that by the time we entered the wards our numbers had been reduced to about half. The survivors looked upon themselves with a modicum of pride, possibly even as the favoured few who had weathered the storm of the pre-clinical years, but there was disillusionment to follow when three months later the Oxbridge contingent arrived. Although less than half our numbers they completely overwhelmed us with their self assurance, and the sharing of their respected alma mater which allowed them a familiarity with the teaching staff that astounded us, because up till then they had seemed more godlike than human. It should be explained that in 1932 most of the consultants were Oxford and Cambridge graduates, and only a few came from London and other universities. The result was that we Londoners were left like stranded whales, and it took a long time to overcome this disadvantage. However two factors came to our rescue, as our group of London students happened to be rather above the average, and at least six subsequently became members of the junior staff, while two were appointed consultants at the hospital. At the same time the various consultant vacancies were being filled more and more by London graduates, and by the time I severed my connections with the hospital the ratio of Oxbridge to London had been completely reversed.

CLINICAL STUDENTS

The obligatory three years of clinical tuition in the wards, out-patient and casualty departments were divided amongst the various specialties according to regulations laid down by the Education Committee of the General Medical Council, which one assumes must have consisted mainly if not exclusively of consultants, since they appeared to ignore completely the fact that most medical students became General Practitioners. Thus no less than nine months of the time were devoted to surgical appointments, though only a very few of our group became surgeons. Six months were spent in the general medical wards, and three months plus three weeks on obstetrics and gynae-cology. The remaining year and a half was divided between all the other departments of the hospital. Some of them such as orthopaedics, ear nose and throat, and paediatrics had definite organised clerkships, with students allocated to the various consultants, but the other subjects could be done on what was called the 'White Card'. This was a document that had to be signed by the consultant at the end of a three month period, and was meant to certify that one had made satisfac-tory attendances. It would be no exaggeration to say that many of the consultants paid but little heed to their teaching responsibilities, and could not have recognised one student from another, with the result that they signed the cards quite automatically even though the student might never have attended the firm's sessions on any occasion. On the other side of the coin when one was dealing with students appointed to a definite firm as clerk or dresser, it would be fair to say that as the overall number of students was so small that the number of clerks or dressers appointed to each firm only totalled about four, the surgeon or physician could if they so wished become well acquainted with the students attached to them. Some of the older men like Charles Hilton Fagg made it a definite cult, and on the first day of a new appointment the junior clerks were lined up and personally introduced by the Registrar. Others like Sir Arthur Hurst never had the slightest idea who his students were, and made no pretence that he knew any of those who attended his rounds.

One is led to believe that before the turn of the century, the consultants concerned themselves very much with teaching, and if that was so the habit, with one or two noticeable exceptions such as Mr E C Hughes, had largely disappeared by 1930. It is a very strange fact that in teaching hospitals, the appointments are rarely if ever influenced to the slightest degree by a candidate's ability to teach. When in later years I became a member of appointment committees, I found that such things as an applicant's erudition, publications, charisma and 'clubability' all rated very highly, but never do I recall any attention whatsoever being paid to their skill at teaching. As a result it is not altogether surprising that, broadly speaking, outstanding communicators tended to be the exception rather than the rule. Certainly at Guy's no attempts were made, nor did any facilities exist to give instruction in the art of teaching, and it all depended on one's natural talent. This meant that about 80% were of average ability, 10% were good or even brilliant, and the other 10% quite appalling. Thus as students we were faced with the fact that as consultants were not often very brilliant teachers, and in addition they rarely attended the hospital more than twice a week, we had to get our tuition from some other quarter, and this was from the Registrars. (There was only one grade of these embryonic consultants before the National Health Service was introduced, where now there are senior house officers, registrars and senior registrars, and they would have ranked as senior registrars of modern times.) They carried the main burden of tuition, and like everyone else they varied in ability, and there is no doubt that where students were concerned the competition was to get onto the firm with the best Registrar, irrespective of whom the titular chief might be. Thus at one stage I was on a firm where the consultant was to say the least, uninspiring, lacking any charisma and to all intents and purposes as a teacher a dead loss; but his Registrar Dr C F Cosin was quite brilliant, and it was everybody's ambition to be on that firm. Incidentally he was never appointed to any teaching hospital, much to their loss.

In another department there was a Registrar, who though most able in all other respects was the most dreadful teacher that could be imagined. His rounds were a painful embarrassment with long periods of silence as he struggled to string a single sentence together, but he was such a nice person that nobody ever thought of complaining. He was elected to the staff of more than one teaching hospital.

Guy's had a considerable and well deserved reputation for producing practical rather than academic doctors, and this must have accounted for the fact that it was probably the last school of medicine to appoint Professors to clinical departments such as medicine, surgery, obstetrics, paediatrics etc., and in fact there had been considerable resistance to agreeing to make the first appointment. This accent on practical training was ingeniously interwoven with a method of providing cheap labour. Students did a great deal of the portering of patients, they were the official writers and keepers of the patients' records, and did many of the lesser investigations such as blood counts, test meals and urinary examinations, and all of the casualty work. It was most instructive to get out old case notes that had been written in the late nineteenth century and compare them with the mid twentieth. They paid meticulous attention to detail and wrote accurate descriptions in a beautiful handwriting, but of course they must have had more time to devote to it, since there was so little else to record other than the course of the patient only too often mortuarywards. However it was the casualty work that provided a wealth of experience, and regretfully it must be said, largely at the patient's expense. Resort to the law courts in actions to obtain damages for accidents or malfunction of treatment had not become the order of the day, and to bring an action for damages against a teaching hospital was unthinkable, something that was reflected in the fact that the annual subscription to the Medical Defence Union was exactly £1 per annum which has to be compared with steeply rising premiums of £1000 and more, which the modern doctor has to pay. The students' first experience of treating patients on their own responsibility was in the 'Back Surgery' where every morning all those requiring dressings for the care of wounds, ulcers and the like were dealt with by very immature junior dressers who were thrown in at the deep end with absolutely no idea of what they were doing. There was theoretical supervision provided by an Assistant House Surgeon who was himself only recently qualified, but the huge number of patients involved made it impossible to supervise what was being done in the name of medicine. There was a profusion of lotions, ointments, creams, powders and antiseptics, none of which we had ever seen before or knew what they were supposed to do, so one simply guessed or chose at random. To add further confusion to the picture, the House Officer and the students changed each day according to a rota so that there was complete absence of continuity in management. There was one unfortunate man who attended on my first day on duty with an abrasion of his knee, and when I departed three months later he had an ulcer covering the entire area. Nobody in those days thought of litigation or even considered that the hospital bore any responsibility.

It was a very different story in the Casualty Department which was known as the 'Front Surgery', which was staffed by senior Dressers who were within six months of qualification, which is the time when students probably have a wider knowledge of medicine as a whole than at any other time of their careers. They could call on the help of the emergency duty House Physician or Surgeon, as well as the Resident Obstetrician, because they could be faced with almost any sort of patient who might be suffering from an acute abdomen such as appendicitis, perforated peptic ulcers, fractures, heart attacks, obstetric emergencies and anything else. The responsibility they carried was considerable when it is remembered that most of these patients were not seen by anybody else before being sent home, and yet disasters were few and far between. It was an admirably conducted department, and anyone who had the good fortune to do this appointment was well equipped to deal with almost any situation in later practice, and it was one of the main factors in producing the typical Guy's man, who no matter with what situation he was confronted was able to give the impression that everything was under control even when any previous experience of having dealt with a similar crisis was entirely lacking. It might be observed that the term 'Guy's man' has been used because at that time, with the exception of one consultant to the female department of venereal diseases, there were no women consultants, registrars, house officers or medical students anywhere to be seen on the horizon.

There was one other appointment, that of 'Extern' which provided a training in practical doctoring that was unsurpassed. It was an arrangement where students' were allowed to conduct obstetric deliveries in an area of Bermondsey and Southwark outside the hospital entirely on their own. There was nothing very unusual about such an arrangement, and much the same thing no doubt went on at many other hospitals, but what was unique, or at least very unusual was the fact that the whole delivery and care of the mother and child from start to finish about a week later, was entirely unsupervised or assisted other than by a Mrs Gamp who was completely unqualified except by experience. As in Dickens's day, their services were hired by the family, not by the hospital, and unlike the original Sarah Gamp they were a helpful bunch of women addicted neither to gin nor 'cowcumber'. All the mothers who were to be delivered by this service were carefully selected at the ante-natal clinic, and were those where the labour was expected to be normal. The students who conducted these deliveries were summoned from the hospital as soon as labour commenced, and they journeyed out on their bicycles, often in the small hours of the morning, and never with any lights fore or aft, into houses that were sometimes little better than hovels in areas where nowadays even the police patrol in pairs. They were recognised by local people as being a normal part of Bermondsey life, and they were never molested. Provided no complications arose they were in sole charge of the labour, delivery and post-natal period, and although qualified assistance was always readily available, it was not usually required, with the result that when the case was finally discharged, the student had a great sense of achievement of being a real doctor at last. Personally I don't think that I ever gave the mothers credit for the not inconsiderable contribution that they made to the process. That sort of experience is no longer possible, because the area was devastated by bombs during the war, and circumstances, social, medical and medicolegal would now make it unacceptable. Added to that is the fact that a strong body of obstetric and paediatric opinion would like to see all forms of domiciliary midwifery abolished, no matter by whom it is conducted.

Although the fraternity of Externs as it was disappeared long ago, they left behind them a memorial in the form of a collection of carved and decorated panels executed over a number of years by some talented people. The nature of the appointment meant that a great deal of time was spent waiting about for calls to action, and this time was occupied in transforming the wooden panels of the Extern's room into topical strip cartoons, vertical rather than horizontal. The subjects which they chose were of course exclusively obstetric, and many were very humourous. Perhaps the best known one was done around the time of the Battle of Jutland, and it showed a cross section of a gravid uterus at term, where the foetus was in a position of ophisthotonus with its umbilicus pressed over the dilated os, and the punchline 'The First Navel Engagement'. The joke here was essentially for the cognoscenti, but in obstetrics the part of the infant that first enters the uterine outlet is said to 'be engaged', and is usually the head and sometimes the buttocks (breech) but never in any circumstances the umbilicus or navel. The Extern's room was destroyed when the College became an air raid casualty during the Second World War, and it was a matter of foresight that the only items to be rescued from the fire were the panels now housed elsewhere in the hospital. When I held the appointment in 1933, no new panels had been carved for a long time, and other diversions had taken their place. My colleagues were much given to gambling and we ran a roulette wheel which netted us a profit of nearly £100, a veritable fortune in those days.

The three years of the clinical course were divided into three monthly periods, and at the end of each one the students moved on to another department. To some extent a similar arrangement still holds, but there is little comparison with the modern medical student. In the first place the pressure of numbers rules out the position where there were only four students to a firm, and they were an integral part of the system to such a degree that the patients thought we were actually doctors, because the student had more contact with his allocation of two or three patients, writing their notes, taking their blood and doing more of the other tests than anybody else. The modern student wears a long white coat, whereas we had no other covering than a mandatory lounge suit, but nobody in the ward would mistake them for anything but students. By the nature of things the pleasure or boredom of an appointment varied according to one's interest in the subject, and the stimulus provided by the consultant or Registrar. As a rule this gave general surgery a big advantage over all the others, and the appointment of Senior Dresser was the apogee of the entire orbit. It was not attained until just before qualifying, and it was the dressers above all others who had the privilege of assisting the surgeon, even at major operations. On occasions they were allowed to perform the repair of an inguinal hernia, under supervision of course. Every fourth week the firm went on emergency duty for a period of seven days during which time they dealt with all the surgical emergencies both day and night, and if it turned out to be a busy week everyone became completely exhausted, suffering from a dreadful lack of sleep far worse than some young people now take steps to advertise after much shorter periods at a salary beyond even our wildest dreams. It was probably not very good from the patients' point of view but it was a thrilling experience for the dressers. Apparently even in those days, other hospitals had shorter periods of duty, and the present arrangement is for something less than three days. There was certainly no question of overtime, as for the duration of the appointment one had sold both body and soul to the hospital, and perhaps another factor came into the reckoning in that apart from the registrar whose salary was £300 per annum nobody else was paid at all.

By an odd quirk of fate it was during this appointment that I had my first encounter with the dilemma that has to be faced when a consultant becomes mentally deranged, and it revealed itself in the following manner. It was the duty of dressers to 'do the instruments' at surgical sessions, and as each consultant varied slightly in their choice of certain things, especially needles, sutures, lotions and dressings, it was routine for the oncoming group to consult with those about to leave the firm as to what would be required. At the first operating list on the new firm we received a series of severe reprimands for presenting to the surgeon the various instruments and sutures that we had been informed were what he required. They were thrown back at us or onto the floor, being told that he had never used such things in his life, and what he demanded in their place was to say the least bizarre; but of course nobody dared question his orders. At the next session he thought we were mad when we offered him those articles he had demanded at the first session, and now he demanded the things he had previously rejected. Everyone was in a dilemma as instruments were being thrown about the theatre, and various pieces of excised material were hurled into the air instead of being placed in the receiver proffered by the nurse for the purpose. Several patients whom one would have expected to recover, died unexpectedly, giving rise to widespread concern and confusion, but nobody had any idea what to do because no guide lines had been laid down as to how to proceed in such a situation, and anyway consultants seemed more like gods than mortals. This appalling situation was fortuitously solved several weeks later when perhaps mercifully the unfortunate man dropped dead from a stroke. Clearly his brain must have had a defective circulation for some time previously. Later in my career I encountered two other similar cases where colleagues went berserk, but by that time procedures had been laid down where it was advised that three senior consultants should get together and hold unofficial and confidential discussions to decide what action to take. Unfortunately, such are the pitfalls and penalties awaiting those who might make an error of judgement (since the government eschewed any responsibility), that the question always arose as to who should 'bell the cat', with the result that once again the resolution of the problem ran a long, difficult and devious course, causing great sorrow, trauma and vast expense to the taxpayer on the way.

Early in the third year of our clinical period the examination season arrived, and we prepared for the Conjoint Board's final examinations in pathology, obstetrics and gynaecology combined, medicine and surgery. Each of these four sections was sat separately at three monthly intervals so that in early January 1934 I found myself with the first three hurdles successfully negotiated and the fourth almost completed with only the final viva to be taken the following day. I went to bed, but sleep was impossible with the thought of what the morrow might bring. It seemed to me, quite stupidly of course, the nearest thing to the last night in the condemned cell, and at 2 am I got up and dressed and walked to the all night coffee stall on London Bridge, where I had a hot dog and a cup of coffee, after which I wandered back to bed and fell into a fitful sleep. Next day, almost paralytic with fear I presented myself at the Examination Hall at Queen Square, and at last was summoned before the examiners. After it was all over I had to wait until 6 pm before the results were announced, after which I left the building and made for the nearest post office where I sent a cable to South Africa saying 'Dr Jacoby sends greetings to his parents with love and many thanks'.

And so from those few pregnant words spoken by the headmaster in 1928, six years had slipped away and I could now set out on my journey through medicine, which like any other similar experience would have so many ups and downs before it had run its course.

THE ROAD TO CONSULTANCY

In order to understand British medical practice it is necessary to understand British medical qualifications which differ from those of almost every other country in the world except for those that were part of the British Empire and Commonwealth. In most places there is just one indication that a person is a medical practitioner, and that is the possession of the letters M.D.. In Britain things are very different in that there are multiple qualifications, some of which are university degrees whilst others are granted by Royal Colleges, and one by a City Livery Company. Three of these qualifications are recognised as entitling the grantee to practise as a doctor, and these are as follows.

1. The bachelorship in medicine and surgery granted by a recognised university (M.B.,B.S.);

2. The diploma of the Conjoint Board of the Royal Colleges of Physicians and Surgeons (M.R.C.S.,L.R.C.P.);

3. The licence of the Society of Apothecaries (L.S.A.); no longer obtainable.

The above all refer to England and Wales, and very similar arrangements with slightly different letters exist in Scotland and Ireland.

This not altogether simple situation is complicated by the fact that the Royal Colleges, in addition to their basic qualifying diplomas all hold examinations to obtain higher qualifications in their own particular specialties. The best known and far the oldest established are Fellowship of the Royal College of Surgeons (F.R.C.S.), and Membership of The Royal College of Physicians (M.R.C.P.): the latter may be later elected to the Fellowship (F.R.C.P.). To all this must be added the fact that the universities grant doctorates in medicine (M.D.) and masterships in surgery (M.S.). The outcome of all these things is that British doctors must have one of the basic qualifications to practise at all, and then one or more of the higher qualifications if they wish to obtain consultant status on a hospital staff. It is all very complex when compared with the simple and solitary M.D. that exists in practically all other countries.

This explanation has been necessary because those setting out on the road to consultancy are required to have the requisite degrees as well as the specialist training and experience, which is, was, and probably always will be a combination of apprenticeship and academe.

It is probable that on the day they qualify, young doctors have a wider knowledge of the whole spectrum of medicine than at any other time in their careers, but on the other hand lack almost everything else that goes to make a competent practitioner, certainly not one fit to be let loose on the public. This is something that is now recognised in law by the fact that full registration to practise independently can only be obtained after a further twelve months of house appointments, and nowadays the majority of General Practitioners undertake a further three year training course. Thus by the time that they go into practice they have some four years or more of previous experience. However in 1934 it was possible to go directly from the Examination Hall into General Practice, and there were a very few people who actually did so. I do not think there was even any legal bar to them setting up as a consultant surgeon or physician, though I never heard of such a case. In after years I occasionally encountered such practitioners, and their lack of post-graduate training stuck out like a sore thumb even after many years, and was generally associated with an aggressive and bombastic manner, which was doubtless necessary to counterbalance their other deficiencies. In practice, even in those days most people spent a further six months or a year doing house appointments before going into practice.

Prior to World War Two, Guy's Hospital had a unique arrangement for its House Officers, and there was intense competition for these posts in spite of the fact that they carried no salary, and only those whose parents were prepared to continue subsidising them could think of applying. The others had to look to non-teaching hospitals where they would be paid the princely sum of £120 per annum plus board and lodging, which was the going rate at the time. Those who conducted affairs at Guy's itself, worked on the principle that people who got teaching hospital house appointments would be potential future consultants who would earn large incomes from private practice, and consequently it would do them no harm to provide their early services free, gratis and for nothing. As a result it was rare in the extreme for any of them to be married because working wives were not the order of the day and there was no kindly Social Service to provide any benefits.

This unique system consisted of an odd arrangement where those considered to be the cream of the applicants were required to fill a series of subsidiary appointments each lasting three months until they achieved the status of a full House Physician or Surgeon, but they were never able to be both. This arrangement was something that turned out to be a serious disadvantage when applying for further training appointments at specialist hospitals, because the other applicants had nearly always held both appointments and were considered to be more experienced and were the ones who usually got appointed. The Guy's system started with the selection of six people as 'Clinicals' for a period of three months, and they shared the use of some thirty beds, acting as House Physicians under the supervision of a full House Physician with the cases under the ultimate care of a consultant who changed every six weeks. The 'Clinicals' had the first choice of taking any case that was for admission, and this provided a wealth of medical experience, because most of the interesting cases found themselves in the Clinicals ward. The appointment carried neither salary nor board and lodging, and at the end of it, only four people were selected to fill the series of subsidiary posts and finally the position of full House Officer in surgery or medicine. The 'dropped Clinicals' and other newly qualified people were able to apply for appointments in the ancillary specialised departments, or had to find positions at other non-teaching hospitals. This strange and somewhat disadvantageous arrangement no longer exists.

In my own case I was one of the fortunate people to be appointed a 'Clinical', but at the end of three months a most unusual thing happened which I had not heard of previously, nor happened subsequently. Instead of only two people getting the chop, three of us were dropped. Of those who survived the holocaust, S H Wass made an interrupted journey to become a very eminent Consultant Surgeon at Guy's, renowned not only for his surgical skill, but also for his unequalled teaching ability. As a matter of record he and I entered Guy's on the same day, qualified as 'Conjoints' on the same day, and likewise the M.B.,B.S., three months later. He gained his F.R.C.S. about the same time that I became an M.R.C.P., and we graduated M.D. and M.S., respectively at the same ceremony. We also combined to write the Residents' play in 1936 and 1937, so I think I can claim to have known him pretty well. His knowledge was encyclopaedic, and he had the enormous advantage that it was all classified and tabulated in his mind, so that his examination papers must have been a joy to the examiners. On one occasion as I was leaving the Examination Hall, my eye was caught by the front page of his paper, and I wondered how, after seeing that sort of work, any examiner was going to bother with my awful scrawl. If Sam Wass achieved great fame, the other two 'Clinicals' who survived with him subsequently entered General Practice where I have no doubt they made excellent doctors. However it seems worthy to record what happened to the three brought down in the unusually large sacrificial act. Gavin Thurston M.D.,F.R.C.P. became one of the best known London coroners, mainly on account of his sagacity, but partly because so many stars of stage, screen, radio and TV, or should one say their remains, passed through his court. Lionel Cosin, M.A., F.R.C.S. also achieved considerable eminence as a consultant geriatrician, where he made a number of important contributions to what was at that time a new speciality, and it all goes to show that even in the best regulated hospitals they do not always get it right!

At the end of my appointment as a 'Clinical' my future at Guy's appeared to have come to an abrupt end, but things turned out otherwise when one of the newly appointed House Surgeons resigned his post in order to enter General Practice, and the vacant position was then offered to me, something that I accepted with alacrity, thus coming to work for Robert Davies-Colley, one of the four senior surgeons. He was a very large figure in every sense of the word, with prodigious hands quite unlike the delicate prehensile organs that surgeons are popularly supposed to possess. What he had in abundance was intellect, probably more than the rest of his surgical colleagues combined, and it was utter unadulterated joy to work for him. To me it seemed that no comparable surgical appointment was made at Guy's until that of R C Brock who was later raised to the peerage. Neither of these two men were great surgeons in the technical sense, but in every other respect decidedly so.

'DC', as he was called, made no great secret of his contempt for several of his consultant colleagues, and this was my first introduction to the fact that at the top of the tree, all was not friendship, light and joy. His closest friend was Professor G W de P Nicholson, the hospital's Clinical Microscopist, who was of Germano-Irish descent, another brilliant brain and quite delightfully ascerbic, irritable and eccentric. His four volumes *Studies in Tumour Formation* was a classic work of the time, but when I tried to read it I found it incomprehensible. He had been brought up in a household where, as a child, he had been required to stand erect and click his heels to his father in the true Germanic style, but when released from this bondage he reverted to the more laissez-faire manner of the Irish. Though in fact he was really a very tolerant person, except where Oxford University was concerned, (needless to say he had been to Cambridge), he also had a pretty poor view of a good many other members of the staff. I was privileged to be allowed to care for him medically for several years towards the end of his life, and stimulating though it was, it wasn't easy.

Having re-established myself on the rungs of the Guy's ladder under the tutelage of so powerful a sponsor, I had no difficulty in progressing further along my chosen path of paediatrics, and after several appointments at other hospitals I returned to Guy's as Registrar in the Children's Department until the outbreak of the War.

Although it was possible, and in fact quite common to be appointed a registrar before one had obtained a higher quali-fication, it would have been impossible to hold it for any length of time without one. Consequently it was essential to obtain the M.R.C.P., and such was the insularity and parochialism of those days that it had to be from the London College, because the Edinburgh Membership would have been a distinct disadvantage south of Watford. The manner in which the examination was conducted was very odd, and possibly unique. There was no primary eliminating examination such as now exists, and anybody could enter provided they had been qualified for two years. Unlike other examinations conducted by the Colleges it was not held at the Examination Hall at Queen Sq. but in the library of the old Royal College of Physicians in Pall Mall, where the candidates sat side by side at long tables. This was possible because only about sixty people had to be accommodated, a figure which our superiors thought was outrageously large, since in their day it had not been much above a dozen. It was also rumoured that whilst the candidates were writing their answers, the College Beadle inspected the top hat of each examinee, and if it didn't carry the label of a respectable West End hatter there was no possibility of that person passing, no matter how brilliant he might be! Apart from hats, things hadn't changed much in 1937, because it was still conducted on the basis of elimination by stages. Every candidate wrote two essay type papers, multiple choice hadn't been invented, and each paper had an addendum in Latin and Greek, or French and German, translation of which could earn a bonus of 5%, but it was not obligatory. It was widely believed that the marking of those sections was a perquisite of the examiner's daughters. Following the papers, there was a 'clinical' held at a teaching hospital, after which there was an interval of about a fortnight, towards the end of which one waited in fear and trembling for the postman to deliver a letter that either invited one to attend at the College for a further viva voce, or informed you that the Censors regretted that on your performance so far there was no possibility of success, and they would trouble you no further. This reduced the field by 50%. The viva consisted of a real grilling in clinical medicine and pathology, and when it was over one had to wait downstairs in the hall until the Beadle brought another sealed envelope which contained much the same message as before. Once again the field was reduced by a further 50%, and those who survived that ordeal were then invited to attend the following day for a final viva where one was arraigned in front of the President and Council of the College, and at which one could be asked anything or nothing at all. Nothing more terrifying can be imagined, and at the end of this ordeal only some ten to fifteen of the original starters were admitted as Members. Everybody knew that the first request that would be made of successful candidates was to pay the fee of £10 to be admitted as a Member, and I recall that before leaving home for the final viva, being in a terrible quandary as to whether it was tempting providence to take one's cheque book.

This might be a good moment to comment on how one climbed the next step up the ladder of the College, which was election to the Fellowship, which was very different from what it is now. The F.R.C.P. is reputedly an honour in recognition of some degree of eminence, and is therefore awarded to those who are supposed to have 'arrived', rather like a private enterprise Honours List. In such a system it is difficult, if not impossible to discover how the privileged are chosen, and why some of the most non-eminent are elected, and many of the other sort are not. With this in mind, I spent many a long hour delving in the Medical Register and the Medical Directory to discover how long it took a physician to become an F.R.C.P. from his appointment as a consultant. In the case of London teaching hospitals the period was under five years, and in provincial teaching hospitals about eight to ten years, whereas in non-teaching hospitals only a few if any were ever elected, and if they were it would not be in less than ten years. I put all these facts together in an article entitled *Apartheid in Pall Mall* and submitted it to one of the medical journals. In due course I received an invitation to lunch at the Athenaeum Club where the editor told me he was in a quandary because he felt that the article ought to be published, but as the College had been one of his lifelong loves he just could not bring himself to attack it, so would I agree to withdraw the article and take no further action. I felt that I had no alternative but to concur and that was that, but not quite. About a year later I was made a Fellow, one of the very few in SE England, and the poacher had become a gamekeeper, but I am happy to record that nowadays almost every Member is elected a Fellow sooner or later, but that still leaves a number of disgruntled people. Why not follow the example of the College of Surgeons and make everyone who passes what is now the Membership examination a Fellow? There would be an immediate loss of income, but this could soon be corrected. Oh yes, the colleges are very much concerned with collecting money.

An M.D. had never been an absolute prerequisite to becoming a consultant, because the degree is usually obtained by the presentation of a thesis, but in 1937 the London M.D. differed from the others in that it was obtained by an examination which was of much the same standard as the M.R.C.P., but instead of being 'killed off' in stages, all the candidates completed the examination, which was conducted in a gentlemanly manner. If you knew your subject you passed, and if you didn't you failed, and I always thought it was a pity that it did not replace the other contest.

But now to return to the original subject. The consultants under whom I worked were Drs H C Cameron, A C Hampson and R W B Ellis. The first of these was the son of Sir Hector Cameron who succeeded Lord Lister in the Chair of Surgery at Glasgow University. Although very much a Scot brought up in Glasgow, he had been to public school in England and then to Cambridge and Guy's, and he lived the rest of his life in SE England, in some ways very like a country squire. He was a wise physician, and though he made no claim to be, he was an outstanding child psychiatrist. He was a founder member of the British Paediatric Association, and its first official historian, as well as the author of a biography of Lord Lister. Unfortunately he never got round to writing another on Lord Byron's feet, a subject on which he used to entrance his firm every now and then, because he was convinced that Byron was really a 'spastic' and not a *talipes equino varus* (club foot) as is generally accepted. His commitment to Guy's was to attend three times a week, and outside those visits he was not to be communicated with about anything. In spite of this he was the main influence in my training, and I always held him in the highest regard. Of my other two superiors I cannot recall that either of them had any effect on me. Dr Hampson had been appointed a paediatrician because there had been no vacancy on the staff for him as a general physician, but as soon as one arose he transferred to that department. Dr Ellis was appointed in his place and remained on the staff for about seven years, very little of which was spent at Guy's. He was away in Spain during that country's civil war, but as a member of the Society of Friends in a completely noncombatant role, dealing with refugee Basque children. Almost as soon as World War Two was declared he obtained a commission in the RAF Medical Service, and was not seen again until after VE Day. Not long after that he was appointed to the Chair of Child

Health at Edinburgh University, but unfortunately his career was cut short by a fatal illness.

With the outbreak of war, the Children's Department of Guy's moved to Pembury Hospital in Kent, with satellite units at Farnborough and at Guy's itself; within a short time I found myself the sole paediatrician in the region, and though some assistance was obtained from retired consultants, I carried almost the entire burden of paediatric teaching and clinical work for the duration of the war. The allocation of manpower during this period was in the hands of the government, and naturally I was 'called up' for military service, but each time that happened, Professor T B Johnstone who had translated from being Dean of the Medical School at Guy's to being the 'Gauleiter' of the sector, and as such had overriding powers in these matters, barred me from leaving as there was nobody left to do the work. When the war was over and everyone was returning from the Services, he forwarded my name for conscription, when it turned out that quite unknown to me, the Act of Westminster had been passed through Parliament, and although I was born a British subject I now carried S African nationality. When the War Office discovered this they had no further interest in my services.

When hostilities in Europe ended, Guy's Hospital terminated my appointment which had been continuous for almost sixteen years. As far as memory holds, I do not think I ever received any official notice that my services were no longer required, let alone any appreciation that for the entire duration of the war the entire burden had rested on my shoulders. I simply turned up for my usual clinic at Guy's and found that Dr Ellis was doing it, and that the miniscule honorarium that I received from the Medical School was no longer paid. I never again had any connection with the hospital, and in the subsequent thirty years passed through its portals on only three occasions. On the other hand, I was appointed an Honorary Physician to the Queen Elizabeth Hospital for Children, which in due course became part of the Institute of Child Health. However my main activities were at Pembury and the Kent & Sussex Hospitals where I had been in sole charge since 1939, and continued as such until 1975. During the intervening thirty-seven years enormous progress had been made in paediatrics, with the result that the heavy work load that had been carried in the early years was reduced almost to the point of disappearance towards the end of my time. Then, almost unbelievably, it was decided by those who ruled the SE Metropolitan Regional Hospital Board, that the correct procedure in such circumstances was to appoint another full time paediatrician to share the work. A year later, I retired.

JOB HUNTING

Prior to the establishment of the National Health Service, getting an appointment as a consultant was a very different matter from the present system. Although the number of candidates looking for posts was a good deal less than nowadays there were infinitely fewer vacancies, because it was only in teaching hospitals, special hospitals and a very few others that such appointments existed. Consequently, practically all of them were to be found only in London and the other major cities which had medical schools. The actual number of vacancies was even further reduced by the fact that most of the consultants at the specialised hospitals were also on the staff of the teaching hospitals. All these appointments were voluntary and unpaid, and the incumbents expected to earn their livings, sometimes enormous and sometimes not, from private practice. On the other hand there were the local authority hospitals which also employed a large number of consultants, but their appointments differed in the fact that they were full-time employees barred from private practice in any shape or form. A great many of these consultants, who were often of a very high standard, had trained in the old Commonwealth countries, with the result that in some hospitals 'Strine' was more or less the only accent to be heard. In contrast to the varied origins of those in local authority hospitals, parochialism and a modicum of nepotism were *de rigueur* in teaching hospitals and their associated medical schools. When I entered the wards in 1931, almost the entire staff of Guy's was home bred, and several were the sons or sons-in-law of previous consultants. It was many years later before the appointment of an outsider was anything but a remote possibility. This position continued with very few exceptions until the establishment of the NHS. There was also a disinclination to appoint a consultant who had trained in some other part of England, and the aversion was even more marked across the national boundaries.

44

In addition to the teaching hospitals there were also a great many smaller voluntary hospitals throughout the land, and almost every town had its own which it supported with a profound enthusiasm. In almost all such hospitals the medical staff were drawn from the local General Practitioners, some of whom had received only the sketchiest of specialist training, whilst others were more than adequately qualified for the positions they held. One of the greatest changes brought about by the NHS has been to staff all these hospitals with properly trained consultants, frequently not one whit inferior to those who have been appointed to teaching hospitals, with the result that medical students are now farmed out to the regions where these hospitals have the staff fully qualified to teach them, as well as the patients on which to do it, a commodity often in such short supply in the centres of excellence.

However, to return to things as they were, anybody with aspirations to become a London consultant had to aim at a position in a teaching hospital, and the routine for the candidates was formidable. They were expected to supply every member of the staff, who numbered between fifty and a hundred, with a copy of their application properly printed and bound. They were also required to call on every consultant unless they declined the offer, and this entailed a great deal of telephoning and writing to secretaries, and then hours spent walking up and down the Harley St area. Most of the people one called on didn't really want you to waste their time because they already had their own home grown favourite or were only interested in their own department, but they felt that they ought to see the applicants to make sure they didn't include any 'shockers'. Naturally, most of the interviews were brief and left one with a feeling of frustration after waiting about for such a long time. It was the period when Hitlerism was in the ascendant, and there was no conspicuous lack of anti-semitism in the UK, and a few consultants felt in no way obliged to restrain themselves. There were, for practical purposes, no Black or Asian candidates and consequently no racism, but some of those doughty old consultants would have found themselves in the hands of the Race Relations Act had they talked to the applicants in these days in similar terms.

The teaching hospital appointment that I did get at the Queen Elizabeth Hospital for Children in London, was most unexpected because I had never worked there as a member of the junior staff, and they could have known very little about me. However, as a member of the consultant staff, I subsequently sat on the committee that made appointments there, and never have I known a fairer or more liberal minded set of people. On one occasion a most unprepossessing individual from overseas, who was incidentally highly intelligent and well qualified, behaved rather aggressively at the interview, and also had such a marked 'colonial' accent that it was very difficult to understand him. At the subsequent discussion, one of the lay members remarked that we couldn't possibly consider him for the post on account of those unattractive features that had nothing to do with his ability or suitability. In all probability he wouldn't have been appointed, but from that moment of what would now be called racism, the medical staff led by Dr Helen McKay and Dr Richard Dobbs saw to it that he got the job, and never in all the years that I was there did any applicant suffer any disadvantage on account of colour, race or creed.

The consultant appointment that occupied most of my time and which was dearest to my heart, was in the Tunbridge Wells area. Strangely enough this was an appointment for which I had never applied, and, like Topsy, 'It just growed'. At the outbreak of war when the Guy's paediatric department was evacuated to Kent, the main base at Pembury came under my care, and I was graded as a consultant in the Emergency Medical Service. When the EMS ceased to exist, the Kent County Council employed me at Pembury; and the Kent and Sussex Hospital, at that time still a voluntary institution, officially appointed me to their staff, so that when the National Health Service came into being I automatically became a consultant under that regime. From then on the enormous expansion of hospital services all over the land has led to a standard of work unknown before the war, and there are now centres of excellence in many places outside the great cities. One of the strange results of this is that it is not unknown for the great and glorious London teaching hospitals to have to tout around in the periphery to find people willing to accept their consultant vacancies, and even to have their offers turned down! Perhaps the most obvious example of this is that those who are in need of a heart or liver replacement have had to go outside London.

Under the old system, candidates for posts were required to provide three testimonials, which of course they could read before submitting them; naturally the sponsor never said anything derogatory, no matter what his personal opinion might be, with the result that these documents had very little influence in making a choice. Thus when I was in the field, hunting for jobs, I had no up to date references at all because my chief mentor Dr Hector Cameron had died, and the only other source that I might have tried was Dr Richard Ellis, with whom I had had no contact for nearly five years. The lack of references seemed to be no disadvantage, but when the NHS took over completely new rules and regulations were introduced, and in general they were a great improvement. In the first place, canvassing was strictly prohibited, and written testimonials gave way to supplying the names of references who could be asked for their opinions on candidates. Their reports were confidential, and consequently the applicants never knew what had been said about them. By this time I was no longer an applicant, but had become a member of selection committees and as a result read a great number of these reports. It is only natural that a person applying for a post gives the name of references who they think will speak well of them, and in general the opinions are laudatory, some *in excelsis* and others less so. Theoretically a sponsor could say very spiteful and damaging things, the apocryphal example being 'If you can get this man to work for you, you will indeed be lucky'. This is not quite so fanciful as might be thought, because on one occasion when we were selecting a surgical colleague his sponsor had written 'This man is suitably qualified and experienced to hold the post for which he is applying. I know nothing else in his favour.' It may or may not have been true but it was absolutely damning, and a complete bar to success. Glowing references won't necessarily get one a job, but bad ones will almost certainly spell failure, something very akin to the 'black ball' in clubland. After the meeting was over, there was an unofficial discussion about this particular case, because it was abundantly clear that the candidate had no idea of the hostility of his reference, had probably used his name in the past, and would do so again in the future. The question was how to inform the man of his predicament, because neither he nor the sponsor were known to any of us personally. One assumes that no candidate in his right senses submits the name of a person without their prior permission, and it is the duty of consultants to refuse the request rather than ruin somebody's chances, so we told the man to check his references in all his future applications, and we hoped that he got the message. This example was, in my experience, unique, and one hopes that the practice has ceased, but human nature being what it is, one doubts it.

PART TWO

MEDICINE FROM 1931
ONWARDS

I began training in the wards of Guy's Hospital in the autumn of 1931. Ever since I had started out in 1928, this had been the cherished vision of the future, when one would actually be dealing with patients. My final year at school, chemistry, physics, biology and then anatomy and physiology had been a necessary and laborious journey, leading like Pilgrim's Progress to the 'Heavenly City'. Now at last I was a recognisable, even if embryonic doctor in training, and I was fired with an enthusiasm and a sense of vocation which remained with me for all the time that I was in practice. This euphoria might have been much modified had it been possible to foresee the amazing progress that was to be made in the next forty-five years, for surely it would have laid bare the fact that by comparison the practice of medicine in 1931 had achieved very little in the way of useful treatment in the preceding two millennia. I doubt whether many people, junior or senior, gave much thought to the extraordinary limitations of their ability to influence the course of events, but as a new ward clerk I believed that doctors, especially those working in teaching hospitals were omniscient, and that their every word and deed would benefit those who were the recipients of their ministrations. That anyway was how it seemed to me, but was it really so? At that time I had not been introduced to the *Barchester Chronicles,* and almost a decade was to elapse before H Oldfield Box and the BBC restored Anthony Trollope to his previous popularity. Had things been otherwise, I should have known that although Dr Thorne was a well loved country G.P., and his rival Dr Filgrave, as his name suggests was not; and that the great London consultants Sir Lamda Mewnew and Sir Omicron Pie achieved their eminence and their wealth by being summoned to the bedsides of the aristocracy, the

51

Establishment and the rich, in order to confirm the inevitability and fairly imminent demise of the patients. It certainly was not safe to die without their prior opinions, but nowhere is there any suggestion that they influenced the course of events. By 1932 matters had advanced quite a lot, but medical treatment still left huge lacunae and much to be desired. Perhaps one might just comment on the fact that in those days, when the medical profession could achieve so little therapeutically, they were held in the highest esteem, though it has to be admitted that even at the turn of the twentieth century, General Practitioners were obliged to call at the tradesmen's entrance of the great houses. Unfortunately those Olympian heights have gradually been eroded until now, when the profession's powers of diagnosis and their range of therapeutics have also reached those same Olympian altitudes, doctors have been downgraded and some even despised.

All this has to be said because, with the benefit of hindsight it is manifest that a very large proportion of those admitted to hospital would have been none the worse off if they had not been, and some would almost certainly have been a deal better off for the omission. On the other hand it would be wrong to suggest that nobody benefited; a great many patients received an awful lot of help and many a life was saved in such conditions as appendicitis, peritonitis, strangulated hernia and other forms of intestinal obstruction. Likewise, many other patients with acute infections of the chest and ears, certain heart diseases, fractures and a number of other things would in all probability have died had they not been admitted. What we did not realise was that in so many other illnesses the treatment was quite useless, and in some cases the patients suffered unnecessarily because of it, and, yes, it has to be added that a few people actually lost their lives from it. It is sad to relate that iatrogenic hospital hazards abounded.

During my time as a clinical student, two remarkable therapeutic advances were made, firstly in the treatment of pulmonary tuberculosis, often referred to as consumption, and secondly in Addison's anaemia, better known as pernicious anaemia, which was quite commonly found, though by no means as ubiquitous as the former.

With regard to pulmonary tuberculosis, it is probably true to say that prior to the introduction of the artificial pneumothorax, there was practically no treatment for this disease. Bed rest and diet played a part in early cases, but when the disease process destroyed the lung tissue and changed it from being a spongy air containing substance into a solid cheesy mass, which the patient coughed up it left behind empty air spaces, known medically as cavities, which made it certain that the disease could never be cured. The victims just had to carry on their lives as best they could, going slowly or rapidly down hill to their inevitable end, and no doubt spreading the disease in the process. The introduction of the artificial pneumothorax, or collapse therapy as it was called, altered all that, because by introducing large volumes of air into the outer lining of the lung it squeezed the cavities until they were obliterated, and as the edges came into apposition it allowed the lung to heal. It should be added that the air that had been introduced in the pleural space not only obliterated the TB cavities, but also acted as a splint directly to the whole lung, thus applying the principle enunciated by John Hilton, author of a major work of the time entitled '*Rest and Pain*' which showed that any inflamed area healed very much more readily if it could be rested by splinting, though he was concerned with diseases of the limbs and the neck. Though introduced long after his death and often by people who had never even heard of him or his book, the artificial pneumothorax was certainly the major factor in revolutionising the treatment of the pulmonary disease, which was the commonest manifestation. Splinting in one form or another was really the only method of treating TB in other parts of the body, and where bones and joints were affected they were encased in plaster casts or other apparatus for months on end. Where local splinting could not be applied the whole body was splinted by keeping the patient in bed for very long periods which might be measured in years. To what extent the treatment was beneficial is conjectural, but certainly it did no harm other than ruin the way of life. Perhaps some people will recognise this state of affairs that was portrayed so often in literature and opera.

Apart from these specific measures it was generally accepted that treatment was best carried out in a sanatorium, and these purpose built pavilion-type buildings were erected in rural sites all over the country. The idea was that the 'better' country air combined with a liberal diet and cod liver oil, would raise the patient's resistance and help bring about a cure. Probably only the diet did any good, and any progress or lack of it would have been much the same had the patient remained in a hospital in the city. For the relatives and friends to visit these isolated places must have been a terrible burden in an age when private motoring was a privilege enjoyed by only a relative few of the rich and middle classes, to which most of the sufferers did not belong. I do not think many of us gave much thought to the matter, and those on the receiving end seemed to take it all as a matter of course.

The most sought after type of sanatorium treatment was that situated in the Swiss Alps, which of course only the rich could afford, though there were limited facilities for less well off patients whose fees were paid by the local authority. To obtain such a vacancy took much time and trouble by the doctor, the social worker and the local authority, and in the few cases where success was achieved, scant thanks were received by anybody. Undoubtedly those who went to Switzerland showed remarkable improvement in a very short time, and had one thought about it, it should have been obvious that a slowly progressive disease like TB could not have altered very much in so short a time. In all probability the high altitude made no difference to the basic disease, but aided by the sunshine and the diet, it was very effective against the other secondary pulmonary germs which rapidly disappeared. All these things, combined with the beautiful surroundings and the marvellous psychological management of the Swiss physicians made the patients seem very much improved. On their return to the UK however, they fairly rapidly reverted to the state they would have reached had they not gone abroad.

Since those days, the whole situation with regard to tuberculosis has changed beyond recognition in the western world. Until the discovery of the antibiotic streptomycin, and other ancillary drugs, which are used separately or in combination, TB constituted one of the major diseases of humanity, comparable with malaria, and in many parts of the world it still is. It was a killer on the grand scale, mostly slowly and remorselessly. Less often, when it manifested as 'Galloping consumption', the lay term for miliary TB, tuberculous bronchopneumonia and tuberculous meningitis, it killed in a matter of days or weeks. Although its ravages caused the disablement and death of countless millions of nameless victims, it seems to have had a special propensity to attack poets and authors, and presumably was the disease of the Brontë family, Keats and Robert Louis Stevenson. Not only did it attack the writers but also their heroes and heroines, leading to their tragic deaths, usually in the last chapter of the book or last act of the opera. Thus Mimi in La Boheme, Violetta in La Traviata, and Smike in Nicholas Nickleby, the last of these inducing floods of tears or acute nausea, according to the reader's susceptibilities. In those days before the advent of x-rays and bacteriology the powers of accurate diagnosis were limited, and it is difficult to be dogmatic about such people, but whereas it is thought that Jane Austen suffered from anaemia, possibly Addisonian, her history might have done for TB.

If for so many centuries tuberculosis was a global scourge that had to be endured, in the late nineteenth and early twentieth centuries it was recognised as a disease that spread from infected persons to healthy ones, and therefore it was considered as a social responsibility, so that public health legislation was enacted to try and decrease the incidence and limit its spread. In the early 1930s we students were frequently told how much progress had been made in that respect, and it was easy to believe because those in teaching hospitals saw relatively little of the disease. Every now and then a case of miliary disease was admitted, and even more rarely broncho-pneumonia, and tuberculous glands in the neck of children was common, and infection of the spine and other bones was not rare. As a student I never saw a case of tuberculous peritonitis where the infection spread from the intestine into the general abdominal cavity. In these cases the germs were originally carried in the milk supply, but because all the London milk had been pasteurised the disease had disappeared. Things were very different in other parts of the country. The thing that gave us quite the wrong impression of the true state of the disease was that if any of the patients admitted to a teaching hospital did not succumb in a short time they were transferred to sanatoria or other hospitals, after which we completely lost sight of and forgot all about them. It was not until I went to Pembury Hospital in Kent in 1939 that I discovered what the real picture was like. The hospital had a small department for adults with pulmonary TB and the state of their disease was such as I had previously thought of only as historic. Huge cavitation, continuous coughing up of blood-stained phlegm and even gross haemorrhages, grave anaemia and grave illness. The thing that seemed quite extraordinary about it all was that so many of these people had not been thought of as really ill until the disease was almost terminal. I shall never forget one farm labourer who was admitted one evening. He had been ploughing all day and was not feeling very well, so he went to his doctor's evening surgery for a 'tonic', instead of which his immediate admission was arranged and thirty-six hours later he was dead. Such a case was by no means unique. In the children's ward there were several cases of gross peritonitis as well as other types of the disease, and nearly always a child with miliary spread and meningitis on its way to eternity. The only thing that lightened the gloom, and which incidentally gave us quite the wrong impression that the treatment we used sometimes worked, was misdiagnosis. This applied particularly to bone and joint diseases where cases were diagnosed as being tuberculous on the flimsiest of evidence, were then encased in plaster casts and kept in bed for months. One of my happiest experiences on arrival was to find that almost all the cases had negative tuberculin skin tests, which meant that they had never ever had any TB infection, so that plasters were removed, bed rest abandoned and the children discharged. The parents were of course delighted, but nothing that I could say could disabuse them of the notion that I had cured their children of 'consumption'! With the benefit of hindsight it is now possible to recognise that what the children really suffered from were the various manifestations of auto-immune disease, which would now be classified as forms of rheumatism, but nobody could be blamed for failure to diagnose a condition that was still some ten to fifteen years in the future before it was identified.

One case of misdiagnosis certainly warrants a description to itself. She was a little girl who was a refugee from Hitler's Germany, and had been diagnosed in that country as suffering from miliary tuberculosis before she came to England prior to the outbreak of the Second World War. She brought her x-rays to prove it. Several more taken in the UK confirmed the diagnosis, and when she came under my care during the Battle of Britain I would certainly have agreed. The only thing was the impossibility of believing that she could have survived for two years, and have so little illness beyond anaemia. In an endeavour to establish the diagnosis, a concentrated effort was made to identify tuberle bacilli in repeated stomach washings, but none were found. Dr W A Taylor drew my attention to the fact that, although there was no TB, every specimen showed large numbers of tissue cells laden with an iron pigment which would of course be radio-opaque, and we wondered whether the miliary shadows might be due to agglomerations of these cells. Surgical removal of a piece of lung tissue would have settled the matter, but such a thing was not possible at that time; several deliberate lung punctures with a syringe and wide bore needle showed similar cells, and our suspicions were largely confirmed when Professor Payling Wright discovered a description of an identical x-ray picture in silver polishers in Sheffield who had inhaled iron laden dust at their work. In our case the iron pigment was self produced from destroyed blood cells. The child was shown at a meeting of the Royal Society of Medicine as a case of 'Idiopathic Haemosiderosis of the Lung', and naturally attracted considerable attention. This led to a hunt for other similar cases; several were found, and thus a new disease was described. Unfortunately such misdiagnoses were rare and tuberculosis itself pretty common, so that if, as we were taught, progress had been made, there was still plenty of room for more of it. How pleasant to record that in a period of less than twenty years consumption as a disease was changed from an ubiquitous disabler and slaughterer to one that has been almost completely eradicated in the United Kingdom. Like so many such events it has been due to a combination of measures such as control of spread from one person to another, vaccination of children, pasteurisation of milk and above all the discovery of streptomycin and other effective drugs that cured the disease even when it manifested as galloping consumption. Elsewhere, in the Third World the situation leaves much to be desired.

The second great advance in treatment that had taken place in the period of my studentship was the cure of pernicious anaemia. The disease had been described originally by Addison, who was probably the most eminent of all Guy's physicians, though it was not given his title till many years later, and was usually described as pernicious anaemia even in his own hospital and in the ward named after him. This ominous title was more than justified by the fact that the disease was resistant to any known form of treatment, and an inevitable downhill course ending in the death of the sufferer from anaemia and very unpleasant complications that occurred in the central nervous system. Before the discovery of the different blood groups not even blood transfusion was possible, though this had been introduced when I entered the wards. The disease was by no means uncommon, and some medical historians think that Jane Austen suffered from it, and that it was the cause of her death. Certainly it was almost as familiar to the lay population as the medical profession, and so it can be imagined what a sensation was caused when quite suddenly it became curable. The new treatment involved the patient in having to eat prodigious quantities of raw, chopped animal liver, a cure that seemed almost worse than the disease itself, though fortunately the rapid and dramatic recovery that soon became evident to all concerned made such a treatment tolerable. In fact it was relatively easy in those days to inflict such ordeals on patients because before the modern era of tablets, injections and palatable elixirs, most medicines that were taken by mouth were expected to taste nasty, with examples such as castor oil; quinine; extract of male fern (Felix Mass) which was the standard treatment for tapeworm and a host of others. The population in general accepted that oral therapy was unpleasant, and some people went so far as to believe that any medicine without a revolting taste could not be doing them much good. On the other hand there are occasions when a dreadful taste can be a bar to treatment. This was shown in the case of a child with meningitis where the newly introduced antibiotic chloramphenicol was essential to her survival, but as she was so young it was impossible for her to swallow the capsules in which it was dispensed. When the contents were removed from the outer covering the drug itself had a taste so bitter that it made quinine seem almost like saccharin, and it was impossible to disguise it; even when emulsified with golden syrup the bitterness was just as apparent. It required a brutal struggle to get it into her stomach by means of a tube. Chloramphenicol (trade name Chloromycetin) proved itself an extremely effective antibiotic, essential for the treatment of influenzal meningitis which is a common affliction of children, and consequently when a very palatable elixir became available it was little short of a godsend to paediatrics. Unfortunately a godsend in one respect can be an invention of the Devil in another, and in the case of chloramphenicol led to its eventual downfall. The disaster lay in the unusual coincidence of two quite unrelated things. Firstly, it is so easy for a palatable medicine to be taken far too often and for far too long a time, and secondly, there are occasions when medical prescriptions are repeated time and time again without the patient being seen or under adequate supervision. In this instance the disease involved was whooping cough which may run a very variable course usually lasting about three weeks, but on the other hand may be enormously extended up to nearly as long as a year, and it was in a few such cases that the catastrophe occurred. As a background to this incident, it has to be pointed out that no drug has much if any effect on whooping cough, but there was a period when chloramphenicol was thought to be helpful. Incidentally just before that time atropine methyl nitrate enjoyed a similar vogue, but it too was quite useless. To return to the subject, it happened that several children were given chloramphenicol for many months on end even though it had no effect on the disease, but it was so palatable that there was no difficulty in getting the children to take it. Undoubtedly as a result of the treatment the children developed a fatal blood disease where the white cell production was destroyed, and it was subsequently shown that even with a normal controlled dosage there was some fall in the white cell count, though with no untoward effect on the patient. Unfortunately this led to a panic situation where the drug got a quite unjustified reputation of being very dangerous, and as a result it is possible that a few lives were lost through its being withheld in cases where it was otherwise indicated.

However, to return to the main subject of this chapter where Addison's anaemia was concerned there were no such difficulties, because the raw liver regime lasted a very short time, after which it was replaced by much less disgusting dried preparations and injections of liver extract, which continued until the identification of the actual substance whose deficiency was the cause of the disease, so that it then became possible to treat it with a synthetic substitute, whereupon liver and its derivatives disappeared from the scene as did the perniciousness of Addison's anaemia.

These two diseases exemplified the fact that dramatic advances were possible, and yet prior to their introduction there was no wringing of hands or donning of sackcloth and ashes at our inability to cure so many other things. At least as students we seemed quite satisfied.

THE CHANGING FACE

No more striking change can be imagined than the pattern of diseases that utilised the hospital beds in 1932, compared with the position as it now exists. The change of course has been due to many factors, chief amongst which are the phenomenal advances in the ability to unravel the true causation of an illness through research in the laboratory with apparatus undreamed of before, and in medical practice by means of investigations that are in the realms of biochemistry, radiology, nuclear medicine and of course the computer. The revolutionary improvement in treatment appears to have kept pace with much of the diagnostic advances, though there are still some yawning gaps to be filled. Two of the diseases, pneumonia and stomach and duodenal ulcers are barely seen in hospital beds these days, and whilst heart and kidney diseases are still very common, the actual nature of the cases is totally different. However the first of the 'Old Brigade' must be pneumonia which historically was to be found at the top of Division One of the league of Killer Diseases, and has now been on the decline for decades, though when it so wishes it can still show its teeth, as for example in Legionnaires' disease. As a more generalised indication of this downward trend, it has lost its attraction for the cinema scenario writers, whereas it used to be a standard potboiler, because in those days every layman knew exactly what the course of the disease should be. It was supposed to last exactly eight days and then end abruptly either by crisis or death. What better cliff hanger presented itself then the heroine, her coiffure done to perfection, her demure sweet smile unaffected by the illness, lying in a bed above which was a 'day by day' tear-off calendar which chronicled the duration of the illness. Would she survive or would she die? And as each fateful moment passed, the camera zoomed in on the calendar; one, two, three, four, five, six, seven and at last the eighth day and the denouement. Generally where the cinema was concerned there was recovery, but definitely not in grand opera where the slaughter of heroines is almost de rigueur. In fact the supposed eight day course was a lot of nonsense, though even in medical circles it had some credence. The whole thing was based on the fact that when, as at that time there was no effective treatment for the disease, the patient's survival or death depended on the length of time that their hearts could stand the strain before they failed and death ensued. In most healthy adults the limit was about a week, and fortunately in most of them the crisis ensued before that time so that they recovered, but for the others it was touch and go, and some 10% succumbed. In children, whose hearts were quite capable of dealing with the toxic effects of the disease for very much longer, the course might go on for several weeks before they recovered or not; but at the other end of the scale, the elderly whose hearts could barely manage at all slipped away quickly, quietly and peacefully, giving rise to the saying 'pneumonia, the old man's friend'.

If the layman's ideas about this disease were somewhat misconceived, they were as nothing compared to those of the medical profession, whose theories about the different causes could hardly have been more erroneous. Whereas nowadays, when it is possible to identify these things, pneumonia is classified according to which particular germ or other agent is the cause of each case, which may be bacteria of several different types, viruses of many very different varieties, other non-germ infections, and even inhaled mechanical substances such as noxious gases and liquids, and certain chemicals. This is very important because in the many cases where there is a treatment, it has to be appropriate to the particular cause in each one. In the 1930s when bacteriology was a little less advanced and virology almost nonexistent, the classification had to be based simply on the shape and distribution of the disease process in the lungs, which was determined by x-ray and physical examination of the patient's chest. This divided the cases into two broad types known as lobar pneumonia and broncho-pneumonia, which did something, though not very much, to indicate the differences of the disease. In the former, as a general rule only one lobe of the lung was affected, but sometimes two were involved and this gave rise to the term 'double pneumonia'. In fact it made very little difference to the outlook, but in lay terms it was interpreted by lay people who understood these matters as something of the gravest significance.

When there was no specific treatment for the disease, the division of cases into lobar and broncho-pneumonia was perfectly adequate, because it was known that the outlook in the latter type was rather worse than in the former and the relations prepared for the worst, but as there was nothing specific that could be done for either type, it was simply a matter of medical semantics. Of course, even at that time it was known which germ caused most though not all cases of lobar pneumonia, and it was even given the indicative name of the pneumococcus, but the ideas about which germs caused the other types was done purely by guesswork, and it turned out that the guesses were unbelievably inaccurate. In spite of that fact, it causes a wry smile when one remembers that the people who taught students singularly failed to point this out, and why should they have done so, since they themselves were deluded into thinking they were telling us facts not fiction. It was only when identification of the causative germ in every case became possible that it could be realised what a load of misinformation and rubbish had previously been accepted as fact.

It has to be remembered that when pneumonia was so common and carried a considerable mortality rate, the only treatment that was possible was based on the principle of maintaining the patient's strength and resistance, whatever that meant. Bed rest of course, but anyway they were much too ill to be ambulant; professional day and night nursing was a sine qua non; at home for those who could afford it, in hospital for those who could not, and a light nutritious diet and lots of fluids which were supposed to allow the kidneys to excrete the body poisons being produced in the lungs. Cough medicines and pain-killers to relieve the painful cough of pleurisy were prescribed in abundance, and above all hypnotics. It was an established maxim that stated 'if the patient sleeps he will recover, and if he doesn't he won't'. It might be observed that at the time there was no talk of sex equality. Where hypnotics were concerned, medical textbooks dilated on the subject, and not infrequently final examination papers might devote an entire question to a discussion of the choice of drugs to be used. At Guy's Hospital this turned out to be more or less exclusively opiates, used with a frequency and dosage that other hospitals could only contemplate with horror. Whereas in those places the standard dose of morphia was grains 1/6th (10 milligrammes) at Guy's it only started at grains 1/4 (15 milligrammes) and in serious cases it rose to grains 1/3rd (20 milligrammes) and even that amount could be exceeded, and not infrequently was. It might be added that it was a practice not always smiled upon benevolently by examiners from more pusillanimous centres of excellence! At that time Guy's doctors were very much under the influence of Sir Arthur Hurst, whose views were that if one used a medicine at all it should be in an adequately large dose, because smaller ones did not produce the required effect and then had to be repeated, with the result that the patient got little or none of the benefits of the drug but at the same time suffered all the unpleasant side effects of the total amount they had been given in repeated ineffective doses. This was a view that I found extremely sound and followed it during all the years that I was in practice.

The effective use of oxygen as a therapeutic agent started in about 1932 by means of an oxygen tent. The original models were very large and cumbersome, had small 'windows', lacked a proper temperature and humidity regulator and gave the patient a sensation of claustrophobia which not infrequently led to manic behaviour. In many cases these bizarre contraptions did more harm than good, and it was a long time before all the disadvantages were overcome.

As quite clearly it was almost impossible to influence the course of the disease, what part did doctors play in the management of the patient and the family? They gave the impression that the treatment was right (remember that they believed it themselves), that everything was under control, and fortunately for them it usually was. What they really knew about was judging the situation from hour to hour and assessing the outlook, because it was necessary to keep the relatives apprised at least daily if not more often. This special aspect of the disease was once again reflected in final examination questions, where something about the prognosis in pneumonia was certain to appear at frequent intervals. It all had to be done by studying the pulse rate, the blood pressure, the respiration rate, the blueness of the lips and face, the height and shape of the temperature chart, the presence or not of any yellow jaundice in the skin and, extremely important, the possible development of heart failure and complications. To add to all those things, some people, probably most, actually believed that having a bowel action was an important factor, and took measures to see that they were opened, which was something that if it affected the outcome at all, weighed against recovery rather than encouraging it. All those factors then had to be weighed against the patient's age, their previous history and lifestyle, their social status and mental reaction, all of which added up to a very complex problem. There were several traps into which the unwary practitioner might fall, and woe betide him if a favourable report was immediately followed by the loved one's death; and even the exact opposite type of prognosis did little to enhance the doctor's reputation locally. Such an unfortunate happening was not uncommonly known to make the attractions of a future life in the colonies, or at least in another part of the country, seem obligatory.

It was the complications of the disease that really governed the outcome, and of these there were a great many possibilities, but two of them were of cardinal importance. Heart failure took pride of place because it presaged impending doom and one knew in advance that 'the Angel of Death was abroad, and one could almost hear the beating of his wings'. As a rule it was first foretold by the body temperature falling and the pulse rate rising; if both of them were falling the outlook was excellent. The use of the stethoscope, nowadays almost unnecessary, played a very important part in judging how matters stood from hour to hour. The second of these complications was the development of collections of pus, known as an empyema between the lung surface and the inner layer of the chest wall. If this happened whilst the pneumonia was still active, it was for technical reasons extremely difficult to deal with and tended to be very fatal. Mostly however, the condition developed a few days after the acute phase of the disease had ended, and it was in fact nothing other than an abscess in an unusual situation within the rib cage, and the treatment required it to be drained just like any other abscess elsewhere in the body. The general rules that governed the surgical management of all abscesses, no matter wherever they were situated in the body, were that the drainage hole must be large enough and sited in the most dependant part to allow the contents to be completely discharged by gravity, otherwise the abscess would not heal. The trouble with applying these rules to an empyema was that the ribs of the chest wall interfered with such precepts, and additionally any surgery within the chest itself was eschewed like the Devil incarnate. Originally these collections of pus were just left alone and allowed to 'point' and finally burst of their own accord. When they did so the discharge always came in the wrong place and through a hole that was much too small, so that the abscess never healed and continued to discharge for the rest of the patient's life. This chronic infection led to the development of a condition called amyloid disease which in the end proved fatal. In view of this grim outlook of masterly inactivity, the next step in treatment was for the surgeon to make a drainage hole in a more dependant situation in the space between two ribs, but it was impossible to make it sufficiently large as the rib edges were so close together, and in effect the outcome as far as the patient was concerned was much the same as before. Eventually the problem was solved by resecting pieces of the ribs to make a large drainage hole, and from then on the empyema healed completely and life was no longer threatened or shortened. The operation was a very unremarkable affair by 1932, and the number of cases requiring it was considerable. Why, one might ask had it not been thought of years before? The answer is distinctly intriguing because its performance broke every rule in the surgical calendar where broken bones were concerned. It has to be remembered that all this occurred at a time when antibiotics had never even been heard of, and fractures were a much graver problem than nowadays. In those days it was a fact that a simple fracture, which meant that only the bone was damaged but the overlying skin remained intact, rarely endangered life, though of course it frequently led to deformity. What everybody feared so greatly was a compound fracture where the overlying skin had been pierced and allowed infection to attack the broken bone, in which case the victims would be fortunate to escape with just the loss of a limb, whereas it was more probable that they would lose their lives into the bargain. Bearing these facts in mind, the proposal to drain an empyema by rib resection meant a procedure of actually and purposely fracturing bone (the rib) where no break had previously existed, and the overlying incision in the skin made it not a simple fracture but a compound one, and then worst of all, not just running the risk of the bone becoming infected, but making absolutely certain that it happened by allowing frank pus from the draining empyema to pour over the broken ends. In theory it was homicidal, and surgical history, which may or may not be apocryphal, has it that the General Medical Council, instead of honouring the surgeon who originated the operation, seriously considered removing his name from the Medical Register on account of an unsound mind! At Guy's it was the generally accepted opinion that this dramatic innovation and major advance had been conceived and introduced by Sir William Arbuthnot Lane, who certainly had many original and not always orthodox ideas, but it is quite possible that other hospitals claimed the credit for one of their own alumni.

There is a tail piece to this story which is almost certainly correct. King George V's penultimate illness was the development of lobar pneumonia, which to judge from the medical bulletins issued by his doctors must have given him something of a rough ride, and to crown it all he developed an empyema. It is sometimes rather surprising to realise that royalty have not always been the recipients of the best medical attention and on this occasion the royal empyema was operated upon by an elderly surgeon who presumably was not very familiar with this particular procedure. The results of his ministrations were unsatisfactory, with the result that a younger man with more experience in these matters had to be summoned to perform a second operation which had the usual excellent result. Although empyemas were really a very common occurrence at that time, nothing similar happened to any of the considerable number that came my way, until the advent of chemotherapy and antibiotics abolished the condition completely. The modern student would be totally unfamiliar with something with which the surgical wards of 1932 were never devoid.

Besides cases of pneumonia, the other disease that was responsible for the occupation of many beds was gastric and duodenal ulcers, and the fact that at that time the patients were kept in bed for very long periods, frequently measured in months, made the condition seem even more common than it really was. Unfortunately so much of the treatment in use at that time was very ineffective, and it is probable that these prolonged sojourns in hospital did more harm than good because they interfered with the patient's normal life and earning ability in an age when their support from the state and other social services was a great deal less plentiful than it is now.

The difficulty lay in the fact that, although the ulcers were confined to the acid-secreting areas of the stomach, and were therefore largely caused by that acid, there were no really effective means of controlling the condition, and consequently all the treatments were aimed at trying to neutralise the acidity rather than prevent it, but nevertheless allowing the ulcers to heal. A number of different regimes were in use, all of which in theory were at least rational in their approach to the problem, and it is only fair to say that a good deal of healing did take place, though in all probability most of this was due to the bed rest, which would have been equally effective at home, because when that part of the treatment was stopped, the relapse rate was high even though the dietary treatment was continued.

Before treatment began, a test-meal had to be done, and it was the medical student's duty to carry it out. The patient was required to swallow some 18 inches (45 cm) of rubber tubing of about 1/8 inch (0.56 cm) in cross section, except at the tip where it was even wider to accommodate a lead weight within. In order to increase the students' awareness of the nature of this procedure, they were required to swallow one themselves, and although to a few it presented no difficulty, others found it a traumatic experience. It was suggested that it would be a good thing to encourage the patients by demonstrating how it was done, but few if any carried out that form of encouragement. However it gave people a valuable insight into what the patients suffered, and a great deal of sympathy for their predicament, which was something entirely lacking in every other aspect of our training. It leads one to wonder why there was such competition amongst the patients to be admitted to a teaching hospital, because it is pretty certain that the students' attitude which lacked much concern for their welfare was only a reflection of the behaviour of their superiors. Whilst in many ways medical education since those days has not been all for the better, it is a pleasure to record that modern medical students are a much more caring group than they were in the 1930s, and they have been known, quite rightly, to chide their mentors if they strayed from the path of accepted standards. Whether this has any anything to do with the admission of women students to what were previously all male citadels is conjectural, but it gives food for thought.

The basis of all the treatments for peptic ulcers was frequent small feeds usually at two-hourly intervals, consisting mainly of milk with perhaps the addition of a farina; or Horlicks or Ovaltine. Between feeds or at the same time, alkaline mixtures of varying constituents were administered, and some of these formulae have persisted into modern times as proprietary stomach powders and tablets. At Guy's Hospital where Sir Arthur Hurst's influence rated very large, there was additional dosing with draughts of olive oil drunk neat. Regimes used by other physicians were not so keen on the latter, and no doubt the patients were grateful for such small mercies. At intervals of perhaps as little as a fortnight, repeated barium meal x-ray screening was done to assess progress, because nobody knew then that this was a very inaccurate method of revealing anything of the sort. What effect all this radiation might have in turning a simple ulcer into a malignant one was never taken into consideration, and if it did happen, it was just considered to be one of the natural complications of the disease, or else it was thought that the ulcer had always been a malignant one, and that a misdiagnosis had been made originally. Incidentally the amount of x-raying done on one patient could be formidable, not only in peptic ulcers, but in pulmonary tuberculosis and fractured bones. What gay abandon we all had.

In about 1935 the flexible gastroscope was introduced, and although only a pale shadow of the modern operating models, it did make it possible to view the stomach wall directly and to assess the true position rather than make indirect deductions. Like all new advances it took some time before the facilities were generally available, and consequently barium meal x-ray examinations continued for many years, especially as the war engaged most of the medical profession on other activities.

In spite of all this extremely dubious therapy, most of the patients were discharged after many weeks in a much improved state of health, and some of them must have remained that way, but unfortunately a high proportion of them relapsed and had to return for another bout of treatment, and perhaps several more after that, provided of course that they did not perforate in the meantime. Can anybody doubt that after so many months or even years of enduring such treatment most of the sufferers were only too ready to submit to surgery, and the surgeons were only too happy to oblige, because they thought they could effect a cure. However, before proceeding to that subject it should be mentioned that there was one voice crying in the wilderness, that of Sir Herbert French. He was the author of a monumental work, *French's Differential Diagnosis*, and by all reports a flamboyant character and extremely able physician whose services were much sought after by both the lay and medical fraternity. Relatively early in his career he retired from practice, had his name removed from the Medical Register and went into the commercial world of manufacturing jams and preserves. Contrary to the almost universal practice of treating peptic ulcers with the sort of regimes described, he used one in which Irish stew figured very large in the diet. It is reputed that when he did his ward rounds he insisted that the empty plates were to be left on the little marble shelves above the bedheads that were a feature of Guy's wards in those days. It is said that in actual fact the patients were never given this diet which everyone in the hospital considered a totally outrageous practice, and the ward sisters merely exhibited the empty plates. If this was so, it was a great pity because it would have saved the patients a great deal of misery, and they would have been none the worse for it. There was another factor that increased the unpleasantness of the disease, and it went unrecognised for a very long time, because in fact it was a result of the treatment and not part of the illness. The trouble was that the almost exclusively milk diets tended to produce the biochemical condition of ketosis, the symptoms of which include a general feeling of ill-being and ill-humour in a person who had quite enough to bear without such an additional burden, and in all probability their ulcers would have been no worse and they would have been much happier on a less rigid diet such as Irish stew. It was generally thought that ulcer patients tended to be irritable and touchy by nature.

It was probably the pain and the treatment that were the cause.

It needs very little imagination to realise that a great many patients with peptic ulcers, whose medical treatment had failed and had been accompanied by repeated relapses were considered suitable candidates for surgical intervention. The operation of choice was gastro-jejunostomy, which joined the stomach to the upper part of the intestine thus by-passing the normal passage through the duodenum. The contents of the latter were strongly alkaline, and when they flowed back into the acid stomach they neutralised its contents and allowed the ulcer to heal. Initially these things did seem to happen, and great was the praise for surgical treatment, to the extent that the surgical wards were filled with failed cases of medical treatment of which there was no shortage. One thing we failed to realise was that although the new treatment caused immediate relief, it had done nothing to deal with the basic cause of acidity. It was also thought that peptic ulcers were in part caused by, or at least made worse by what was called 'focal sepsis'. It was a topic that entered into many aspects of diseases other than ulcers, the causes of which were obscure or unknown, and it was supposed to be due to a low grade infection elsewhere in the body, the site of which was conjectural because of course most of them never existed. The places where these infections were supposed to exist and were imagined to be producing bacterial poisons that prevented the main disease from healing were in the teeth, as in 'pyorrhoea' of the gums, in the kidney and the gall-bladder or even a grumbling appendix. In the state of knowledge at the time it seemed logical to suggest that the patient was continually swallowing the pus surrounding the teeth, and that it irritated the ulcer and prevented it from healing. Pyorrhoea was a disease so common that almost every patient in the hospital was supposed to suffer from it, and yet suddenly the diagnosis disappeared from the calendar without any intervention from the dental profession. However, be that as it may, it was considered essential that these sources of infection should be eradicated, and as far as the teeth were concerned, it usually meant a complete dental clearance producing the disability of a toothless mouth to add to the misery of the ulcer. With regard to the other supposed sites of infection, the patients were lucky if they didn't lose both their appendix and gall bladder and they might well have lost their kidneys into the bargain had it not been a fatal procedure.

It was easy to see why the operation was so popular with surgeons, because it was such a satisfactory procedure to perform. The great clamps, the various suture lines and the many sutures held in Spencer Wells forceps looked at first like chaos, but as the operation progressed everything fell into place, all the loose ends joined up, practically no blood flowed, and as the abdomen was closed everyone present felt that a good job had been done. The immediate relief to the patient was most gratifying, and loud was the praise of surgery, and as not infrequently happens, the humble physician was most unfavourably compared with his more extrovert colleague. However that was not the end of the saga, and for many worse was to befall. As pointed out earlier, the theory was that the operation would allow the ulcers to heal, and this they did, but in their place there tended to develop a new ulcer where none had been before, on the edge of the artificial opening that had been created by the operation. If ordinary peptic ulcers were difficult to cure, they were as nothing compared to these new ones which were the devil to treat, and in most cases the old operation had to be undone and the previous anatomy restored. This operation was more difficult and more time consuming than had been the original gastro-jejunostomy, and was much disliked by surgeons who heaved a huge sigh of relief when the whole concept of this type of treatment was abandoned, but it was a gradual process over many years. Before this stage was reached it was not unknown for a surgical list to figure both one patient having a gastro-jejunostomy performed, and another in whom there was the restoration of the normal anatomy, not of course the same patient, though it might have saved a lot of time had it been so.

In the mid-1930s a completely new operation was introduced which was much more logical because it removed all or a large part of the stomach from which the causative acid arose, and a much more satisfactory result was obtained. Removing the entire stomach is by any standards a major operation, and when first performed was not without its risks, especially when the understanding and control of the body's fluid and chemical balance were in their infancy, and although some progress in anaesthetics had been made from the 'rag and bottle' regime, it fell far short of modern practice, so that initially the mortality rate of the operation was rather high. However it continued as the standard surgical treatment with ever decreasing risk until the introduction of Tagamet and Zan-Tac and other similar drugs which were able to control acid secretion just by swallowing a few pills, thus achieving the same or better results than ever before. The wheel had turned full circle, and the humble physician with his pills and medicine had superceded the surgeon with his knife, and in practically every case there was no longer any need for a hospital admission. The whole transition had covered a period of more than four decades.

If the picture painted so far reveals a rather grim situation, there were and still are for that matter, two surgical procedures that unquestionably saved many lives. The first is when an ulcer perforates, spilling the intestinal contents into the perito-neal cavity causing agonising pain, and if unattended to kills the patient from peritonitis. It might have been thought that such cases were always in people where prolonged medical treatment had been tried and had failed, and of course most of them were, but it is rather surprising that sometimes the perforation was the first intimation that the patient was suffering from an ulcer. The condition was by no means rare, and most surgical teams on emergency duty expected to deal with at least one such case in the week. The immediate results were very satisfactory and the mortality rate was low. The other life threatening complication was when uncontrollable haemorrhage occurred. Initially the cases were treated in the medical wards with blood transfusions and, at Guy's, large doses of morphia. If this treatment failed, surgery was indicated, but the operation could prove to be very difficult, and sometimes an emergency removal of the stomach had to be performed, which in the circumstances then reigning was something of an heroic undertaking.

With the benefit of hindsight it would indeed be a bold spirit who claimed that the treatment received by ulcer cases as here described did more good than harm, and it is possible if not probable that most of the great host of sufferers would have been wiser never to have passed a hospital's portals. Fortunately such doubts never entered anybody's head, and the patients seemed equally uncritical. Not even the government was blamed.

NEW WINE IN OLD BOTTLES

Part 1. Diseases of the Heart

There may be, and in fact there undoubtedly is considerable doubt as to where in the body the soul may reside, but from time immemorial it has been known that when the heart stops functioning, life ends. It therefore causes no surprise that heart specialists and their subject cardiology, are one of the oldest specialties in medicine. In 1932 Guy's Hospital had appointed an Assistant Physician as a part time cardiologist, though this did not entail him dealing exclusively in heart diseases, nor did it preclude the other physicians from caring for their own cardiac cases. Consequently there was no separate cardiac department, but just tacit admission that it was a very important subject. Except for the fact that it dealt with the same vital organ, the cases of 1932 bore almost no relation to their modern counterpart. The diseases of yore now mainly no longer exist, and their modern replacements were either unrecognised, or where they did exist were hardly even considered worthy of attention, as there was nothing that could be done about them. A bigger change is difficult to imagine.

It is probable that Hippocrates's emblem of the serpent climbing his staff is in modern parlance what might be called the logo of the medical profession, but it is surely the stethoscope that most readily brings to mind the image of a medical practitioner. It was one's most treasured badge of office on entering the wards, and it promised to unlock all the deepest secrets of mankind, but it was a false promise. The reason was that, rather surprisingly, the understanding of diseases of the heart and the blood vessels had made relatively little progress from the era of Hippocrates up to the introduction of McKenzie's polygraph, which was a forerunner of the present day electrocardiogram. The stumbling block that hindered the cardiologist lay in the fact that the heart did not lend itself to any form of direct examination until after death, so that as a result everything had to be deduced indirectly from nothing more than feeling the pulse and the radial artery, laying a hand and then an ear on the chest wall, the latter subsequently upgraded to the uniaural and then the binaural stethoscope. However by 1930, when x-rays were proving increasingly helpful, it was possible to diagnose many cardiac diseases quite accurately, though after that had been done it was very largely a matter of simply watching the natural course of events without being in a position to do very much to influence them.

At that time the two diseases that were the most important in cardiology were rheumatic fever and syphilis, both of which are nowadays extremely uncommon, and have been replaced by the diseases due to hardening of the arteries, known technically as arteriosclerosis and atherosclerosis. Of course the latter diseases were known to exist, mainly at autopsy, but as the life expectancy was less than now, and as they were essentially conditions of the elderly, they seemed less important when compared with the other two that afflicted the young and active in the prime of life. It may be surprising to learn that coronary thrombosis, which is now such a scourge of the western world, was only gradually being recognised as a disease at all, let alone as one of major importance. There is little doubt that coronary disease was common even then, but it was only just being differentiated from angina, which was the diagnosis of that period. Certainly it was no discredit to the physicians, as the differentiation of the two conditions largely depends on the electrocardiograph. This was only just being introduced and was taken with only three leads, as opposed to the multiple chest leads that are now employed. Presumably the reason for the relative lack of importance of the conditions was that they were the diseases that increased with age, where anyway the old had to die of something. That at least seemed to be the attitude of the students and staff of teaching hospitals, an attitude that happily has undergone an enormous change in the intervening fifty years. When a diagnosis of angina and coronary thrombosis was made, it almost constituted the end of the story because beyond treatment with nitrites to relieve the pain of angina, there was little else that could be done. Drugs to reduce high blood pressure were still some way in the future, and the universal panacea of heart disease at that time was to restrict exercise even when it was not really necessary.

The second of the cardiac diseases common in 1932 and now almost, if not completely nonexistent, was the result of previous attacks of rheumatic fever. As a rule the sufferers were young or middle-aged adults showing the effects of the disease contracted in childhood, but only giving rise to serious symptoms some years later. The original heart involvement took place during attacks of the acute disease in childhood, and these were rare or ceased altogether after the onset of puberty. Although they infrequently caused any symptoms at that stage of the disease, they led to chronic inflammation which thickened and deformed the valves and narrowed the passages from one heart chamber to another. The disease also damaged the mechanism that regulated the heart's rate and rhythm causing gross irregularities, some of which were very fast and others very slow. The outcome in either case was progressive incapacity of heart function until the heart failed, and although it could be helped in the early stages, finally led to the patient's death at an early age. It was pathetic to watch these young and middle-aged people progress on the path to mortality, because beyond controlling the abnormalities of rhythm, there was nothing that could be done to help them. It is a matter of some interest that amongst the palliative measures that were used were the two very old remedies of blood-letting and attaching, or more accurately trying to get leeches to attach themselves to the skin over the swollen and painful liver. It should be recorded that in spite of their age as therapeutic agents, they were both very effective in relieving the conditions for which they were used. There were very few other diseases in which these remedies were still indicated. Viewed from a modern stance it was all very gloomy.

And then suddenly a 'white knight' appeared on the scene in the armour and accoutrements of the very newly introduced specialist, the cardiac surgeon. From very small beginnings they had created the operation of open heart surgery, the developments of which have been of immense benefit to mankind. At the beginning they were confined to dealing with the obstructive lesions caused to the heart valves by the scarring of the old rheumatic fever. A normal heart valve is made up of thin, very flexible diaphanous material, but the scarring turned it into a thick unbendable contracted mass, and they devised operations to either bypass the obstruction, or to cut a larger pathway through the scar tissue. Either way, they did great good to many people, and at the same time the basic disease which had originally caused these troubles disappeared, with the result that what had been a very large part of the cardiologists' work was no longer seen. It had to be replaced by a new vintage.

Another common cause of diseases of the heart was syphilis, and the ways in which it could manifest itself were manifold. The incidence of the basic disease itself was on the decrease because a moderately effective treatment with organic arsenical drugs had been introduced. However, as far as the heart was concerned, there was no treatment other than for the general disease of the body, and once again it was a matter of watching things take their natural course. With the introduction of penicillin and other antibiotics the incidence of syphilitic heart disease was greatly reduced; though it did not disappear, it was no longer one of the cardiologists' main preoccupations.

Another extremely important condition, especially where rheumatic and congenital heart diseases were concerned, was the ominous possibility of developing the complication of subacute bacterial endocarditis, a type of blood poisoning which was invariably fatal, and amongst its victims claimed the lives of Lord Northcliffe, the greatest press baron of his day, and also Reginald Mitchell, the designer of the Spitfire fighter aircraft that played such an important part in the Battle of Britain. It was no respecter of persons, and smote both the mighty and the humble. It was a frequent occurrence though perhaps not quite as common as it appeared, because it was one of the few chronic diseases that were kept as in-patients in teaching hospitals, partly to try and control the symptoms, but mainly as teaching cases that exhibited excellent and constantly changing physical signs. This meant that there were always one or two examples in the medical wards at any given time, and that must have made it appear so common. Once again there was no real treatment for the disease, which ran a slow course over months to its final conclusion. Though still amongst the diseases affecting the heart, the cases are no longer fatal, as they respond to treatment with antibiotics, and usually respond very well. It must be obvious that at this time there was very little that could be done for heart disease other than palliative measures. With hindsight, one wonders how the cardiologists justified their existence, but at the time no such thoughts entered their heads as they busied themselves with diagnosis, prognosis and restricting the patients' activity to add to their other troubles.

The possibility of a normal heart producing abnormal sounds or having irregular rhythms was barely considered, and the presence of an abnormal heart sound was nearly always taken to be a manifestation of some sort of heart disease: an assumption that led to the misconception of such supposed cardiac diseases as athlete's heart, heart strain and weak heart. All these conditions were treated so rigorously by rest and restricted exercise that they put an end to many a promising career on the games field, the Services and other active careers which, though distinctly unfortunate, was by no means as catastrophic as it would be in these days when huge financial gain for sportsmen is at stake. It was the day of the true amateur who played without material reward, though even so there were rumours that some outstanding international Rugby Union players expected to discover treasury notes in their football boots hanging up in the dressing room. It was also the age of the annual Gentlemen v Players match at Lords cricket ground, where the former entered and left the field of play through the main portals of the Members Pavilion, whilst the latter perforce had to use a separate small gate, or should one use the much older English word 'wicket', which was tucked away in a much less obvious position, well to one side. I once attended one of these matches and felt ashamed.

It must have been the diagnosis of these non-existent diseases that was the origin of the many cases where people were told that they had 'six months to live', and then confounded everyone by surviving for a further sixty years, at the end of which they were so inconsiderate as to succumb to some other completely non-cardiac disease. It was also an example of the saying 'It's an ill wind that blows nobody any good', because on these same grounds many men were rejected as unfit for military service in the 1914–18 war; but had their murmurs been ignored and the men conscripted, their prognosis of six months to live would have been over optimistic, since the life expectancy of those in the trenches on the Western Front was vastly less than that, heart disease or not.

Congenital heart disease is the condition where an infant is born with some mechanical abnormality of the heart, and whilst it was very commonly encountered, played a very small part in the study of both cardiology and paediatrics (there was no such thing as a paediatric cardiologist), because there was absolutely no treatment for the many affected children. The mortality rate in infancy was very high, and for those who survived the outlook was generally rather grim. Accurate diagnosis was rarely undertaken, and the cases were divided into just two groups according to whether they were 'blue babies' or not. When attempts were made to try and identify what exactly was mechanically abnormal, the answer was usually hopelessly wrong because it was surprising how very little attention was paid to the post-mortem findings, if one was performed at all, and trying to correlate them with what had been found during life. Very often the generally accepted medical views were so inaccurate that if, for example, a student at the final examination had diagnosed a case as suffering from congenital narrowing of the pulmonary artery, he would probably have been failed on the spot for suggesting so rare a disease, which incidentally is now known to be one of the commoner abnormalities occurring in congenital heart disease. In 1888, Fallot had described a special type of congenital heart disease now associated with his name and recognised as a very important condition; but almost nobody recognised it in 1932. In fact, the diagnosis of the actual abnormality in a child with a congenital abnormality of the heart played practically no part in our knowledge, and one suspects that there was just as much ignorance in the minds of those who taught and examined us. There were only a very few people who had any interest in the subject, and one of these was Maude Abbot, who was responsible for sorting out what had been until then a tangled web of the different anatomical abnormalities that did occur. This put the subject on a firm foundation and cleared away the previous fictitious ideas. The direct result of this was undoubtedly when Helen Taussig's work, led to the Taussig-Blalock operation, once again an operation of the developing open heart surgery, which for the first time treated Fallot's disease with enormous improvement. Once it became possible to treat one type of congenital heart disease surgically, the flood gates opened and led to a new concept of the whole subject. Until that point was reached, the views of Roger, expressed in 1897 held sway: 'that any treatment of congenital heart disease was useless and could do great harm'.

It was much the same in all forms of heart disease, where treatment was very limited. In all these diseases, rest in bed and restriction of exercise were the key words, and it seemed reasonable enough in the light of medical knowledge at the time, but it was often carried to such extremes that it must have ruined many lives except for those who either ignored the advice, or like Florence Nightingale directed affairs from their beds. Anybody who was diagnosed as having a weak heart was turned into a chronic invalid until the end of their lives, which could be many years hence. On the other hand, there must have been hordes of patients who ignored their doctors' instructions without coming to any harm, but for some reason or another the significance never seemed to register with the medical profession, who continued in the same old way. It is perhaps surprising to the modern physician, and even more to ASH that at no time were cigarettes or tobacco in general thought to be a health hazard, and this fact at least must have been of some comfort and solace in counterbalancing the other restrictions that were placed on the unfortunate sufferers.

Cardiac failure, which was very common, could only be treated with palliatives since nothing could be done for the basic disease. From the patient's point of view the painful symptoms of heart disease were well controlled. Nitrites in various preparations were, as they still are, the stock remedy for anginal attacks, and when they failed to give relief morphine was readily prescribed. Cardiac asthma, which is a singularly unpleasant thing to suffer from, was often treated with asthma type drugs such as ephedrine, but it was once again morphine that really gave blessed relief.

Perhaps this might be a good place for a philosophical discussion on the merits and demerits of the poppy, because from all that has been stated here it might be supposed that in the years 1930—40, Guy's Hospital was a hotbed of opium addicts, with students, doctors, nurses, ancillary staff and hordes of patients huddled in groups in the extensive underground passages enjoying the delights of the hubble bubble. Indeed it was not so, nor were there any emigrés from the Ear, Nose and Throat dept indulging in crack, because at the time cocaine sprays were the standard method of local anaesthesia of the mouth and throat. If there were addicts, and there must have been some, they were few and far between, since they never appeared in the medical wards, nor was there any mention of them during the course in psychiatry which was held in one of those dark satanic mental hospitals that abounded in the outskirts of London. Although much of what has been written must seem strange and even dangerous to the modern physician who abjures the opiates as he does the very Devil himself, these practices did not produce addicts in any significant numbers. Conversely, when the apparent laxity in the use of these drugs has been put down with great force, what, might one be permitted to ask, is the present position? Drug addiction throughout the world is rife, and nobody seems able to stop it spreading and spreading and spreading, and any idea of containing the problem and then reducing it is really only a pipe dream. Maybe the pipe in this case is a hookah!

Finally we come to the disease which is now probably the main concern of the cardiologist, and was not known at the turn of the century. As stated elsewhere, it was not until the advent of the electrocardiograph that coronary thrombosis was identified during a person's lifetime, and in 1932 it was still thought of as rare, whereas nowadays it is as well known to the lay population as it is to the medical profession, and many a patient announces 'I have joined the coronary club'. When smitten by an attack, many a person succumbs within half an hour, but many more survive and return to an active life, supervised only by drugs to reduce high blood pressure and collections of fluid in the tissues, and where required, dietary restrictions on animal fats and other things, though once again some people are not impressed with restrictions which have such a history of ill repute. Strangely enough angina pectoris, which was common enough and well identified amongst the old vintages, is still much the same nowadays, and the treatment has not altered very much, being essentially nitrites under the tongue. On the other hand the treatment of coronary artery disease has changed out of all recognition, because the obstruction to the flow of blood down them occurs mainly at the point where they originate from the main blood vessel of the body, and this has led to the surgical skill of bypassing the obstruction using the patient's own veins from the leg. Cardiac surgical wards are full of such cases, as well as others where defective valves can be replaced instead of simply watching the patient die.

Finally, in a selected group of cases where there was previously no hope there is now the possibility of a cardiac transplant which is continually improving in its results.

To sum up, in 1932 the cardiologist was mainly concerned with rheumatic disease, syphilis, bacterial endocarditis, angina, blood pressure, all of which he could barely influence, and in all of them the outlook was death. Now his cellar has been cleared to be replaced by congenital heart disease, coronary disease, bacterial endocarditis and certain other troubles, practically all of which he or she is able either to cure or so modify that the evil angel is debarred from his due until several or many years later. For once, the new vintage is far preferable to the old.

Part 2: Diseases of the Kidneys and Renal Tract

If the diseases that occupied the heart specialist have changed so radically since 1932, exactly the same can be said of those who specialised in the ills that befell the kidneys. There was however one considerable difference in the fact that, although there were a great many genito-urinary surgeons long before I entered the wards, the number of physicians who were concerned full-time as what are now called nephrologists could be counted on the fingers of one hand, and might have been as few as two. Their numbers did not really increase until after the Second World War, when the subsequent growth was enormous, with a schism into those who dealt with adults, and others who confined themselves to children; and professors now abound where'er the eye might fall.

A retrospective view of what was known about diseases and treatment of the kidneys and their associated structures in the early 1930s would reveal that the surgeons had far outstripped the corresponding state of knowledge of the medical conditions. This was simply due to the fact that unlike cardiac surgery, none of the organs involved lay outside the range of the genito-urinary surgeon who was able to approach them, discover what was wrong and treat them accordingly.

With medical diseases on the other hand everything had to be done by indirect means using such limited tests and investigations as were possible, and then make reasoned deductions which could so easily be wrong, leading to errors of diagnosis and misconceptions as to the causes. All that could be done by the physician was to take the blood pressure, examine the urine, and make use of a limited number of estimates of the blood chemistry, and certain tests that had been devised to judge the state of the kidney function. One very considerable advance that had recently been introduced was a new x-ray technique where the kidneys, ureters and bladder could be visualised after the intravenous injection of a radio-opaque dye which was excreted by the kidneys. Although it was a great help to the physician, it was even more applicable to surgical diseases such as stones, obstructions giving rise to back pressure destruction of the kidney and ureter, and the characteristic appearance in tuberculosis and malignant disease, but it had to be remembered that the operative approach to any part of the system was a major procedure, not lightly to be undertaken.

Amongst the diseases that affected this area, gonorrhoea (known to most of its victims as clap), was rife and largely untreatable, so that strictures within the penis were common, and were treated by the passage of catheters and dilators, but sooner or later gave rise to acute urinary retention. The relief of this very painful and distressing condition required very skilled catheterisation, although it far too often received exactly the opposite, and in the end a great many such patients had to be relieved by an artificial opening of the bladder onto the lower abdominal wall. This nearly always proved permanent and led to a thickened, contracted, heavily infected bladder for which no really satisfactory method of controlling the urinary incontinence was ever devised.

The situation with regard to the other common obstructive lesion, enlargement of the prostate gland, was less gloomy, though the modern very safe operations had not been thought of or were not then technically possible. The only thing that could be done was to remove the offending piece of the prostate by opening the bladder, and this led to a very long and difficult convalescence, especially when compared with the modern practice of 'out of bed in two days and out of hospital in a week or less'. In nearly all the prostate cases there was a long history of increasing difficulty in passing urine, often leading to bladder infection, something that was largely due to the patient's natural disclination to submit to the inevitable surgery until it could no longer be avoided. A high proportion of the cases did not present themselves until the sudden subvention of complete urinary obstruction, by which time the long period of back pressure had damaged the kidneys and caused generally poor health. In such circumstances and the state of surgery at the time, the operation had to be done in two stages. The first was an emergency measure to provide an artificial opening in the bladder, and then after an interval during which it was hoped to improve the patient's general health, another major operation to remove the enlarged lobe of the prostate gland that was causing the obstruction. This entailed two prolonged anaesthetics of chloroform and ether, and a long post-operative period confined to bed. Naturally the patients were all either elderly, rather old or very old, and it is surprising that so many of them survived, though of course large numbers fell by the wayside. In fact, the actual operations of genito-urinary surgery at that time had already reached a very high standard, but the anaesthetic drugs and techniques, as well as the pre- and post-operative management left much to be desired when compared with modern times. Mortality rates have fallen dramatically, and the pain, discomfort and period of hospitalisation that the patients have to endure have been enormously reduced.

There have also been two further developments never dreamed of in 1930, namely renal dialysis, which is in effect a sort of external artificial kidney, and kidney transplantation, which have transformed the treatment and the outlook in a whole range of diseases. In the olden days, if any doctor had so much as suggested such a thing as removing both kidneys, he would have been despatched to Bedlam, *quam celerrime, magna celeritate*, never to have darkened a hospital door again!

Since 1932 the medical, as opposed to the surgical management of kidney diseases has also altered out of all recognition, especially in its two major afflictions, pyelitis and nephritis.

Pyelitis

It may surprise many to learn that in the early 1930s this extremely common disease, which is a bacterial infection of the urine, and now considered rather a minor affair, was either difficult, very difficult or impossible to cure. So-called urinary antiseptics existed in profusion in the form of herbal extracts, chemical dyes and synthetic drugs, but their curative effect was minimal. The various preparations containing dyes had more psychological importance than any effect on the bacterial intruders, especially methylene blue which turned the urine a vivid greenish colour, just the hue that a patient might expect when ridding the body of a noxious poison, and to have visual confirmation was indeed a bonus! It was a favourite constituent of proprietary medicines at a time when the legal restrictions on the claims made in advertisements were slight. In general, these antiseptics found little favour in medical circles. The ketogenic diet was moderately efficient but, as in epilepsy, it was so difficult for the patient to tolerate or afford, that its use was limited. If, however, there was no simple cure, the activity of the disease was easy to control by means of alkaline mixtures containing potassium citrate, but unfortunately, as soon as the treatment ceased the symptoms returned, and many patients had to endure very long-term or even permanent treatment. Then quite suddenly the whole picture changed with the introduction of mandelic acid which was a treatment that actually cured the disease rather than simply acting as a palliative. As in so many other matters, what is a benefaction on the one hand is a malefaction on the other, and here the trouble lay in the fact that the treatment was only effective in the presence of a strongly acid urine. This necessitated giving large doses of ammonium chloride, which is a remarkably nauseous substance that the patients found difficult to swallow though they had to manage it as best they could, until other methods of overcoming the difficulty were found. When this new and remarkable treatment first came into use, we students were told that it was the result of the research work by a Dr Max Rosenheim and, as in the pre-Hitler era the eminence of Austro-Germanic medicine was thought to be supreme, it was naturally assumed that this benefactor must be another bearded, heel-clicking Central European. What a surprise we all got when we learned that far from being a Hanseatic Professor, Dr Rosenheim was in fact only a Medical Registrar at University College Hospital in London, and that relatively humble station proved to be just the beginning of a brilliant career that brought him every medical honour and a peerage.

It was fortunate for the taste buds in particular and mankind in general that the mandelic acid and ammonium chloride treatment did not last very long, because less offensive preparations of the same drug were discovered, and the imminent introduction of sulpha drugs and later antibiotics provided an even more effective means of treatment. In spite of all these advances, it usually happens that no single medicine cures every case, and though the use of mandelic acid was largely superceded, a derivative, hexamine mandelate is still available and is used occasionally. All these very efficient treatments have reduced pyelitis to a relatively minor, though still extremely common affliction.

Nephritis (Bright's Disease)

There have been relatively few diseases that have been so well described, so easily recognised, so extensively studied, and yet remained so ill-understood as to what exactly was going on in the kidneys where the trouble was situated. The difficulty lay in the fact that, except in the very few cases that proved fatal at the onset, and those who died of the chronic disease many years later, there was no way in which the kidneys themselves could be inspected and examined microscopically to allow a doctor to correlate the clinical condition of the patient and the actual condition of the kidneys whilst the patient was still alive. To complicate matters even further, it was discovered that a number of people who at one time were thought to be suffering from Bright's disease were in fact suffering from a number of quite different conditions in which the outlook and even the treatment might be quite different, and yet only direct examination of the kidneys or the death of the patient would deliver the answer. The former of course was impossible.

It might be thought that the state of affairs already described above made things difficult enough, but there were even more complexities to be encountered, because a patient suffering from Bright's disease might run a course lasting twenty years or more. During that time there could easily be periods of remission when there was nothing to suggest that they suffered any illness at all, and later, when it did relapse, their symptoms, their bodily condition and the findings in their blood and urine bore no relationship to those they had suffered previously. This in spite of the fact that it was the same disease they were suffering from all the way through. As in so many cases, the disease started in childhood and ended in middle age, and it was probable that the medical care fell to different doctors in different places at different times, and not only might the patients be unaware of their previous troubles, but their old case notes were more than likely to be missing or lost. Thus only too frequently it was impossible to obtain a comprehensive picture in a given case, and all this led to great uncertainty and confusion as to the true nature of the diagnosis. An outstanding example of this sort of thing is well illustrated in the book *Testament of Friendship*, Vera Brittain's biography of Winifred Holtby, who in 1913, at the age of fifteen had an attack of scarlet fever with complications, which in the light of subsequent events probably included acute nephritis, something which was by no means uncommon in those days. It is strange to relate that although scarlet fever at the time was a very serious and greatly feared children's disease, no further medical attention was paid to this episode after her apparent recovery. There was no follow-up, because such medical procedures did not exist, and to all intents and purposes she was assumed to have made a full recovery and regained her previous health. During World War One, she served in the WAACS, and at the end of hostilities when she was twenty-one went up to Somerville College, Oxford where, at their first meeting Vera Brittain was mightily impressed by her superb beauty and physical fitness. There was most certainly nothing to suggest an underlying chronic illness, but rather a state of radiant health, though in fact her disease was on its inexorable journey that was to end only fourteen years later. After graduation she led an extremely active life, primarily as an authoress, but also as a back room politician, an active propagandist for the

League of Nations, a worker for the Labour Party, a supporter
of Trades Unionism in S Africa, and in addition was appointed
a director of the journal Time and Tide. She accomplished all
these things without any inking of ill health, until aged thirty-
three, which was some eighteen years after the original attack
of scarlet fever, when she began to develop severe headaches,
nausea, vomiting and lethargy, which were symptoms previously unknown to her. In spite of this, little attention was paid
to her troubles, and it was not until a further year had passed
that a diagnosis of chronic nephritis was established. She came
under the care of Dr Obermeyer who was one of the very few
physicians who specialised in kidney diseases, and she was
treated with a regime of drugs, diet and graduated exercise,
which was thought to have had a beneficial effect and perhaps
lengthened her life long enough to allow her to complete her
best known novel South Riding. It must have been a Hercu-
lean task, because during all that time she suffered from
constant pain and chronic illness until her death four years
later at the age of thirty-seven.

If the natural history of this disease in one VIP has been
recorded for posterity, it can be assumed that many tens of
thousands of other less eminent persons must have travelled a
similar path, and yet there seemed to be no general recognition
of what a common and important disease nephritis really was.
As a result, little heed was paid to it or its treatment and
sufferers were left to run their alloted course without undue
concern by the medical profession. In 1932, Guy's Hospital
would have considered nephritis to be very much its own
disease, on account of the fact that the original description of
it had been made by Richard Bright, one of their most famous
alumni whose name provided the title by which it was generally known, and the kidneys that he had studied were there in
the Gordon Museum for all to see. It was therefore appropriate
that amongst the very few physicians who specialised in
nephritis in the 1930s, was Dr A A Osman. I first encountered
him when appointed to one of the posts of 'clinical' at Guy's
Hospital, where amongst our duties we acted as house physicians to the four beds he had been allocated for his 'kidney
cases' as they were vulgarly termed. His personal (though I
must declare unconfirmed) history related that during the
1914–18 war, although a qualified doctor, he had been in

Turkey engaged in espionage on behalf of the British Empire, and at the end of hostilities it was said that he had stood upon the Hellespont and tossed a coin, saying that if it came down heads he would specialise in nephritis, but if it was tails he would make the violin his career! Fortunately for a great many people it must have come down heads, and in due course he was appointed to the position of Clinical Assistant in charge of the Renal Department at Guy's Hospital. It was a strange limbo-like status, not altogether dissimilar to the one that was given to Thomas Hodgkin many years earlier. Both of them were in effect full consultants, but neither of them were ever appointed to be members of the Hospital Staff. Osman had full control of the four beds with the one proviso that the patients who occupied them had to be suffering from some kidney disease, and yet in spite of these limitations he never appeared to bear any resentment against the fact that he was not a full consultant. He was an academic nephrologist rather than a clinician, as we discovered when one of his patients was examined and found to have a previously undiagnosed cancer of the prostate gland. On his next round we were all bursting to enlighten and probably confound him with our clinical acumen, but his response was unexpected, because on receiving the news he merely gave a grunt, moved on to the next bed and took no further interest in, nor visited that patient again. As far as I know he never examined any of his cases, leaving that to his House Physician, and he conducted his ward rounds almost entirely from Sister's office. He studied enormous charts that plotted all the parameters that he required to be measured, and they were thought to be vast in numbers when compared with the practice of those days before the transatlantic habit of multiple investigations on every patient spread to the UK. He believed that bed rest played an all-important part in treatment, and he kept his patients in hospital for very long periods measured in months or even longer. On one occasion I lent him a bed in the Children's Ward for one of his twelve-year-old patients, and he visited her every now and then. She was an introverted little girl who hid herself and her property under the bedclothes if anybody entered her room, and it was clear that she was engaged on some secret activity. After nearly a year in the ward she was discharged to her home, whereupon she got hold of her father's hand gun and blew her brains out.

It was a ghastly episode, but after the initial shock had passed, her father published as a private venture the book she had written unbeknownst to us all when she was in hospital, and it was of course what she had been hiding under the bedclothes away from prying eyes.

Thus far this introduction sounds distinctly unpromising, but in fact Osman made a very great contribution to nephrology at a time when it was an arcane subject. Before the war he had been limited to that miserable complement of four beds, which grossly restricted his activities, but when in 1939 Guy's Hospital was largely evacuated from London it brought him to Pembury Hospital in Kent, where the foresight and wisdom of the Superintendant Dr E D Y Grasby made available to him the undreamed-of bounty of a unit of some forty beds exclusively for patients with renal disease. It would be untrue to say that the other members of the hospital staff welcomed this arrangement, not because of the number of beds, of which there was a plethora. The trouble was that his unit absorbed such a large proportion of the nursing staff to care for his patients, who came not from the local area, but from all over England and Wales. However our protests were to no avail and he managed to preserve his kingdom.

As far as the country in general was concerned, it could be said that due to the overall lack of interest in this disease, the orthodox medical treatment of chronic nephritis consisted of a vague reduction of protein in the diet coupled with various placebos, and an ample supply of analgesics including opiates to alleviate the headache, nausea, vomiting and general ill health that was associated with the retention of waste products in the blood. The object was to keep the patient comfortable until the inevitable end. Osman took a very different view which was based on the fact, as he used to teach, that in the ultimate extremity of the disease, if a person's kidneys were reduced to just one of its functioning units, of which it was normally supplied with myriads, they could be kept in perfect health provided they could manage each day to drink and excrete a volume of water equivalent to that in the river Thames! By such a feat they would get rid of all the waste products necessary in a dilute form, whereas in normal health the kidneys' main function is to concentrate them in the urine. To carry out his treatment, which he called renal compensation, he reduced the dietary protein intake to the minimum compatible with health, and then encouraged the patients to drink as large a volume of fluid as they could, some apparently managing as much as twenty pints in twenty-four hours. This regime was supplemented with massive doses of an alkali which acted as a safe diuretic for prolonged use. In view of the very large doses he employed, there had to be constant supervision of the blood chemistry to avoid the patient becoming overdosed with alkali and developing fits and tetany. There can be no doubt that the patients' general health was dramatically improved, though the extent to which their life expectancy was increased is uncertain, but the quality of that life was improved out of all recognition, and many who had been previously totally disabled were able to return to work and a normal lifestyle. One such beneficiary later became a Member of Parliament, and he worked very hard to try and get the Government to support and extend Osman's work, and to make the country more aware of the widespread extent and neglect of chronic renal disease. Unfortunately it was a subject in which they showed a remarkable lack of concern, though subsequent events such as renal dialysis and transplantation achieved the recognition and publicity that was so singularly lacking during his career.

Dr Osman held very strong views that most of the cases of chronic nephritis were preventable, and were due to the fact that when the acute attacks of the disease occurred they were inadequately cared for. It was perfectly true that they had just been allowed to drift back to a normal unsupervised life until the symptoms of the chronic stage supervened, very much as had happened to Winifred Holtby. He demanded that in an acute attack all his cases were to be kept strictly in bed until all the symptoms and signs had disappeared, and all the special blood tests had returned to normal, something that could take many weeks or months to achieve. Subsequently, after discharge from hospital everyone was subject to a strict follow-up for an indefinite period to identify any case that might be developing early evidence of chronic disease. I was a devoted disciple of this teaching, and certainly kept in touch with all my cases until they were too old for a paediatric department. Up to the time of my retirement, almost all of them remained perfectly normal, and it was a natural reaction to attribute this to the original Osman treatment. In retrospect there is room for the greatest doubt about it all, because it now seems very probable that a great many cases of chronic nephritis are not a result of an earlier acute attack of the disease, but are due to quite different causes.

There was another renal condition known as the nephrotic syndrome which could be caused by several different diseases. It caused abnormal amounts of fluid to collect in the body leading to gross disability, and it ran a very long course often measured in years. The usual treatments were most unsatisfactory, but the one devised by Osman was a great improvement though it was difficult to carry out and needed the patients in hospital for long periods. Fortunately the discovery of steroids overcame all the difficulties of treating the condition and replaced all the other therapies.

This all leads back to the fact that in those days it was difficult if not impossible to be certain what actual disease of the kidney one was dealing with, and in view of this unsatisfactory state of affairs, an enormous amount of energy was expended by academics in devising differing classifications of the various types of kidney disease. All of this was supposed to make it easier to identify each case, but it did not quite work out in practice for two main reasons. In the first place, some of the theories on which they were based were incorrect, and sometimes two different classifications used the same term for different conditions, leading to even greater confusion. However after all those years, in fact some two centuries of them, groping in the dark was brought to an end by the development of a technique known as renal biopsy. This was done by inserting a special type of needle into the kidney and removing a small piece that could be examined under the microscope. This enabled physicians to discover exactly what disease process actually was going on in the kidneys, instead of the inspired, or sometimes less than inspired guesswork that had so frequently been misleading in the past. At much the same time, enormous advances were made into much more detailed investigation of body chemistry and other essential functions, all of which led to a position where it became possible to make an accurate diagnosis in every case. Finally two new methods of treatment, renal dialysis, which in effect acts as a type of artificial kidney, and renal transplantation which is a true replacement, brought hope and succour to those who previously had no other prospect than the grave.

It can be seen that the type of work undertaken by the heart specialist and the nephrologist underwent enormous changes between 1932 and the modern era. Either the diseases that had once been their main concern disappeared, or else the whole prospect for those that remained improved out of all recognition. Viewed with the aid of the retrospectoscope, one might have thought that the old time specialists would have been gloomy and humbled by their limitations, but this was not so. Some even seemed, to me at least, rather pompous. It was an age when ignorance was bliss, but it would not have been foolish to be wise. The latter had to be awaited some years in the future.

THEY CERTAINLY SPELT
DEATH

It used to be a ploy when teaching by the bedside, to ask a group of students which of them had suffered from pneumonia,meningitis or appendicitis, and without fail four or more would have held up their hands causing no surprise. The punch line was to point out that before the turn of the century all or most of them would have been dead. All of those diseases are now eminently curable, and it is proposed to trace the history of two of them, i.e. meningitis and leukaemia, which though not yet quite in the same category is heading that way.

Part 1. Meningitis

Meningitis is a disease which may occur in either epidemic or sporadic form, and has never been noted for its rarity. With very few exceptions, it is uniformly fatal unless very vigorously treated. It is only in those cases where the infection is due to a virus that spontaneous recovery can be expected, and as no effective treatment of any sort was available until about 1930, anyone who developed any other type of meningitis was almost certain to die. Even in the early 1930s when some sort of treatment was possible, it was essential to make an early diagnosis if there was to be any hope of recovery, but unfortunately meningitis in its early stages is not an easy condition to recognise, especially in children who are amongst the most frequently affected. To illustrate this point, it is interesting to note that of all the cases suffering from meningitis who were admitted to the Children's Ward at Pembury Hospital, the diagnosis had not even been considered as a possibility in 60% of them prior to admission, and of those cases that were referred by their doctors with a tentative diagnosis of meningitis, 50% were not subsequently confirmed, and this in an area which was very fortunate in being served by a very high standard of General Practitioners. In such circumstances it is not surprising that the battle to conquer a disease carrying a near 100% mortality rate, and bring it to the position of almost universal recovery took about thirty years. Of course the situtation can be looked at from quite another point of view when one recalls that the universal mortality had existed for millenia, so that by comparison the duration of the struggle to abolish death was, relatively speaking, little more than the winking of an eye.

The term meningitis simply means an inflammation of the tissues surrounding the brain, and though not really included in the word there is also an inflammation of the brain itself. Within that definition, meningitis constitutes just one disease, but from the patients' point of view with regard to treatment and chances of recovery, it is really of several different types according to the actual bacterium or virus causing the infection. Thus medically the various types of meningitis are classified according to the particular germ involved in each case, and for convenience may be divided into the following groups meningococcal; influenzal; septic; tuberculous and viral. From all points of view this classification is very helpful, since each type requires its own specific treatment, all of which were introduced at different times over the period of thirty years mentioned above. This meant of course that during that period some cases of the disease were treatable and recovered, whilst others had no such succour and very sadly died. It is therefore proposed to deal with each type separately.

Meningococcal Meningitis

This is the commonest type of meningitis that occurs, and is sometimes known as spotted fever especially when it manifests in epidemic form, when the patient may be covered with small blood spots in the skin. In 1932 this was the only type of the disease that was treatable and, let it be said, the treatment was horrific. Fortunately, very soon after the onset of symptoms most of the patients were either comatose or so drowsy that they were unaware of the manoeuvres to which they were being subjected, but if they happened to be conscious the treatment was surely unbearable, for they had the unpleasant procedure of a twice daily injection into the spine. This enabled the doctor to withdraw a specimen of the cerebro-spinal fluid (CSF) which surrounds the brain to be sent to the laboratory for examination, and at the same time provided the route for the injection of anti-meningococcal horse serum into the spinal canal, thus bringing it into close contact with the inflamed, infected tissues. At the start of this treatment the CSF, which in health is normally crystal clear like pure water, was already cloudy and swarming with germs, but as the serum injections were continued the fluid withdrawn become daily thicker and more like frank pus, but the injections had to be continued until the CSF was sterile on culture in the laboratory, a process that might go on for several weeks. At that point treatment was stopped and the patient made a slow recovery. That at least was the theory, but it was by no means the universal result, and as far as children were concerned it just *never* happened. They simply lingered on and progressed to a condition that was called 'post basic meningitis' where the head swelled alarmingly, and at the same time the spine curved backwards until the back of the child's head came into contact with its buttocks. Eventually death brought relief. This dreadful situation came to an end when a therapeutic revolution occurred with the introduction of the sulphonamide drug M & B 693, which when simply administered by mouth in a dose of several tablets thrice daily, miraculously cured the disease in but a few days, though once again it had almost no effect on children, who were of course the main group affected. This was due to the standard practice whereby, at that time, the size of the dose for children was calculated. In those days nobody controlled drug dosage by estimating how much of it was circulating in the blood, nor was the blood-brain barrier which controls the passage of drugs from the blood stream to the brain known about. In modern times such matters are routine, and are relevant whatever the condition being treated, but when M & B 693 was first introduced, the dose of any medicine given to a patient was usually one or two teaspoonfuls, or one or two tablets, three times a day and incidentally nearly always all of them were administered in the twelve hours of daylight, a practice which must have produced a high blood concentration for half the time, and a very low figure for the remainder. The corresponding dose for children was calculated by a formula in which the adult dose was multiplied by the child's age, and then dividing that figure by the child's age + twelve. Thus if the adult dose was 500 milligrammes, a child aged five years would be given about 150 milligrammes, and in most diseases this rough estimate worked quite well, but where meningococcal meningitis was concerned, young children continued to die as before until Dr Banks of the London County Council Fever Service showed that a dosage at least two to three times as large as that being used was necessary to cure the cases. After this information, the results in children were just as dramatic as they were in adults. Later on, the introduction of penicillin and other anti-biotics proved even more effective than sulphonamides, but never completely replaced them. It was extremely unfortunate that before those new drugs were discovered all the other types of meningitis failed to respond to sulphonamide treatment, and continued to be just as fatal as they always had been.

Haemophilus Influenzae Meningitis

This is the second commonest variety of the disease, and is caused by a bacterium called haemophilus influenzae; it has absolutely no connection whatsoever with the much commoner universally known disease also called influenza (flu), which is caused by a virus. The similarity of names can give rise to some confusion, and it is a pity that steps were never taken to prevent it. The disease proved extremely resistant to treatment before it was finally brought under control, because disappointingly the causative germ was not in any way sensitive to sulphonamides. It was not until penicillin became available that any progress at all seemed possible, even though its use turned out to be perhaps the cruellest episode in the whole thirty year battle against the entire disease of meningitis. The reason for this was the fact that in this type of the disease, as soon as penicillin treatment was started it produced a rapid and dramatic improvement in all aspects of the patient's condition, and it seemed certain that he would recover; but this was not to be. The first indication that all was not well was the fact that the temperature never quite settled, and towards the end of the first week of treatment it was clear to the expert eye that the infection was reactivated, and as the days passed the patient's condition continued to deteriorate until once again it became obvious that death was inevitable. It seemed that victory had been snatched away just at the very moment it was about to be grasped, an outcome even crueller than one where there had never been any hope of recovery. The anguish and distress of the relatives is only too easy to imagine. The treatment with penicillin seemed to be so near perfection that it was clear that if only some additional drug could be found to supplement it, a cure would be possible. The natural choice was to try a combination of both sulphonamides and penicillin, but it failed in its objective and no other preparations from the pharmacopoea proved any more efficacious. In the USA. a specific rabbit anti-serum was said to be effective but its use appeared to be very limited, and at much the same time salvation arrived in the shape of a new antibiotic called chloramphenicol (Chloromycetin). This extremely effective and life-saving medicament had a stormy career, which has been described elsewhere in the book, and the fact that it was probably the first of the antibiotics to be patented by the discoverers before being made available for general use, did not endear it to a profession that had been reared in a more liberal tradition. Of course nowadays all new drugs are patented, and in many cases where the trials appear favourable, the shares of the manufacturers can make spectacular advances on the Stock Exchange even before one tablet, capsule, phial or bottleful has been sold. Personally, the reaction of a large section of the medical profession to the use of chloramphenicol was a cause of wry amusement to me. In the treatment of all other diseases where it was effective they shunned it as though it was an agent of Lucifer himself, campaigned against anybody else using it, and yet in cases of influenzal meningitis happily prescribed it in the required large dosage for many days on end. They were quite delighted with the patient's recovery which was due solely to the drug they so vehemently decried, and which could have been achieved by nothing else. Even when good naturedly taxed about their evident inconsistency, it seemed to make no difference.

Pneumococcal Meningitis

It is somewhat suprising that in the treatment of this condition sulphonamide drugs such as M & B 693 were disappointing, because they were so very effective against the same germ, and had built their reputation in the treatment of all the other diseases caused by it. In fact it was in the treatment of pneumococcal pneumonia that they had made their overwhelming impact. The trouble lay in the fact that, in this particular infection the area surrounding the brain, known as the subarachnoid space, rapidly becomes filled with thick pus, and at autopsy the brain surface looks as though it has been spread with green butter. If treatment was started early, things went well, but if at all delayed, the drug could not penetrate the tenacious pus and circulate to all the places where it was required. Penicillin stood more chance of getting to the necessary area, but even so it still required early diagnosis, and in some ways pneumococcal meningitis has remained a difficult therapeutic problem, though most cases make a satisfactory, if sometimes stormy recovery.

Septic Meningitis

This group includes those cases due to the other germs that give rise to pus formation. They are all eminently treatable with the antibiotics already mentioned, and with other newer discoveries that are even more effective.

Viral Meningitis

This condition has always been the one variety that recovered without any treatment, and at this point it can now be seen that all the acute types of meningitis had become both treatable and curable, but there was one extremely important exception which was tuberculous meningitis.

Tuberculous Meningitis

TBM as it is commonly called, was a disease that from time immemorial had been totally untreatable, inevitably fatal and was not infrequently diagnosed when the patient was still not very ill and completely conscious. There were very few more awful experiences for the family and their doctor to go through than to watch the remorseless progress of the disease to its inevitable conclusion with an unrelieved feeling of utter helplessness. Thus, whilst the other types of meningitis had become readily treatable, TBM remained completely resistant to all or any therapy until the advent of the new antibiotic streptomycin. Unfortunately it took a very long time to learn how best to use this drug, and in the process almost as much damage was done by some of the methods of treatment, as any benefit that might have been received by the patient. In the earliest cases to be treated the supplies of the drug were limited, and the knowledge of how to use it was to say the least minimal, and consequently very little or no progress was made. Tuberculosis, wherever it occurs, is by nature a chronic slowly progressive disease, so that no rapid or dramatic response to treatment could be expected. Responses, such as were to be seen in the acute types of the disease described above, left one in no doubt that the patient was getting better, and the lack of such evidence made it very difficult for the pioneers in the treatment of this disease to judge whether the regime they were using was being effective or not. They simply had no previous experience by which to judge. This was made yet more difficult since it was known that even in successful cases the treatment of TBM had to be continued for weeks or months rather than days, as was the case in all the other types of meningitis. This led people to devise a host of different regimes where the size of the dose, and the frequency and duration of direct spinal injections (intrathecal) of streptomycin varied widely, as an indication of how little was known; one school of thought advised that no streptomycin should be injected into the spaces surrounding the brain and spinal cord (intrathecally), but only systemically into the muscles of the legs and arms, and at the other end of the scale there was a

French regime that advised that intrathecal injections should be continued at intervals for as long as a year. This latter regime was an unmitigated disaster, because when any substance is injected into the spaces round the brain and spinal cord it has a tendency to cause the development of adhesions which interfere with the circulation of the cerebro-spinal fluid in those spaces, with the consequent development of water on the brain (internal hydrocephalus). The response of those who perpetrated this awful iatrogenic malfeasance was not, as one might have expected, the abandonment of the practice, but the devising of courses of cortisone treatment to combat the ill results produced by the original injections. Unfortunately they proved just as ineffective in curing the trouble as the rest of the regime had been effective in causing the damage, and in the end, most certainly not before time, the practice was abandoned.

Most of us pioneers who were involved in the early stages of devising a satisfactory regime that could be accepted for general use agreed on limiting the number and the frequency of intrathecal injections, combined with ordinary systemic injections of streptomycin treatment. Later on other anti-tuberculous drugs were developed and added to the course of treatment, until at long last nearly all cases of TBM made a full recovery, provided that they were diagnosed in time. The greatest danger to the final result lay in the fact that the disease has never been an easy one to diagnose in the early stages, and in the era before the procedure of lumbar puncture was developed and made it possible to examine the cerebro-spinal fluid during life, the condition was not even recognised as a manifestation of tuberculosis. This by a medical profession which, though limited in effective treatments, was superb in clinical observation, and the disease was considered to be a rather bizarre cause of water on the brain, until a post-mortem examination revealed the true nature of the disease. Thus even when modern methods of diagnosis and effective treatment became available, it still happened that some cases were not diagnosed until they had lapsed into coma, at which stage of the disease it was generally supposed that recovery was almost impossible. However, such was the efficiency of the new treatments that had been devised, that in fact even most of these patients did get better, though unfortunately their recovery was sometimes associated with blindness or deafness or both.

Thus finally the stage was reached where, apart from a few examples of rare esoteric infections or particularly virulent epidemics of meningococcal infection, the dread history of meningitis was brought to a very happy conclusion within a period of about thirty years. Personally it seems strange that when this position was reached, it took almost no time to forget the awful situation that had faced the profession but three decades previously. To recall those days may perhaps prove interesting though certainly not nostalgic.

Part 2. Leukaemia

Although not in quite the same successful class as meningitis, leukaemia is struggling, and not without some hope, to achieve a similar status. Those who developed this ominous disease in the decade 1930–40 saw only writ large the sign 'Abandon hope all ye who enter here' because, to put it bluntly, there was almost nothing that could be done to help them. Blood transfusions alleviated the symptoms of anaemia, but because neither they nor any other measure could slow down or moderate the actual disease process to any degree, it was effective for only a short time. Deep therapy was useful in reducing the size of the spleen and glands in chronic types, but it was in no way curative of the disease which not infrequently ran a spontaneous course of several years. In spite of this unhappy situation, I cannot recall that we were imbued with the idea that leukaemia was a major medical problem, except of course for the victims, because it seemed relatively rare, though in all probability this was once again just relative to the far greater numbers of other serious and fatal diseases that filled the hospital beds.

From the medical point of view, there was great interest in classifying the various types of the disease according to the particular cells involved, the rapidity of the course and the nature of the blood examinations. Thus when one had diagnosed chronic lymphatic leukaemic leukaemia, or acute myelogenous aleukaemic leukaemia, or any of the other variants, one had a sense of personal achievement, whereas it made very little difference to the unfortunate patient, and not much to anybody else for that matter. All it did was enable one to pronounce on the probable length of life that could be expected. Presumably the physician had to take refuge in this sort of activity in order to blind himself to the fact that he was powerless to help. The whole situation was very forcibly brought home to us students on a ward round with our chief, Dr (later Sir) John Ryle. In those days, Guy's and other medical schools admitted a small number of undergraduate students from the US, and their presence certainly added a refreshing wind to our otherwise sedate world. On this occasion we enjoyed the company of a certain Martin Harris, and he was asked the question 'Now Mr Harris, how do you classify the various types of leukaemia?' to which without a moment's hesitation he replied 'Well Dr Ryle,' (none of us would have dared address him other than Sir), 'in the States we only recognise two sorts and they both die, so what the hell'. The crude truth of that statement struck us all like a thunderbolt, and it was something that not even the master could cope with as the firm moved on hastily to the next patient. Leukaemia is not and never has been a subject for humour, and none was intended here, but it was simply an essay into bringing us all, including consultants, down to earth from the ivory-towered castle where we were taking refuge from our sense of impotence.

Later on my experience of the disease was confined to children, where the chronic varieties were non-existent, and the only merciful thing about it all was the rapidity with which the inevitable end was reached. Instead of a course of perhaps three or more years as in an adult with chronic leukaemia, children lasted rarely more than a few weeks, and the longest survival of an untreated case in my experience was six months, and that was considered quite remarkable at the time. At the other end of the scale, one child under my care lived less than twentyfour hours after its first admission for investigation of a fever where the diagnosis of leukaemia had not even been considered. That sort of thing was not thought of as at all unusual.

The only hope for those suffering from this disease was a mistaken diagnosis, which unfortunately was a pretty rare occurrence. I once had a case of a boy who was discharged home to end his days there, as there was nothing that could be done for him in hospital. Some weeks later his GP rang me to say that he was taking an unconscionable time a-dying, and he had just seen him dash past the surgery window on his bicycle in apparently robust health, and what ought he to do about it. I promptly invoked the aid of my friend and colleague Dr Barnet Levin at the Queen Elizabeth Hospital for Children, whose formidable brain power was equalled only by his knowledge of diseases of the blood, and it turned out that we had got the diagnosis wrong, and the boy had a rare but non-fatal disease of quite a different kind. Naturally the parents were delighted at the news, something that would seem not unnatural, though one cannot but conjecture what might have happened in modern times, and for what tort, malfeasance or other offence might we have been taken to court, and what damages might have been awarded? Perhaps we should have escaped the worst rigours of the law, because I had been taught, and certainly taught others, never to give an absolutely hopeless prognosis in any case of leukaemia in view of the possibility of a misdiagnosis. The chances were always remote, and I regret to say that I never had another similar experience.

With the passage of time, treatment that did have some effect on the course of the disease began to appear, but as the basis of it was the use of very toxic drugs, the treatment was very unpleasant in almost every respect. The sole exception was the use of steroids, which not only removed all the symptoms and signs of the disease but induced a feeling of remarkable well being. If only, but if only, the effects could have been permanent, what a wonderful thing it would have been. There was one other non-toxic treatment that I encountered in a drug trial with a derivative of royal jelly, which was imported by a continental drug firm. It smelled like honey and it tasted like honey, but regretfully its effect as a form of treatment appeared to be nil and it disappeared from the scene with some rapidity.

Whilst no specific drug was found that cured the disease by itself, treatment was developed using a number of different ones in various combinations and permutations, and by varying routes of administration. These things combined with total destruction of the bone marrow by radiation and subsequent marrow grafts have led to the position where a number of cases have survived well beyond the five year period, and the use of the word 'cure' seems justified, which is a truly remarkable and wonderful thing by any standards. Unfortunately such treatments require facilities that were not available in ordinary hospitals, and my subsequent cases were referred to special units set up for the purpose. In this disease it was the natural and obvious thing to do, but it should also be remembered that we ignored the enormous inconvenience to the relatives, and the trauma to a child of being in solitary isolation in a strange hospital in a vast city. For quite different reasons, this time financial, it would appear that deep therapy treatment is to be made available in only a few regional centres, and once again patients will have to travel faster and further.

Leaving the scene of paediatrics, and in the position of senior citizen, leukaemia has once again entered my consciousness, not as a diagnostic or therapeutic problem, but in the fact that a not inconsiderable number of contemporaries have developed the disease. That fact now causes it to appear as a relatively common condition and certainly one of major medical importance, as opposed to the views that we held many years ago. In spite of all the advances that have been made, the length of survival in these people has not been all that remarkable, often no longer than those cases for which there was no treatment when I was a student. We must just hope.

PERHAPS MORE HARM THAN GOOD

Part 1. Acute Osteomyelitis

It is doubtful whether the history of the disease has ever been much discussed because it is assumed by doctors in general, and surgeons in particular that whatever treatment they have undertaken has been for the patient's benefit. Oh that it always really had been so. The condition no longer looms very large in the category of disease, though it still occurs, but at the turn of the century it was the commonest surgical emergency admitted to hospital, outnumbering acute appendicits. By 1932 the positions had been reversed, but the treatment had not changed. What then is this disease, and what was its treatment? The disease, as the name indicates, is an infection of the bone marrow leading to an abscess formation within the rigid confines of the bone itself. It matters not at all in which part of the body it occurs, but any acute inflammation from a simple septic spot to a full abscess always gives rise to a painful swelling of the tissues in and around itself. When it is the bone marrow that is involved, it is surrounded on all sides by entirely rigid bone which will not allow any swelling to take place, with the result that the pressure within the bone rises, causing not just pain but excruciating pain. Any child, and they are the main ones affected, will scream on the approach of anybody in a white coat, because they know they will touch or even move the affected limb, either of which causes terrible suffering. When that is added to all the other symptoms associated with an acute infection and fever, it becomes clear what an awesome disease this is. Prior to the turn of the century, it was a condition not only of extreme gravity but also of frequent occurrence. By the 1930s that invidious position had given way to acute appendicitis, but even so it was anything but rare, and at Guy's Hospital some one or two cases could be expected to present themselves each week, compared with perhaps ten to fifteen people with acute appendicitis. The decrease in the incidence was due directly to the rising standard of living, and the cleanliness and improved personal hygiene associated with better housing. The reason why those factors played such a direct part in reducing the frequency is due to the fact that in acute osteomyelitis the entry into the body of the staphylococcus, the main germ concerned, is nearly always through the skin, and whilst it is fortunate that only a small percentage of children who have skin infections develop osteomyelitis, the incidence of the disease is bound to be proportional to the numbers of children in the area who are suffering from such skin diseases as scabies, impetigo, furuncles, boils, infected wounds and carbuncles. Such was the situation before the end of the nineteenth century that almost every slum child had some variety of skin infection most of the time, and consequently the potential reservoir of candidates who might develop osteomyelitis was immense. The physique, health and hygiene of the modern child bears no relationship whatsoever to the Dickensian pauperised waif, and acute osteomyelitis has largely disappeared with that change. Naturally the vast proportion of cases occurred in children, but sometimes adults were affected, though mostly they were people who were suffering from recurrences of an original attack in childhood dating back many years.

With the benefit of hindsight, when it comes to a consideration of the way these cases were treated, it is now possible to realise how really dreadful it was, though nobody recognised the fact at the time, or they would not have carried it out. This must have been due to the fact that the disease posed a considerable risk to life, and the surgeons who dealt with the cases assumed that they were trying to save it by what appeared to them to be sound surgical principles, and it took many years to persuade them otherwise. It would be difficult to say with any certainty just how many children actually lost their lives because of the treatment, but probably it was not inconsiderable, though many would have succumbed anyway, but all of them whether they survived or not would have suffered rather less had treatment been a great deal less drastic.

In view of the fact that classical examples of the disease, once so common, are now almost unknown in the UK, it is necessary to describe what they were like, because only then is it possible to understand why there were treated as they were, and why it was almost impossible to persuade anyone to modify it.

The extremely ill child presented with a very high fever and all the symptoms that went with it, but especially vomiting and dehydration, with the addition of an acutely inflamed limb, red, swollen and tense with the overlying skin shining under the pressure. To the child, those things were relatively unimportant compared with the ghastly pain it was suffering and the terror that it would be made worse by people, especially doctors, touching the affected part and making the agony even worse. Their fears were well founded because for one reason or another, some of them essential for diagnostic purposes, and others less essential for instructing students, a good deal of manipulation was inflicted on the unfortunate victims. It needs little imagination to realise that these were some of the most ill and most miserable creatures that it was possible to encounter. To the medical mind the position was quite straightforward, for here was a condition where there was an acute abscess with the pus under pressure, and every surgical principle taught that the undoubtedly correct procedure was to drain it as soon as possible. It was what had always been done in the past, and much the same as one did with abscesses elsewhere in the body, though in fact in the latter matter they were not quite correct. It seemed obvious that if such an established and orthodox treatment was carried out and the patient survived, it must be due to the treatment. How wrong can one be?

The routine arrangements for this treatment were to prepare the child for surgery by witholding all food and fluid (once again standard pre-anaesthetic practice), ignoring the fact that the previous vomiting and fever had already produced dehydration, which in modern times would have merited an immediate intravenous infusion. The unfortunate victim, now in this very sad condition, was then anaesthetised with chloroform and ether, which by their nature were both toxic drugs. The operation consisted of an enormous skin incision along the complete length of the affected limb down to the bone where, using a gouge and a hammer, the entire front aspect of the bone was chipped away leaving the marrow cavity bleeding and exposed so that no further pressure abscesses could form. The wound was then packed with vaseline gauze and the patient returned to the ward. Provided that the child survived the operation, and most of them did, the wound had to be dressed daily, when the pus sodden gauze was removed, the area washed out with an antiseptic Eusol solution and repacked with fresh vaseline gauze. This unhappy procedure, which was excruciatingly painful, fell to the lot of the reluctant surgical dresser to carry out, and even before he reached the bedside pushing the tell-tale dressing trolley, the child was bellowing and screaming with apprehension, which none of those who carried it out are likely to forget. Some exaggeration, it may be thought; but *I* think not because I was there. Post-operatively some cases died from the toxic effects of the illness, combined with blood poisoning and the shock of the operation, but the others endured a long and gruelling convalescence of many weeks until they finally healed. Sometimes that was the end of the disease, but many cases suffered one or more discharging sinuses due to retained pieces of dead bone which had to be surgically removed, and were also subject to further recurrences of the acute disease in other limbs. In such an event, the local appearance was exactly as it had been in the first attack, but with the astonishing difference that the patient was hardly ill at all, and the pain minimal. It was wrongly assumed that all these things were due to the natural course of the disease, but they were quite wrong and those who thought otherwise were considered to be slightly mad.

What then was wrong about the standard treatment? It lay in the fact that when the child was admitted to hospital it was still suffering from an active blood stream infection, something that ought to have had much more attention paid to it, because finding the germs in a blood culture was a well known diagnostic feature. At that stage what the body's natural defensive mechanism was desperately trying to do, was to wall off and localise the infection out of the blood stream and into the bone, and had there been no surgical interference a localised abscess would have formed there, provided of course that the child survived. The trouble was that everyone assumed that an operation was life-saving, and if the child died without one it would be a case of gross negligence. It was difficult, or more accurately, impossible to get a surgeon to withold his hand until the condition could have been dealt with by a limited surgical procedure. What the operation described actually did was to counteract everything that the body's natural defences were attempting to achieve by removing in its entirety the area of bone that was trying to localise the abscess and, if that wasn't bad enough, it also allowed pus to pour all over the exposed bone marrow, which with its very liberal supply of open blood vessels made certain that far from localising the trouble, there was now pus circulating in the blood stream to every part of the body as a condition known as pyaemia. It no doubt accounted for some deaths that might not otherwise have occurred, and certainly was responsible for the development of secondary abscesses in other parts of the body, all of which led to further operations. A small number of people tried very hard to persuade surgeons not to operate at the stage when the bacteria were still circulating in the blood stream, but to leave the child alone when it could be treated with fluids and analgesics until a much less extensive operation could be performed. Amongst the arguments put forward to support this unpopular view was the incontravertible fact that when osteomyelitis happened to occur, not in a limb but in a spinal or a pelvic bone, certain anatomical difficulties made it impossible to operate in the acute stage, and even the most enthusiastic surgeon had to wait until the position of the abscess revealed itself; only then could it be drained with safety. All that was being asked was that they should treat the very same disease in the long bones in exactly the same manner. Regretfully, the success we achieved was minimal because everybody was irrevocably wedded to the much respected aphorism, 'that the operation had been a great success, but unfortunately the patient died'. Naturally the relations believed it, and so did the majority of the medical profession. The possibility that the treatment might have been lethal was rejected out of hand, and it was many years before subsequent events proved that those who advocated surgical restraint were correct.

Salvation came in two quite unrelated happenings. The first was during the Spanish Civil War, where as in all wars, osteomyelitis is the hand-maiden of battle wounds. On the Republican side, which was almost always on the retreat and short of medical supplies, one of their surgeons, Dr Trueta, apparently found that he had neither the time, nor the facilities nor even the materials to carry out what was considered the correct treatment, and all that he could manage was minimal surgery and then encasing the limb in plaster of Paris, after which the soldier was sent back to base, where it was assumed that he would certainly die. As the retreat continued, Trueta caught up with these patients and discovered that, far from succumbing, they had done very much better than they probably would have had standard treatment been possible. Whether he knew it or not, his treatment was on exactly the same principles that had been devised by the Guy's Consultant Surgeon John Hilton and delivered in a series of lectures during 1860–62 at the Royal College of Surgeons, *On the Influence of Mechanical and Physiological Rest in the Treatment of Accidents and Surgical Diseases, and the Diagnostic Value of Pain*, and subsequently known throughout the world as Hilton's principle of rest and pain. Following the defeat of the Republican army, Trueta moved to Oxford where he achieved great eminence as the Professor of Orthopaedic Surgery, and was responsible for the introduction of treating acute osteomyelitis with just the minimal surgical interference, which consisted of drilling a few holes down to the marrow cavity and then encasing the limb in a plaster cast. Fortuntely, the introduction of penicillin further revolutionised the treatment and made it possible to control the blood poisoning stage very rapidly and safely before any operation was undertaken. Even so, this idea was not easily accepted by some surgeons, and the mere sight of an acutely inflamed limb made them feel that immediate operative interference was paramount, and they were not easily restrained, if at all. Personally I was fortunate in that I worked in close co-operation with Mr J H Mayer at Pembury Hospital, and we agreed that any operation should be delayed until after the blood poisoning had been controlled by the antibiotics. This led to a greatly reduced local deformity and scarring, with the additional bonus that a number of cases escaped operation altogether and made a full recovery without one. Thus another chapter in the annals of unwise surgery, done with the best of motives, came to an end, but 'The road to Hell is paved with good intentions.'

Part 2. Serum Treatment

I hope I am not doing this subject an injustice including it here because in 1932 some of the diseases such as diphtheria and spotted fever for which serum was the basis of treatment were no longer as common as they used to be, but even so, what I observed of their usefulness was not impressive. The trouble is that there can be few if any doctors still alive who could give an expert opinion on the difference the introduction of this form of therapy made to the diseases for which it was used, because they were conditions for which there had been no treatment at all previously. Those who like myself entered the scene towards the end of the era could only make their own judgements, and there are not so many of us around these days. A further difficulty arises, as will be discussed later, where a new serum was introduced that left us in no doubt as to the balance of therapeutic good and evil, but it unquestionably tends to warp one's judgement.

The serum which was used was obtained from animals, mainly horses which were inoculated with a vaccine until they had developed a high degree of immunity to a specific disease, whereupon the serum was used as injections to treat the same disease in humans. The Wellcome Foundation laboratories at Beckenham, amongst others, kept a large number of horses solely for the production of serum, and as the active life of these animals was several years, the amount of serum produced and distributed was very considerable. It is now probable that most of if not all such manufacture has ceased, and when the balance sheet for this period comes to be struck, there may perhaps be something on the credit side, but not a great deal. Just how effective this treatment really was is not easy to assess, because it can be done only on a personal judgement in conditions where scientific investigations with controlled trials were out of the question. It is impossible to do that sort of thing where the risk to life is great and there is no alternative treatment for the control group.

Anti-sera, as they were called, were available for the treatment of diphtheria, typhoid, tetanus, pneumococcal and meningococcal infections and anthrax. Later there was a so-called anti-streptococcal serum which will have to be dealt with separately. In this list of diseases I never had any experience of treating typhoid fever either directly or indirectly, and it would be presumptuous for me to comment on it.

Diphtheria

At the turn of the century and for ages previously, this was a common and terrifying disease, so much so that it continued to leave its mark on medical practice long after it had ceased to be common. Thus, when as students we attended the twelve compulsory sessions at the South Eastern Fever Hospital, the Superintendant, who was the tutor and an authority on diphtheria, devoted no less than ten of those sessions solely to diphtheria, and compressed all the other infectious fevers into the remaining two. However, during the three months that the course lasted he was unable to demonstrate a single case of the disease, and subsequently only a very few appeared in practice. All of these were promptly transferred to isolation hospitals, so that one never really got to know what the treatment actually achieved.

Although the disease had been very rare for a good many years, it was still the routine procedure at Guy's for every case of sore throat that presented at Casualty to have a special swab taken to exclude diphtheria. If the Medical Officer was at all suspicious that the case might be a true diphtheria, (bearing in mind that none of us had ever seen a case) a prophylactic dose of anti-diphtheritic serum was injected. In a long experience I am unable to recall a single positive case, though the practice continued unabated for many years. Another relic of the past was the diphtheria alarm bell which was activated from the porters' lodge in the Residents' College. It had been installed so that it could be rung if there was a case of respiratory obstruction in the front surgery, and whoever heard it had to rush there to perform an emergency tracheostomy. Nobody in my time ever heard the bell ring, and nor were any of us called on to emulate 'The Prooshian Bates', the headmaster in Kipling's Stalky & Co., who heroically sucked a diphtheric membrane from Stetson Major's throat, presumably in a mouth to mouth operation. It is clear that diphtheria had been an extremely serious disease that loomed large in the minds of both medical and lay personnel, and many a doctor must have had to deal with such cases.

I did in fact once perform an emergency tracheostomy, but that had nothing to do with diphtheria. I was Resident Medical Officer at a small London Children's hospital when an infant suffering from laryngitis was admitted in great distress, showing all the signs that a tracheostomy was going to be required. Urgent phone calls all over London failed to locate the Ear Nose and Throat surgeon, who anyway was very much a part-time appointment making infrequent visits, nor could any other surgeon be contacted, and as the respiratory distress grew progressively worse I had to do the operation myself. This was an operation that in theory at least I knew perfectly well how to perform, but had never had to put it to practical use. Even now after some fifty years I can still remember the essential details that I had drummed into my head in case the need should arise, because it is not one that would allow a quick visit to the library for reference purposes. In theory the operation should be quite easy to perform since the windpipe lies just beneath the skin of the neck, but in fact there are two great difficulties. In the first place the obstruction to the respiratory passages causes great congestion of the blood vessels in the head and neck, and intense cyanosis from lack of oxygen, so that once the overlying skin has been incised the entire operation area disappears in a sea of dark blood which cannot be stemmed until the windpipe has been opened and respiration restored. Consequently the rest of the operation has to be done blind, and unless one remembers to keep identifying the landmarks it is easy to miss the windpipe. The second difficulty lies in the fact that, when having opened the trachea there is a natural tendency to withdraw the scalpel, and if one does, the cut edges override one another, and in such a bloody scene it is nigh unto impossible to reopen the wound. It is essential to insert a tracheostomy tube before the scalpel is removed. Assuming that the procedure has been successfully completed, the patient, who incidentally is not anaesthetised, is able to take a huge gasping breath, and there lies the rub, because it not only takes in very much needed air, but also a very much unwanted quantity of blood that enters the lungs and can have disastrous results. Some days later, regretfully this was the outcome in my solitary essay into emergency tracheostomy. Many years later, with the co-operation of a very skilled Ear Nose and Throat surgeon, Mr John Clark, I ran a special unit for cases of laryngitis, where obstruction to the respiration can be very severe and very acute. No such smash and grab operations such as I have described were allowed or even contemplated because, as he always said, an emergency tracheostomy was just as fatal as cutting the patient's throat! By that time he had devised other means of dealing temporarily with the acute obstruction until a theatre had been prepared and a set operation under general anaesthesia with complete control of the bleeding could be done. They weren't very often necessary, and happily none of the cases died. Needless to say that none of these many cases suffered from diphtheria.

Pneumococcal Infections

The serum treatment of this disease was an odd affair, because unlike the other diseases in this group, there was not one serum, but no less than ten, each specific against its own particular type of pneumococcus, though useless against any of the others. To complicate matters further, there were an almost equal number of other types for which there was no active serum. This meant that it was first necessary to identify the germ involved, a procedure that might take several days, and sometimes no definite organism was ever discovered. This might well have meant that the patient had died or recovered before the specific serum treatment could commence, so the practice was to inject sera against types one and two on a purely speculative basis, as they were the most common types involved. It is very doubtful how much benefit this treatment conferred in cases of pneumonia, and in pneumococcal meningitis it was probably nil. This is not surprising because even when modern and very effective antibiotics are available, even they prove ineffective unless treatment is started very early in the course of the disease.

Finally there was one case of pneumonia that seems worth mentioning because it shows the very different attitude to experimental treatment in those days, compared with the present time when there are ethical committees and other safeguards to control such actions. A middle-aged woman with pneumonia had not responded to serum treatment, and the consultant decided to try the effect of an intravenous injection of bile salts, based on the fact that as pneumococci were soluble in bile in the laboratory, they might well react in the same way in the blood stream. As I was a student at the time I was unaware of the details of how the treatment was carried out, but the following morning the unfortunate lady was intensely jaundiced and stone dead. No comment was made by anybody, and it all seems like a bad dream nowadays when treatment is so efficient.

Meningococcal Infections

This is dealt with in the section on meningitis.

Tetanus

Anti-tetanus serum was considered to act specifically on the nervous system rather than on the tetanus bacilli themselves, and was supposed to limit the extent or even totally prevent the toxic effects on the nervous system. The disease then as now was relatively uncommon, but had a very high mortality rate, and it is dubious as to what extent the serum affected the course of the disease. Although it is a quite an infrequent occurrence in ordinary civilian circumstances, it was a very common complication of wounds on the Western Front in the 1914—18 War where the battles that caused such terrible slaughter were fought over argicultural land that had been cultivated for generations with animal manure, a rich source of tetanus germs, and the disease must have added many thousands of deaths to the total of that holocaust. In my own experience only a modest number of cases came under my care, and if there was any beneficial effect of serum treatment it was not clinically very obvious, so that the unfortunate patients had to endure the horrors of the disease until they either recovered or died, regretfully rather more in the latter than the former category. It was more than obvious that what was required was some means of controlling the spasms and convulsions, and prior to the introduction of curare and its related drugs it was almost impossible. I treated several cases with bromethol (Avertin), which had been introduced originally as the first of the basal anaesthetics. It was administered rectally and produced a semi-comatose state that lasted some four to six hours, after which further doses could be given for several days. It was a great improvement on anything previously available, but nothing like as effective as modern paralytic regimes, though these required very specialised management in special departments. Avertin certainly controlled the worst of the symptoms and several cases recovered, but they were always the ones where the general outlook was known to be less serious. To indicate the extraordinary progress that has been made in the treatment, the last case that came under my care had a wound on the face and, as a case of cephalic tetanus, would almost certainly have proved fatal. He was transferred for treatment to the special unit in Oxford, and in due course reappeared in our out-patient department none the worse for wear nor considered to be anything unusual. Serum played no part in his treatment.

Anthrax

Sclavo's serum, which was produced from donkeys rather than horses, was the standard treatment for this disease, and it was injected into the abdominal wall on account of the large volume that had to be given. As a disease affecting human beings it is not very common in the UK, but in the area around Guy's Hospital there was a large hide and leather industry, with the result that occasionally employees became infected, and I saw two cases, both of which were fatal. The first was when I was a student and I saw very little of the patient, but the second was a burly porter with a classical anthrax boil on his neck caused by an abrasion from carrying infected hides on his shoulder, and even now I recall the fierce intensity of the inflammation. It was like a huge boil with a gangrenous centre, surrounded by a fiery red iron hard swelling, and beyond that, tissue fluid swelling that spread far and wide. He didn't seem so very ill on admission, but the course of the disease was rapidly downhill in spite of heroic doses of serum. This so distressed the House Physician looking after him, that he kept on phoning the consultant to ask if there was anything more that could be done, and eventually he was told that there was nothing and that he was to go to bed. With the greatest reluctance he complied, but the next morning the man was dead.

Anti-Streptococcal serum

This form of treatment had a meteoric career, and there is no other word that can so accurately describe it. The appellation 'streptococcal' was misleading, because most of the cases where it was used had no definite evidence of such an infection, and it was all based on an assumption that streptococci were the cause. It would appear that by some odd quirk of fate its introduction must have coincided with an outbreak of a self-limiting virus infection that was not recognised as such, but the cases seemed to respond dramatically to the treatment, though it is impossible to think that it really could have had any effect, and yet on one ward round, a consultant physician described it as the greatest advance that had been made in therapeutics. Unfortunately it was after only a short period of time that the apparent benefits from its use became less and less obvious, and consequently it was administered in larger and larger doses, but still without benefit, and it was only a matter of two or three years later that Sir J J Conybeare, on one of his ward rounds, observed that in his opinion the serum had never done anyone the slightest bit of good, and on the contrary an awful lot of people had suffered a great deal of harm. What he was referring to was the syndrome that came to be known as serum sickness.

Serum Sickness

Nobody ever regretted the disappearance of this condition which was clinically dramatic, and above all extremely unpleasant for the victim. It was purely and simply the result of injecting large amounts of a foreign protein, in this case horse serum, which produced a condition with the highly dramatic clinical picture of a very ill patient with a high fever, widespread skin rashes and swellings which could make the face unrecognisable, and intestinal, pulmonary and neurological involvement with their related clinical symptoms. Skin irritation was intense, and so was the misery it caused, to which could be added abdominal pain, vomiting and diarrhoea, as well as painful swollen joints which, if associated with heart murmurs as they often were, caused difficulty in the differential diagnosis from various forms of arthritis as well as organic heart disease. The reason for this was that the sera were used to treat infections which could have their own complications exactly the same as those found in serum sickness, and it could prove quite a diagnostic problem. There was no very satisfactory treatment except to stop the injections and administer adrenaline, because no other antihistamine drugs were available. Even if they had been, it is doubtful whether they would have had much effect on such an overwhelming reaction, and only modern day steroids would have been able to cope with the situation. Unfortunately they were still many years in the future, and there can be no wonder that the moment alternate treatments became available serum therapy was rapidly abandoned. Doubtless the overall idea that generated the regime was a good one, but in practice it turned out quite the opposite, and in retrospect it was not one of the happiest experiences in the history of medicine.

To be fair it must be admitted that this chapter has been an almost exclusively subjective description of the state of affairs, drawing only on memory and not on fact, yet the picture remains clear of many cases of awful serum sickness

and very few of an impression that serum made much difference to the outcome of the disease for which it had been used.
However it was once again a matter where these volumes of
serum were pumped into patients in the belief that it was
doing good, and possibly it might have been; but nowhere was
there anybody who seemed to question the truth of their belief
and perhaps Oliver Cromwell should have been invoked once
again: 'Considerist thou that thou mightst be wrong'.

Part 3. Rheumatic Fever

There can be no doubt that this subject more than earns its
place in this section of ill repute, though there was never any
doubt in anybody's mind that we were engaged in a beneficial
act for a large section of the population. We were not.

The first thing is to define exactly what is being discussed,
because there is no such medical disease as rheumatism, even
though the term is widely used as though there were. If it has
any meaning at all, it simply indicates that a person suffers
from pains in the joints or the back, or both. However, with
certain suffixes and prefixes it indicates definite diseases often
bearing no relation to each other except for the pain. Thus for
example, rheumatic fever and rheumatoid arthritis have much
in common, but they are totally unrelated conditions. What is
being discussed here is the disease *rheumatic fever*, which in 1932
and for generations previously, and for at least ten years to
come was one of the greatest scourges of Britain. It is now
either almost or completely unknown. It was essentially an
affection of children and young adults, and unlike other similar
diseases it never caused any permanent damage to the joints,
and consequently no deformity, disablement or crippling, but
on the other hand it was the cause of awesome and widespread
heart disease, an organ that the other types of 'rheumatic'
disease broadly speaking tended to eschew. One of the major
difficulties that the medical profession had to face was the
difficulty of diagnosis, because although nobody could miss a
full blooded acute attack, it was the so called sub-acute attacks
that, if they actually did exist, were reputed to be just as
dangerous to the heart. It is simply a matter of record that in
those times the differentiation between all the possible diseases

was not very well done, with the result that when it came to statistical surveys, and there were many, about the causes, incidence, complications and the effect of treatment of rheumatic fever, a good deal of error crept into the results and led to many false assumptions.

As mentioned above, one of the greatest changes in the pattern of disease in the period under review is the fact that rheumatic fever is now a rare and relatively unimportant disease, whereas in the 1930s it loomed very large indeed in the field of medicine. Its manifestations and its machinations extended like tentacles into many different areas of health and education, including children's wards, general wards, convalescent homes and the public health departments of local authorities; and had there been such things at that time, it would also have been a major, if not the major cause of those attending cardiac units. Thus where rheumatic fever was concerned, it was the possibility of developing heart disease that made everyone ultra-cautious, especially as there was the widespread though erroneous belief that if the patient was subjected to a prolonged period of bed rest, it lessened the chances of heart disease developing or if it did occur it reduced the amount of permanent damage that might be done. Consequently, in any case where there was any suspicion of such a diagnosis, it seemed much wiser to call it rheumatic fever and treat it accordingly. Had it been known that most of the treatment that was used, and there was no shortage of it, did absolutely no good, and in many of the cases, especially those that had been misdiagnosed, a great deal of harm, things would have been very different.

Once a child had been diagnosed as suffering from rheumatic fever it came under a regime that took control of its life for many years to come, and certainly until the end of its school days. This disease and tuberculosis were the only conditions which were subjected to continuous medical supervision in the days before the modern ubiquitous follow-up clinics became the rule. The whole attitude to the management of rheumatic fever was based on the undoubted fact that as a disease 'it licked the joints and bit the heart'. This was a convenient way of reminding people that, although the joint pains were a major feature of an acute attack, and could be extremely distressing, they never caused any permanent damage or disability, whereas the involvement of the heart, which at that stage hardly ever gave rise to any symptoms of which the patient or the parents were aware, was the cause of the subsequent grave disability and an early death. Consequently the entire management of these cases was directed absolutely to all forms of treatment that were believed to be beneficial to the heart, both immediately and with the future in view. The former might possibly have done some, though not very much good, whereas on balance most of the latter was harmful.

Although nowadays, with the benefit of hindsight it is easy to be critical of the way things were done in those days, it has to be remembered that the effect of rheumatic fever on the heart could be disastrous. There was not only the immediate attack, but the high probability of recurrent episodes causing further heart involvement, and even when the acute attacks had passed and the rest of the body was unaffected, the disease continued in the heart as a chronic process. It damaged the heart muscle, scarred, deformed and narrowed the valves, causing obstruction to the blood flow, or they became incompetent and diminished the ability of the heart to maintain its output; and it also interfered with the nerve control of the heart's rate and rhythm. Sometimes it produced a lot of scarring of the tissues surrounding the heart, causing the entire organ to become attached to the ribs, which added a huge burden to an already damaged heart, so that the difficulty of pumping was enormously increased. All these things were of common occurrence, and they not only greatly shortened life, but equally limited the physical activity that was possible in the few years of it that remained. It is no wonder that the disease and its machinations loomed so large in the physician's mind, because they knew that once any of those conditions developed there was nothing radical that could be done to alter the state of affairs, and one just had to watch the patient's downward progress to the inevitable end. Because of these grim possibilities, the treatment was aimed at trying to limit the amount of heart damage, and once again heroic measures were invoked. It was an unquestioned fact that recurrent attacks of the disease were the main cause of the heart damage extending, and therefore treatment was aimed at two things, firstly to try and prevent the recurrences, and secondly to protect the heart muscle if they did occur. With regard to the former, epidemiological study made it obvious that the incidence of rheumatic fever was commoner in those families who lived in a damp environment, and in one of the most dramatic surveys ever made of the disease, a map was drawn showing the incidence and the areas where the cases in London occurred. This revealed a concentration along the banks of the Thames and its tributaries, but with one mystifying exception. Even this apparent aberration proved to be in the same mould, because it was subsequently discovered that these cases were occurring along the course of the Fleet river, which was no longer visible since it had been covered over many years previously, and houses built along its course as it continued to run subterreanally. As a prophylactic measure, efforts were made to try and improve the housing conditions of those who developed the disease, and where possible they were moved to other and better accommodation elsewhere, though in fact it was an achievement more often hoped for than attained. The disease was not by any means confined exclusively to such damp environments, and it even occurred in places where drought rather than dampness was the order of the day, but they were much rarer. In general it was an affliction of the poorer section of the population, but it was not unknown for it to rear its ugly head amongst the more affluent of the population and even, if rarely, in public schools.

Although very little was known about the actual cause of the disease, it was an undoubted fact that each attack was almost always preceded by a throat infection with a specific germ, the haemolytic streptococcus, and this led to the most unscientific, illogical and ill-conceived bit of therapy that can be imagined. They removed the child's tonsils in the pathetic belief that they were the *fons et origo* of the infection, whereas they were really nature's first line of defence against it! Truly the medical profession has much for which to rend its garments and don both sackcloth and ashes. The trouble here was that it was done on such a massive scale, that in the end the London County Council's Statistics Department became cognizant of the fact that it was absurd, and they set about discouraging the practice, though only with moderate success. In order to accomplish this operation the children were admitted to Ear Nose and Throat wards, where nobody seemed to bother about the fact that most of the other patients were suffering from acute mastoiditis. In practically all those cases the main infecting organism was the dreaded h. streptococcus, which had spread to every nook and cranny of the ward, with the result that not infrequently the unfortunate rheumatic children, now *sans* tonsils, were reinfected with disastrous results. When this is added to the fact that removing the tonsils is nearly always a useless operation, and that it carries the risk of a small mortality rate on its own account, (not so small in those days), it is probable that this aspect of the prophylactic treatment did nothing but harm. Finally there is an addendum which highlights the absurdity of certain practices that were carried out for years without anyone recognising the fact. Although not directly related to rheumatic fever, it was to be found in ENT wards where, as already mentioned, a very high proportion of the patients were suffering from diseases due to the haemolytic streptococcus, and although there was much cross infection nobody took any notice of it. If, however, one of the cases developed a red skin rash, then it was obvious that the diagnosis was scarlet fever, which was a notifiable infectious disease, so that the case was sent to an isolation hospital and the ward was then closed to all admissions until no further cases had occurred for at least seven days. What was bizarre about the procedure is the fact that the only difference between scarlet fever and the other cases with the h. streptococcal infection was the development of a rash, which made it neither more nor less infectious than the other patients, and yet the ward was closed for the one but not the other.

The actual treatment of an attack of acute rheumatic fever could be summed up in two words, salicilates and rest, and in what extremes they were used. The drug of choice was sodium salicilate, a close relation of aspirin, which seemed almost specific because even in small doses it brought down the temperature and cured the joint pains and swelling within twenty-four hours, but it was thought that if used up to the maximum dose that could be tolerated, it had some curative effect on the disease itself. To achieve this state of affairs, the dose was raised until the amount of salicilate circulating in the blood was brought perilously near the level where it was poisonous, and sometimes if there was a lot of sweating and dehydration the blood level did actually go over the top, producing some remarkable examples of what was called salicilism, where the symptoms were most unpleasant, and could be fatal, though things rarely went that far. It should be added that nobody imagined the treatment had any effect on the streptococci, which anyway had not been active for ten to fourteen days before the onset of the rheumatic fever. The second part of the treatment was forced bed rest, and the manner in which it was carried out was to say the least, heroic if not horrific. The children were made to lie flat in bed, often without even a pillow, usually wearing a canvas restraining jacket that prevented almost all bodily movement. They were not supposed to move at all, and were even fed whilst still lying in the supine position, and were never allowed to sit up. By the time this absurd regime was abandoned, it was generally agreed that the struggling it engendered caused a greater output of energy than if the children had simply been kept in bed as in any other disease. These methods were rigorously applied whilst there was any fever or fast pulse rate, and when that stage was over it was followed by a further period of simply being confined to bed for at least a further six weeks. When in later years a new test called the sedimentation rate was introduced, it was accepted as a much more accurate method of judging the activity of the disease than the clinical thermometer and general observation, so that the duration of bed rest was decided by its results, but even so it was very rarely less than six weeks, and was frequently very much more. No one surely ever doubted but that these measures were doing the patient a great deal of good! It was a long time before that dubiety arrived.

It should be apparent that the object of the treatment in the acute phase was to reduce to a minimum the amount of work that was put on the heart muscle, and the same general principle governed the subsequent management of the cases for the rest of their lives. This meant that any child who was diagnosed as having had rheumatic fever, and once again it must be stressed that a great many of them had never even had the disease, came into the clutches of the local authority Rheumatic Fever Service, and amongst these organisations it was generally agreed that the London County Council ran one of the best in the country. The Children were collected from their homes in special buses, taken to special schools for the physically handicapped (they were called physically defective in those days), and transported back to their homes at the end of the day. At any sign of their general health being not quite normal, they were sent to convalescent homes for long periods, where the physical and mental effort required of them was even less than before. They lived a life far removed from the realities of the hard cold world, but nobody at that time would have questioned this method of dealing with the disease. Now with the benefit of modern knowledge and hindsight, it is obvious that it could not have done any good to any of them, and in many ways did a great deal of harm by forcing them into unnecessarily restricted lives. However no blame can be attached either to the local authorities or the medical profession of those days because all the statistical surveys showed that no less than 60% of all the cases when they were discharged from the service never had any further trouble, and remained well and free from rheumatic fever and its complications for the rest of their lives. These were certainly impressive figures which seemed to justify the great expense involved, and it was not until the consultant paediatrician to the London County Council revealed the fact that, in his opinion 60% of the cases that were dealt with by the authority had been misdiagnosed, and had either never had nor ever developed the disease. In his opinion, the remaining 40% who had actually suffered from rheumatic fever were in no better condition than they would have been if all the treatment they had undergone had never taken place. As a footnote to all this, one might mention that some of the misdiagnosed children received a very rude shock in 1939, when they were drafted as physically A1 into the army, having previously lived a sheltered and protected existence, only to realise that in fact the world was not really a bit like that.

When the children reached the end of their school days they were discharged from the special service, and as it so happens this is also the age at which recurrences of rheumatic fever tend to become less frequent and disappear. The combination of these two things removed them from continuous medical supervision, and even most of those whose hearts had been affected suffered no symptoms from them because, in spite of what had happened, they worked perfectly well and allowed them to lead normal lives for a number of years. They only reappeared in hospital when the more or less inevitable progress of the heart disease or complications from it gave rise to trouble. One of the commonest manifestations was acute heart failure brought on by a combination of two factors. The first was the result of gradually progressive scarring and narrowing of one of the heart valves, the mitral, which caused progressively increasing obstruction to the blood flow, and this in turn made extra work for the heart muscle which had to overcome it, and which as a rule it managed to cope with for a number of years. The final straw was the loss of control of the nerve mechanism that governed the heart's rate and rhythm, and this produced a grossly irregular and extremely fast heart rate that rapidly led to heart failure. Although the first attack was relatively easy to control, the episode presaged the beginning of the end. Purely by chance the very first acute emergency that I had to deal with in my very first house appointment after qualification was just such a case, of a girl aged twenty who was not known ever to have had an attack of rheumatic fever, but when admitted to hospital she was extremely ill, breathless, blue and swollen. She was treated by a method called venesection, a very old established procedure with which Pepys would have been totally familiar, though in the vernacular of his time it was just called blood-letting. The result was dramatic. At one moment she was apparently moribund, and very shortly afterwards enormously improved, and I always felt that the incident had, in foxhunting terms, well and truly blooded me into my new status.

In many of these cases of congestive heart failure with which that unfortumate young lady was smitten, they also suffered from severe abdominal pain which was caused by the swelling of a congested and swollen liver, and the recommended treatment to obtain symptomatic relief was to apply leeches to the skin over the affected area. These intriguing little creatures were still in occasional use, and they were delivered from the dispensary where, according to legend, they had been kept in a well-starved state so that in theory they would be ravenous for blood. They arrived in their personal narrow corked test tubes, and the recommended procedure was to put some milk and sugar on the patient's skin, uncork the tube and place the open end where one wanted the damned thing to bite, attach itself and start blood sucking. I am afraid that personally I never managed to persuade a single one of the wily creatures to do any of those things, no matter which end of it I offered to the supposedly appetising skin, not being sure which was the cranial or the caudal end. I never encountered anybody else who had more success than that, and consequently it is impossible to say how effective a treatment they proved to be.

However the main method of treating these cases was to control the gross disturbance of the heart rate and rhythm with the drug digitalis, a measure which is still just as routine at the present time. The only real difference was that in those days the only preparations available were either a tincture or pills made from the dried leaves of foxglove plants. Although their active constituent had been only roughly assayed, with the result that the potency varied from batch to batch, they both worked very well, though of course not with the speed or consistency of modern preparations. A new accurately standardised remedy, Nativelle's digitalin, was just coming into use, and another drug called strophanthin was also available; but sadly one other called veratrone viride, which was derived from lily of the valley, had very recently been deleted from the British pharmacopea. It seemed an awful pity, as it would have been so much nicer and more romantic to have been able to prescribe something infinitely more exotic than foxglove leaves.

The subsequent progress of these cases was progressively downhill until death from terminal heart failure, or they developed a superadded infection of the heart valves and heart lining called subacute bacterial endocarditis, which was inevitably fatal and for which there was no real treatment. It was not until open heart surgery made it possible for surgeons to relieve valvular obstructions that any real progress was made, but it was the advent of antibiotics that proved to be the greatest benefactor, for not only did they make infective endocarditis treatable and non-fatal, but their ability to control h. streptococcal infections abolished the incidence of rheumatic fever almost completely. Surveyed from this distance and with the benefit of hindsight, it is probabably true to say that the hospital treatment here described did very little if any good, and perhaps a great deal of harm. What a mercy both for doctors and patients that those who carried it out with so much care and dedication were blissfully unaware at the time. It is difficult to think why none of us gave much if any attention to the fact that unnecessary and prolonged stay in bed did the patient no good, and the measures that were resorted to must have been very hard to bear. Patients in those days had a pathetic confidence in what the doctors in teaching hospitals were doing for them, something that has disappeared with the years until those doctors' successors really can produce miracles of treatment. The recipients are of course universally grateful for those efforts, as the unending string of court cases demanding huge damages readily testifies.

THE BOTTOMLESS PIT

Part 1. Blood Transfusion

There is a story, in all probability apocryphal, of a Pope in the Middle Ages who suffered from anaemia, and his Jewish physician who hailed from Padua treated him with a transfusion of ox blood. Needless to say, it proved fatal, and the prognosis of the physician was none too good either when it was decided to sever his head from his shoulders as a reward for his troubles. This must have been one of the very few, possibly unique occasions where a medical procedure had a mortality rate of 200%. It is just worth conjecturing the fact that, had the two procedures been reversed in sequence, the physician's blood might have been used for the Pope's transfusion, and he might have survived and been much improved or even cured, because there was always the chance that the two bloods might have been compatible. It would not have made a lot of difference to the physician, though possibly he might have been the posthumous recipient of some Papal award. However the point of this story is that the idea of pouring various fluids into the veins as a method of treatment is very old indeed, but much more important is the fact that its unwise use can be, and still is very dangerous. Nowadays the risks are small, but it remains true that once a drip has been set up any liquid can be poured down it, either by accident, ignorance or with malice aforethought as in Hitler's death camps, and as a method of judicial execution in the United States. It would be nice to think that apart from those incidents, all the others have been beneficial; but regretfully this is not so, and iatrogenic intravenous fatalities have been anything but rare.

Obviously blood transfusion was not a practical proposition until the various different groups had been identified. In those days when a patient at Guy's Hospital required a blood transfusion, it fell to the students to do the grouping, and the facilities such as they were, existed in a rather gloomy clinical laboratory situated at the top of the medical block far removed from the main laboratories. The ampoules of grouping sera were undated, unrefrigerated and, I suspect, inactivated, because almost every patient turned out to be a universal recipient blood group 4/0, but even when on rare occasions they didn't, so little did I trust my technique that no matter what happened on the microscope slide, every case that I dealt with was reported as group 4, and much the same thing held for all the other students! Incidentally it was also our duty to do the routine blood counts in the same laboratory, and the results were equally unreliable. Fortunately, when the result really mattered a further count was done by the haematologist.

When the patient had been grouped, the House Officer rang the London Blood Transfusion Service to supply a suitable donor, because there was no stored blood available. In small country hospitals, there was no transfusion service on which they could call, but there was a list of grouped voluntary donors who could be contacted, and the house officer had to telephone around until a compatible one could be found. No matter by what means they were procured, these donors were a most noble band of people, even more so than those of to-day, because in addition to needing a social conscience they had to be brave as well. It has always been the practice in the United Kingdom for blood donors to serve in a purely voluntary capacity, but prior to the outbreak of war in 1939 instead of attending blood-taking sessions staffed by skilled operators, held at special clinics at convenient times, they were prepared to have their lives interrupted at any hour of the day or night, and then make their own way to the hospital and submit to a blood-letting by people of very varying skill and experience. Some people can and some people cannot get a needle into a vein, and though mainly things went well there were a good many bruised and battered donors' arms, often after a long and bitter struggle, which at its worst 'did naught availeth'. Lack of dexterity to that degree was rare, but in the transfusion service of that time those noble people who offered their blood knew what they might be facing.

The techniques of transfusion were not all that different from the present time, though there was perhaps more bias towards syringes than gravity. At the North Middlesex Hospital there was a very different technique in use where the donor and the recipient lay alongside each other on stretcher trolleys separated only by screens. Their arm veins were connected to each other by a long rubber tube at the centre of which was a most ingeniously designed all-glass, two-way syringe that contained absolutely no valves or taps of any kind, and the only moving part was the grooved piston. It had one possible disadvantage, and that lay in the fact that if the piston was rotated in the wrong direction, blood could be transfused in the reverse direction from the recipient into the donor by mistake, but I never knew this to happen. As a method of transfusion, there was nothing to be said for having such a close conjunction of donor and recipient, but it seems surprising that this entirely tapless type of two-way syringe never came into popular use. It certainly would have lent itself to manufacture in plastic form in the modern era of disposables.

Naturally, when conditions such as these prevailed, blood had to be used much more circumspectly than is fashionable nowadays, and it was unusual to transfuse more than a single pint to a patient at any one time. It would have been extremely uncommon to have had a bottle of cross-matched blood ready pre-operatively, and if there were sudden calls for large amounts in cases of real emergency, gum-saline was infused until a donor could be obtained, though sometimes the hospital staff gave blood if there was no other source available. In fact neither doctors or nurses were encouraged to act as donors, because it was considered that the natural hazards of their occupation should not be increased. Personally I only acted as a donor on two occasions, which was partly due to the fact that I was not a Group 4, and that after an attack of infective hepatitis (yellow jaundice), nobody showed any further interest in using my blood.

When in about 1937 it was obvious that war was approaching, a profound change in the donor system took shape. A national system was set up to have as many as possible of the population blood-grouped both with a view to their being donors or possibly recipients in case of air-raids; and this information was subsequently added to their identity cards when these were issued in 1939. The central committee also discussed setting up a blood bank and even designed the shape of the storage bottles, which seemed to have undergone very little change since that time. I was a very junior member of that committee, and was put in charge of the grouping centres for part of SE London. These were staffed by student and nurse volunteers from the hours of 6 to 9 p.m., but the public response was minimal. No doubt the publicity had not been very good, and in an effort to improve it we tried to get the local cinemas to show information slides with their other advertisements during the interval. Here again the co-operation was poor, and I recall getting a very dusty answer and a blank refusal from the manager of a picture house in Lower Rd, Bermondsey. Equally, it came to pass a couple of years later during the Battle of Britain, that the very same picture house received a direct hit from a bomb during a night attack and as I motored past the following morning, I conjectured as to who the manager was at the time. It brought to mind a quotation from Tennyson's *Morte d'Arthur*, 'and God fulfills himself in many ways'. As this shamefully poor response of the people to get themselves grouped was moving towards a national scandal, Commander Stephen King-Hall made a radio appeal, and such was the force of his style that suddenly the clinics were overwhelmed with attenders and the whole operation was completed in about four weeks. Out of this beginning there grew the National Blood Transfusion Service, still entirely voluntary and the envy of a great many other countries.

As said previously, blood transfusions used to be much less commonly undertaken, but when the supply is free and available in almost unlimited amounts, the list of indications for its use become longer and longer, possibly too long, but it is only fair to point out that there is nothing new about it, and it has been the position for a long time. In 1935 one of the consultants to the Children's Department at Guy's Hospital insisted that all his cases of pyloric stenosis had to have a blood transfusion on the two successive days prior to operation, irrespective of the clinical condition. As the main risk of life in this disease was contracting a hospital infection rather than any hazard of surgery, he must have imagined that the extra blood would have some protective effect. It certainly had no such action, and apart from being a waste of blood the practice was just an odd quirk of that particular paediatrician. As his House Physician I was trained so to do, and it was a great surprise subsequently to discover that it was used nowhere else.

Substitution transfusion which may be used in several diseases had not even been thought of at that time because Rhesus blood groups were unknown, and leukaemia was hardly thought of as a treatable disease. The condition that is now called haemolytic disease of the newborn was then known as icterus gravis neonatorum, and its cause was completely unknown. It manifested itself by destroying the newborn infant's red blood cells at an horrendous rate, as a result of which the baby became very anaemic and very very jaundiced. There was no treatment for it except for that devised by Dr A C Hampson, which was thought to be very effective and had a wide vogue, and was even described by Mr G F Gibberd, an eminent obstetrician, as one of the great advances in paediatrics. The procedure was to take a pint of the mother's blood into a sterile jam jar, place it in the refrigerator until the clot had separated and then inject 20 ml of the supernatant serum into the infant's buttocks for three to four days. It was made clear that a donor should not be used as there was something in the maternal blood that affected the condition! Indeed how right they were about it having an effect; but what an effect, because it was exactly the wrong thing to do, and instead of helping matters it gave the infant an extra dose of the substance that was causing all the trouble, and could only have made the position worse. The fact that this treatment was not only thought to be beneficial when actually it was very harmful, and remarkably in addition it remained in vogue for a number of years, goes to show how difficult it can be to judge the effect of a treatment without at least having a comparable control group. In the end it was the treatment of repeated substitution transfusions, devised by Louis Diamond at Harvard, that transformed the prognosis by removing the antibodies that were causing the destruction of the infant's red blood cells, and at the same time replacing its blood with non-susceptible cells that would not be affected. The number of infant lives and the damage to their brains that have been saved by this method must be enormous, because the treatment is and was the only recognised way of dealing with the condition. Even this major therapeutic achievement was superseded by Sir Cyril Clarke, who devised a prophylactic measure that has led to the disease becoming extremely rare, though substitution transfusion remains the treatment in such cases as do occur.

At this point a not unrelated anecdote would not be out of place. One of the pleasanter occupations of a paediatrician is to be asked to care for one's colleague's children, and amongst these was a dental colleague's American-born wife, who early on in our association said to me, en passant, 'Say Norman, I wonder whether you have ever heard of my uncle, Louis Diamond, who's a paediatrician in the States?' After making her a triple obeisance I could only reply that it was rather like asking one of the Apostles whether they had ever heard of Jesus Christ.

In the early days of substitution transfusion the actual procedure could be a nightmare, because each paediatric department had to devise its own apparatus which involved a lot of tubing, several syringes and three way taps, which finally connected to an umbilical catheter which was in fact a gum-elastic ureteric catheter borrowed from the genito-urinary department, and it had a very small internal bore quite unsuited to the injecting and withdrawing of a viscous fluid like blood. It was obvious that polythene plastic tubing such as was used in the insulation of electric flex would be much more suitable, and I wrote to a British manufacturer to see if it could be procured. Their most courteous reply stated that there would be no difficulty at all in manufacturing what was required, but we would have to accept a minimum of one complete run of the machine which was some 6000, or was it 60,000 miles at an horrendous cost that immediately ruled it out of court, when only a few yards would be required annually. As is usual in these matters, it was left to the United States of America to get any sense of co-operation out of their industrialists, and they cornered a worldwide market leading to the production of complete plastic substition transfusion sets ready packed and sterilised for immediate use. Taking all things together, blood transfusion has come a long way since the anaemic Pope, and just when everything seemed set fair a hurricane called AIDS appeared, threatening to blow the ship off course, though the British transfusion service was very quick off the mark to remove the risks, but the country's eminent persons and their like now have to travel to the more exotic places equipped with their own supply of blood and the means to instil it if and when required.

No doubt can be cast upon the fact that blood transfusion is one of the greatest therapeutic measures in medicine, possibly the greatest, and it has opened up new vistas in the practice of surgery undreamed of in 1934. With the passage of time and the advances made by the profession, the demand for blood will increase unless or until some other substitute for it can be found. Indeed the quantities required will be, like so many other good things, an attempt to fill a truly bottomless pit.

Part 2. Non-Blood Intravenous Treatment

In the world league of great killer diseases, dehydration and an unbalancing of the various salts of the body's chemistry, in association with their handmaidens cholera, typhoid, dysentry and various other forms of intestinal upset must surely rank very high amongst the top ten together with tuberculosis, malaria, influenza and trauma. Diseases such as cancer and heart and blood vessel disorders which cause so much alarm and despondency in the western world, and very much less elsewhere, would no doubt be comfortably settled at the foot of the table. That at least was the situation until early in the 1940s when an understanding of the importance of blood chemistry gradually unfolded, and has since completely transformed the entire situation. It is known technically as fluid and electrolyte balance, but the term need concern us no longer.

In order to illustrate what this subject is all about, it has to be understood that blood is an extremely complex substance that is responsible for a myriad of different functions. It is a well known fact that it is made up of red cells, white cells and platelets, but in fact its greatest constituent is water, in which there are dissolved various salts and proteins, and it is these salts and the water that this subject is all about. The concentration of these substances in the blood is normally very closely controlled, and their levels show only minor variations, but when the body suffers a severe and unusual loss of fluid, complications occur. The reason for these great losses of fluid are mainly vomiting and diarrhoea, though in diabetes it is via the urine, and on occasions excessive sweating can be important. An example of the latter occurred when at the turn of the century an investigation was held into the condition known as miners' cramp, which was found to be caused by excessive sweating during long sessions in poorly ventilated coal mines. Sweat contains large amounts of common salt, and it was loss of this substance that gave rise to the symptoms, and the disease was cured by adding salt to the local beer. Much the same condition affects soldiers in hot climates and is indirectly the cause of so-called sun stroke. Until this was understood, the efforts to deal with the condition in the British army were based on the idea that the cause was the sun beating down on a soldier's neck and pictures taken in Victorian times show the soldiers with tunics buttoned up to their necks and cloths hanging down over the same area suspended from the rear of their pith helmets. Poor devils, and the treatment was useless into the bargain. The proper preventative was to make the men take a salt tablet each day, and how the Duke of Wellington would have been shocked to see the pictures of the troops in North Africa stripped to the waist in shorts, and possibly not even wearing a hat.

Similar situations arise, but in infinitely more serious forms, when the loss of fluid is brought about by vomiting or diarrhoea or, as is very common, both together in such diseases as cholera and dysentery. Here the loss of fluid may be prodigious leaving the body looking like a skeleton as so often protrayed on TV. These diseases have really come into their own in times of war, and it is probably true to say that until the Second World War, disease in one form or another, but especially gastro-enteritis was responsible for far more deaths than actual battle casualties. This was certainly true of the Crimean campaign and the South African War, in the latter of which those who were killed or died of wounds numbered about 5000, whereas disease was the cause of death in something like 25000 cases. All this happened before the time when it became possible to restore the fluid loss via the veins, and all that could be done was to give drinks by mouth, but it was self-defeating in view of the fact that most of it was vomited back again, and what remained down irritated the bowel and made the diarrhoea worse. The only possible remedy, and not very effective at that, was to try and semi-paralyse the intestine by means of administering opium in some form or another. In the Crimean war, pictures of the scenes in the wards of the hospital at Scutari are ubiquitous, though they do not portray it as I have always imagined the true picture to be. I think that as Florence Nightingale did her nightly rounds with her personal illumination in one hand, as the 'lady with the lamp' I feel sure that in the other she carried an outsize bottle of laudanum, the name for tincture of opium at that time. With that she would have calmed the wretched soldiers' fevered brows, and their even more fevered bowels, thus earning their eternal gratitude. I do hope that she did.

Since those days the enormous advance was made of supplying the lost fluids via the veins, thus short-circuiting the need to use the patient's intestinal system at all. However this method is not without its perils, and in the early days they were great. Once an intravenous infusion has been set up anything can be poured down it at any speed that one chooses. There are two essential dangers to be avoided, neither of which was realised at the beginning, but are now simply part of the general management of such things. When a patient has lost a great deal of fluid there is a natural inclination to replace it as quickly as possible, but the rate at which it can be done is not just at the whim of the physician's wish, but the fact that if the speed is too great it embarrasses the heart's ability to deal with the matter so that the patient, instead of dying of dehydration, dies of heart failure. The second danger lies in the fact that the patient has not only lost water but salts as well, and unless their replacement is carefully monitored disaster can ensue. Just as an example, because it happened so often in the early days, too much sodium chloride waterlogged the tissues and sometimes proved fatal, whereas too much potassium stopped the heart and definitely proved fatal. Originally all these things were done by guess work and rule of thumb, and in most adults their own body-regulating mechanisms corrected the human errors, but in children this was not so, and it is possibly true to say that intravenous drips in that group were more often fatal than therapeutic. Succour arrived in the form of laboratory estimations of the state of the blood, by which means the nature of the replacement required could be judged very accurately. Even nowadays laboratories require a minimum of ten millilitres (two teaspoonfuls) to carry out a full blood analysis, and this is a lot of blood to collect from a small dehydrated infant, especially as it may be required several times a day. This difficulty was solved by the late Dr Barnet Levin, who was pathologist at the Queen Elizabeth Hospital for Children in London, who devised methods by which it was possible to get a complete blood chemistry analysis on as little as one-tenth of that amount, with the results returned in an hour or less. It could now be claimed that intravenous treatment of that type was both safe and sound, and its transition from an almost lethal weapon to an ubiquitous life-saver in a period of less than thirty years was another modern miracle which was never really recognised as such and entirely missed by the media.

The advantage of using a patient's veins rather than their mouths is very attractive to doctors, and the method is being used more and more, so that it is now commonplace for drugs to be given that way and in addition it is possible to provide a complete diet for small premature babies, and some others by the same route. Once again we have a bottomless pit into which more and more will be poured as techniques continue to advance. At times one just wonders whether it cannot be overdone, because intravenous drips tend to be set up as a routine even in cases where the mouth could easily be used instead. Nowadays TV has brought all the gory details of accidents and violence into viewers' homes, and whenever a casualty is being removed on a stretcher there is one ambulance man in front, another at the rear, and a third at the side supporting a bottle of some intravenous fluid. May one be allowed to wonder whether they are all really necessary?

ASTHMA

Asthma is an awful disease, and yet in spite of its horrors it is difficult to get students and even doctors to appreciate just how unpleasant and dangerous it can be. The trouble is that the worst symptoms occur in the small hours of the morning when few people are about, and unless the attack is life-threateningly severe patients are not admitted to hospital, but suffer their distress at home because they are reluctant to call out their practitioner at that time of night. If the attack is so severe that they have to be admitted to hospital, they are usually much improved by the time the consultant physician and the students do their morning round, so that relatively few doctors get a picture of the disease as it really is. Were this not so, far fewer of them would tell their patients that they will have to learn to live with their disease, whereas the exact opposite is true and far too many of them or their families learn that they will die from it.

Mercifully I am not a sufferer, but I have had one attack and would not wish for any more. It happened at the end of the war when the blackout restrictions were removed, and domestically we found ourselves with many yards of black cotton cloth for which there was no apparent use. As clothes rationing remained in force for several years afterwards, it seemed a good idea to bleach this gloomy material and recycle it back into use as clothing. In order to achieve this end we filled the bath with an hypochlorite solution and immersed the blackout material, and within minutes I realised that I was inhaling a good deal more chlorine than was good for me, and so I donned the gas mask that had been issued to everyone at the outbreak of war, but which had never been needed. This was extremely fortunate because what little protection it provided lasted less than a minute and after that it was completely useless. In a short time I had developed a full blown attack of asthma, or as it would have been called, chlorine gas poisoning. I had asked for trouble and I certainly got it, but it did lead me to look up the literature on chlorine gas warfare in World War One, and there it was in the description of a hyperacute attack of asthma going on to pulmonary oedema and often death.

An asthmatic attack is really a symptom complex which can be set off by one or more of three triggers, each of which in themselves have multiple constituents. They are allergy, infection and psychological factors. Consequently the ideal way to treat the condition is to avoid or abolish the triggers, but such a thing is more easily said than done. An enormous amount of time and energy has been devoted to the allergic aspect, even to the development of full time allergists, all of which has helped but could hardly be claimed as an overwhelming success. In the early days this was partly due to a lack of a sense of proportion in interpreting skin tests, but it was also a fact that in addition to the genuine specially trained allergists there were a large number of offbeat practitioners who added nothing to the reputation of this speciality. Of course the ubiquitous house mite had not been identified, but one's experience of desensitisation against it even after its discovery has been, to put it mildly, unimpressive. Thus in the battle against protein sensitivity as a cause of asthma, much remains to be done. A great deal of progress has been made in the treatment of respiratory tract infections, and also in the understanding of mental processes, but in spite of all that, the conquest of all the factors that set off asthmatic attacks has been by no means complete. Consequently the treatment of the disease remains what it has always been: drug therapy aimed at prophylaxis, and when that fails, relief of the distressing respiratory attack. It is in this aspect that enormous progress has been made.

Even as students, it was obvious that the therapeutic armamentarium was very limited and largely ineffective. In addition to courses of desensitisation injections to real or imaginary allergens, there was adrenaline, ephedrine and the inhalation of the vapours of burning herbs, or taking them orally. It was one of the rare occasions when the medical profession actually encouraged smoking! Apart from adrenaline, it is probably true to say that all the other therapy had very little effect. The one really useful treatment was adrenaline injections, and their effect on an acute attack was quite dramatic especially in the early stages, but unfortunately its other side effects were exactly the opposite of what was needed. An attack of asthma is, goodness knows, frightening enough without the addition of those produced by adrenaline, and the tachycardia and hypertension are extremely undesirable, so its use was a mixed blessing. Sir Arthur Hurst, himself a severe asthmatic, devised his own technique for severe attacks. He started with a hypodermic injection of adrenaline 5 minims (0.4 ml) and then left the needle in situ, giving further amounts of 1 minim (0.08 ml) at intervals of one minute up to a total of 25 minims (2 ml) which was a pretty heroic dose. There was and still is one other drug, opium and its derivatives, which is of immense value in severe attacks, but its use gives rise to extreme argument, and even arouses passionate protestations in some people.

As a background to these views it should be said that at Guy's prior to 1939, morphia was freely prescribed in a vast variety of diseases, medical and surgical without any ill effects, and what is more the dosages used were larger than at other London teaching hospitals, where the standard amount was 1/6 grain, (10 milligrammes), whereas at Guy's it was 1/4 gr (15 mgm), and this was often increased to 1/3 gr (20 mgm), without anyone so much as raising an eyebrow, though some of the examiners in the final medicine viva voce blinked a bit if a candidate suggested such a thing. It was in such an environment that one could realise the great benefit that could be bestowed on suffering asthmatics without the disaster of addiction. However it is only fair to add that in every other respect asthma appears to be the classical disease in which opium should be avoided. Firstly because some patients have a disturbed psychological background only too ready for addiction, secondly it is a disease subject to recurrent attacks and therefore repeated dosage, and thirdly it is a drug that gives blessed relief where all else fails, a set of circumstances that must surely give rise to addiction. In fact this would be the case unless it is used with circumspection, an element of subterfuge, and even then administered only to the severest attacks. Dr Charles Cameron had decided views on this subject and worked on the basis that the British would believe anything about their bowels, so that when faced with an adult having a

severe attack he told them that what they needed was a good
bowel action, and then prescribed a combination of an opium
preparation combined with an anthracene purgative. The
former could be expected to have a continuing effect lasting
about six hours, whereas the latter had a latent interval of
approximately the same duration before exerting its effect.
Thus after taking the cocktail, the patient sank into a blissfully
sound sleep only to be awoken some hours later with ominous
rumblings in the lower bowel, and after a rapid visit to the
WC and a modest attack of diarrhoea the attack appeared to
have evaporated round the U bend. The patient's comment
was 'How right he was about my bowels'! A slight complication
lay in the fact that in the next attack, the patient wishing to
avoid a physician's fee might dose himself with a purgative
and end up with an unrelieved asthmatic attack complicated
by diarrhoea.

It was the general practice of the physicians at Guy's to use
opiates in adults with severe asthma, and in the paediatric
department it was routine, as there was no danger of addiction,
and the other supposed dangers of using it were, as they have
always been, imaginary. It is one of the odd quirks of medical
teaching that students are always told how dangerous it is to
use opiates in asthma, and for generations I taught the students,
undergraduate and postgraduate, that there were several ways
in which to ensure that they would fail their examinations.
They could physically attack the examiner, rape his wife or
state that they would use morphia in the treatment of asthma!
Thus it was with the greatest of pleasure that I was told by a
very capable Australian lady doctor to whom I had given such
a warning, that she had done just that and had nevertheless
passed the examination for the Diploma in Child Health.
When I enquired how this had come about she related in her
very best Strine that the examiner had, as expected, looked
very shocked and asked where she had learned such nonsense.
Having revealed the *fons et origo*, she told the examiner that
her own child suffered severely from the disease and that she
had tried everything else, all of which seemed quite useless,
but the opium was 'bloody marvellous' and that she proposed
to use it again and again. There was yet another unusual
occasion that goes to show that the supposed dangers of this
treatment are unreal. I was phoned by my HP in London to

say that there was an infant but a few weeks old, with very severe asthma who had been given all the usual treatments without response, and it was surely going to die. Was there anything more that they could do? I advised the administration of a large injection of steroids, and 2 mg of papaveratum, after which I heard no more, and so assumed that the worst had happened. On my next visit to the hospital I enquired of my HP what had happened to the baby, to which the reply was 'Your reputation has gone to the very top of the tree, because the infant went into a deep semi-coma for forty-eight hours and then woke up cured', but then as a sort of back handed compliment added, 'Of course we always did think that you were a bit mad; but what an enormous dose to prescribe'. In fact the 2 mg dose that I had advised was quite within the therapeutic range, so I asked what was meant by that remark, only to find that in error the HP had given the baby a dose of 20 mg! I only quote this, not to suggest that it is a good practice, but to show that even ten times the supposedly dangerous dose, had had no untoward effect in that particular case. It seems a pity that people continue to teach something which is manifestly untrue, and which many of them don't believe themselves, simply because text books copy one from another. In a career constantly bombarded with criticism for this treatment, my response was always the same: 'Have you tried it?' and the answer is always 'No'. 'Then how do you know that it's dangerous?' 'Because the books all say so', and at that stage my mind goes out to my 'disciple' somewhere in Australia, and I bless her for her courage to have tried and won.

The greatest advance in the treatment of asthma is the use of steroids, but they too have become embroiled in controversy and their use unecessarily restricted. Many people avoid the problem by favouring sodium cromoglycate, but as far as I was concerned it was in no way comparable to steroids, and neither did I have much use for isoprenaline, aminophylline or diazepam. My views have been developed from the fact that I was in a very unusual situation of being a consultant at both a London children's hospital, and a provincial non-teaching unit. At first sight there is nothing unusual about that, for many a London consultant makes pastoral visits to country hospitals, but I did exactly the opposite and was basically a countryman who paid, dare I call them pastoral visits to London? Let us now consider what happens in night emergencies, (and most severe asthma occurs at night), in these two different organisations. In the teaching hospital there is an HP in immediate control, who can call on the greater experience of the resident Medical Officer, who can then turn to the even more experienced Registrar or Senior Registrar. The consultant may or may not even have been informed as to what is happening, but in any case is very unlikely to be summoned to attend in person. I doubt whether anybody would disagree with the statement that consultants are but rarely found in teaching hospitals in the small hours of the night, and therefore don't see such cases until the following morning at the earliest, or even some days later when the emergency has passed, thus tending to lose touch with the realities of the situation. In the country hospital things are different, and until relatively recently there was nobody between the HP and the consultants, who consequently tended to find themselves at the bedside in the middle of the night helping to deal with these emergencies. As a result I was only too familiar with the true nature of severe nocturnal asthma, and of the limitations of the treatment available. Consequently, when steroids came on the scene it was obvious that a new and powerful weapon was at hand, and for the rest of my career I saw to it that cases under my care were treated with steroids whenever necessary.

Steroids in themselves are perfectly safe, and unlike almost every other drug there is no known dangerous top dose. The trouble lies in the side effects from continuous use, and sometimes these are unavoidable in the treatment of certain malignant diseases or surgical transplants; and in my view there are also a few asthmatics who are so severely affected that the side effects are preferable to death. I think that I can claim a little credit for drawing attention to the fact that asthma can be and is much more of a killer disease than is generally recognised, and that the old idea that it was just something that one had to learn to live with, was now out. In this matter I received some encouragement from the insurance companies who know much more about these things, because they have to put their money where the prognosis really lies. However, the vast proportion of asthmatics can be steroid treated and given enormously improved lives without any side effects, but it does mean constant medical supervision and regulation of the dosage. It is when patients are allowed repeat prescriptions without being seen that produces the awful side-effects that give rise to its bad reputation. The prophylactic use of steroid inhalers revolutionised the lives of most of those who used them properly, and having weighed up the efficiency of steroids against all the other supposedly less dangerous non-steroid inhalers and injections, I never again found any use for the latter group. Although I am now out of the active theatre of practice, word reaches me that more and more people are now turning to steroids, and I hope that it is true, but however one looks at things, this is a disease whose treatment has come a very long way from the days of ephedrine and fuming herbs.

ANTERIOR POLIOMYELITIS

It would be extremely difficult, in fact probably impossible to convey to those who have never experienced it, the horrors of an epidemic of this fell disease. It made a very considerable impact on my consciousness on two quite separate occasions separated by some twenty years. The first was at the age of seven or eight years old, when all the schools in Johannesburg were shut on account of an epidemic of infantile paralysis, and the children found their holidays extended by several weeks. Naturally we had no idea what the disease was or what it did; even the ominous words of the title meant nothing to us, and even though our area of movement was severely restricted, we had each other as playmates, and consequently we thought that anything which extended school holidays was an entirely good thing and ought to be encouraged. These facts are merely related to show that at a time when parents are extremely anxious and even terrified, their children, who are the potential victims, have no such qualms.

After that epidemic, polio as it came to be known seemed to disappear, and for the remainder of my schooldays, my time as a medical student and through all my junior hospital appointments it was a rare condition. Every now and then a sporadic case would appear and create a good deal of interest but nothing more, and it was soon forgotten. It was not until at least two or more years after the start of World War Two that it suddenly reappeared and presented itself again in epidemic form, and thereafter there were similar outbreaks every year. After the passing of high summer and the advent of autumn one's heart sank into one's boots as the prospect of another savaging of children hove into view. It was anything but apparent why the outbreaks always came at that time, and many theories were put forward, including one where a person had noticed that they seemed to coincide with a sudden increase in the mortality of hedgehogs run over on the roads, in spite of the much reduced wartime traffic, and it was suggested that these attractive little 'Tiggy-Winkles' might be the vectors of the virus. Of course it was not so, and in fact any epidemic of any kind can always be shown to coincide with some other phenomenon with which it is totally unconnected. In a very different context, there was once a group of public health experts who discovered that epidemics of summer diarrhoea in infants broke out when the six foot ground thermometer reached 68 deg F, and they were convinced that something happened at that depth and at that temperature to spark off an epidemic. Whether they conducted further work by excavation is not known, but Dr Charles Cameron, very much with tongue in cheek, pointed out that this was also the moment when Victoria plums turned from green to red, and he was equally 'convinced' that this was the cause! However, ground thermometers, Victoria plums or anything else for that matter, the appearance of flattened hedgehog corpses on the highways always gave me a jolt, presaging the frightfulness to come.

For the disease itself, there was nothing that could be done to prevent it, and nothing but palliative measures for those afflicted. The bare comfort that one could give the parents was that only a very small proportion of children who contracted the disease actually went to the stage of paralysis, and only about half of that group were seriously disabled. This knowledge did help a bit as I discovered when one of my own sons developed a fever during an epidemic, and the following morning had neck rigidity. Fortunately he was not one of the paralytic few, but the pangs of parenthood have never been greater.

When a case became paralysed there was nothing that could be done except to try and limit the damage in the affected muscles and assist recovery as best one could. It is in the nature of the disease that it has what might be called a retrogressive onset, in that after the initial paralysis there is no further spread, just the prospect of recovery of function, usually only partial, but it can be complete. This is a very important factor in dispensing what comfort one can to the parents at the stage where they are shocked by the paralysis, but even so have an even greater horror of creeping paralysis, which as the name suggests is where the damage increases, so that one is able to assure them that this will not happen. In order to achieve the maximum recovery it is necessary to have the co-operation of an orthopaedic surgeon who takes control of the necessary splinting and rehabilitation, because extra damage can be done if the muscles are stretched either by gravity or imbalance, and most surgeons demand to see the patient at the earliest possible moment. There was one occasion which can now be related because all those who were involved are dead, which concerns a child I was asked to see in a hospital other than my own. There was quite extensive paralysis and I sent an urgent request to the orthopaedic surgeon to see the case, but after some forty eight hours there had been no visit, nor would the surgeon concerned communicate with me, so in desperation I asked my usual colleague to stretch a point and advise on the child even though it wasn't in one of his hospitals, and he most readily agreed. In due course I managed to contact the erring party who informed me that he wouldn't see any case of acute poliomyelitis because he had a child of his own, and was unwilling to risk carrying the infection to it. I suppose that in some ways one can see a point in his attitude, but I had to inform him that against his one sibling, my orthopaedic colleague and I could muster no less than seven children, all of whom were at risk. This was the only occasion when I came across a doctor who eschewed the normal and admittedly not inconsiderable risks of our profession, and in my view he was despicable. Never again did we exchange a word.

Bulbar poliomyetitis, although it is not a different disease, has to be separated from the other varieties because it can and often does paralyse the muscles of respiration, and artificial ventilation is required. A good many years before there was any obvious or widespread need for such machines, Lord Nuffield had presented every hospital in the land with a box type, negative pressure respirator, and these had lain unused and unloved wherever a space could be found to store them. In any polio epidemic a few cases with bulbar paralysis can be expected, and in one such outbreak which started in a hoppers' camp at Paddock Wood in Kent, some 80% of the cases had this type of involvement, though fortunately most of them were not seriously embarrassed. Now of course was the moment to bring the respirators out of their long retirement and into action, and they proved to work very well provided they were not needed for more than a day or so. This was because these unfortunate patients had the added disability that they couldn't swallow their saliva or cough up any sputum, and so tended to drown in their own secretions, and consequently only those whose respiratory muscles recovered quickly survived. It was obvious that these secretions could be drained by the force of gravity, but to do so the patients had to be tilted to a precipitous sixty-degree head-down position because of two factors. The first is that when the body is lying flat in the supine position the trachea is running at an angle of twenty degrees in the *antigravity* direction, and consequently tilting the bed only twenty degrees just brings it level and nothing will drain. The extra forty degrees is needed because the bronchial secretions are somewhat viscous, and everyone knows that when trying to get tomato ketchup out of a bottle it has to be held almost vertical and given a sharp bang on the base before it will deliver its contents. Draining the bronchi is not dissimilar, and fortunately we had a considerable experience of this sort of thing with bronchiectatic children. At such an angle the danger of the patient slipping and dislocating the neck is very great, but we were well-prepared in having a supply of suspensory jackets that were made of sailcloth and webbing, and would have supported a large adult safely at any angle of tilt. There was one complication to our plans, and this was that the Nuffield respirator could only tip to an angle of twenty degrees, but the Works Department came to our aid and modified the machine so that it could obtain the necessary degree of inversion. This was a great improvement and most of the cases now survived, though there was one further complication to overcome, and that was the fact that when cases had to be treated for very long periods their general condition started to deteriorate, and this was due to the artificial respiration altering the blood chemistry, especially the acid/base balance, and so constant monitoring of the blood chemistry and the necessary therapeutic adjustments was required. This was difficult when the entire patient was enclosed in a box, but the problem was solved by the use of jacket-type positive pressure respirators, and bronchial drainage by suction. This required the services of an oto-rhino-laryngologist, and so the treatment of these cases passed to units where combined specialist care was available.

The box respirators went back into retirement and are probably no longer in existence, but there is a tailpiece that bears repetition. The Nuffield respirators were of course made in the factories of Morris Motors Ltd, and no doubt made use of various components that were common to the cars as well as the respirators. In some hospitals, when the machines were brought out to be got ready for use it was found that they were not fit for service, on account of the fact that they lacked various essential parts that had been removed surreptitiously over the years by hospital staff who wanted them as spares for their Morris cars.

The country was relieved of the horrors of the annual epidemic of polio by the introduction of prophylactic vaccination, and the disease has since disappeared, one hopes for good; but it should be remembered what fearful havoc was wreaked on the Allied forces in North Africa when a large susceptible population was introduced into an area where the disease was endemic, but largely masked by the high resistance of the locals. Great vigilance will always be required because once a disease becomes rare, people are less and less concerned about vaccination, and it could be that once again an unprotected population will be at risk. It must be hoped that this does not happen, even if it prevents some children getting an unexpected holiday bonus when schools have to be shut because of the infection.

FITS, CONVULSIONS, EPILEPSY

Between the years 1931 and 1976 the knowledge and understanding of the various types of fits, epilepsy or convulsions,
call them what you will, made enormous advances, and the
armamentarium of therapeutic drugs increased ten or twenty-
fold. Yet in spite of all this, treatment of the condition can still
present a difficult problem, so that the benefit reaped for the
afflicted has been comparatively small when compared to these
advances. The perfect treatment is nowhere in sight.

It is a somewhat rough and ready procedure to lump
together the very diverse ways in which fits manifest themselves
as though they were a single entity, because most certainly
they are not, but that is how things were in the past, and they
have not changed all that amount since. Provided that the
sufferer had no obvious primary cause such as a brain tumour,
disease of the kidneys, inflammation of the brain or a great
number of other less overt diseases, the fits were deemed to be
a disease in their own right and were therefore called idiopathic
epilepsy to distinguish them from the others which were
symptoms of those diseases just mentioned. The fits are again
further divided into groups according to the nature of the
attacks which can vary from a dramatic collapse into unconsciousness, lying on the ground with shaking and salivation
(grand mal), to a brief transient loss of consciousness that may
not even be observed by an onlooker (petit mal). Sometimes a
fit affects only a limited area of the body (Jacksonian fits), or
worst of all there are major attacks running one into another
which if not stopped can prove fatal (status epilepticus). The
above descriptions are based on happenings that can be
observed when the patient has an attack, but that is by no
means the end of the story, since there are a number of further
variations according to what happens in the brain; but these
were only identified after the invention of the electro-encephal-
ogram (EEG). All these facts have been mentioned only to

153

demonstrate that epilepsy is an extremely complex condition made up of many different facets, and a lot of lay people are reluctant to accept this fact, quite apart from the revulsion which the word epilepsy causes. 'The Falling Sickness' as it was originally called, is one of the oldest described diseases and it dates back to biblical times at least; since when there have been many eminent people, or 'personalities' in modern parlance that have been afflicted: Julius Caesar and Beethoven just for starters. Despite this very long history and the frequency and the ubiquity of its sufferers, the progress in treatment had until recently been anything but remarkable. No doubt in its time a mass of different remedies have been tried, from extract of toad's foot to mustard plasters, and incidentally a mustard bath was and still is a very good way of dealing with status epilepticus in the home, until more complex treatments are available. Surely arsenic and divers herbal extracts must have been tried, and it is probable that anyone with homeopathic leanings was tempted to prescribe a strychnine-type tonic. As a student in 1931, bromides were the basis of treatment, and they continued to play a major part for many years to come. As is the rule in any anti-convulsant treatment, some cases respond very well, some quite well and others not at all, and when the latter happens and the available drugs have all been tried, the natural tendency is to continually increase the dosage in the hope of a better result. This procedure has to be associated with another point of importance, which is that treatment, whatever its type, has to be continued for periods measured in years, and this when combined with a high dosage leads to cumulative effects, and in fact overdosage. As might be expected when using drugs that are acting on the brain, any such overdosage tends to manifest itself as mental symptoms, but this has not always been immediately recognised as such. The difficulty in assessing the cause of the deterioration is the fact that epileptics with uncontrolled convulsions can also produce very similar mental changes, due to the actual attacks themselves and not related to any treatment. It is not surprising that doctors faced with such a situation are more inclined to attribute any deterioration in the patient to the disease rather than the treatment they have been using. In the case of the drug potassium bromide, this was shown in an extraordinary way when a very considerable number of cases had deteriorated mentally to such an extent that they had to be admitted to mental hospitals, under the impression that their fits had produced major brain degeneration and they could no longer be managed at home. Sometime later, a research worker investigating these unfortunate people discovered that the level of bromide circulating in their blood was inordinately high, and when the treatment was stopped their mental state returned to normal. This type of error still occurred in isolated cases when I was in practice, and I have no doubt that it still does.

About this time phenobarbitone, which had been available for some years, was beginning to be more widely prescribed, alone or in combination with bromide, and in the end it replaced the latter completely. In fact all subsequent treatment has been along similar lines using combinations and permutations of the much greater range of medicaments now available, with a preference for certain groups of drugs according to the type of tracing revealed by the EEG. However there is still the tendency to increase the dose when the response to treatment is unsatisfactory, and some patients are so troubled by the side effects and overdosage that it makes one wonder whether the treatment is not worse than the disease. However, these relatively infrequent cases apart, it could be said that most people who suffer from fits respond well to treatment, and can manage a normal life, and where children are conerned it would be true to say that the vast proportion of those who suffer from fits, provided they are adequately treated, grow up to be adults who do not have them. A difficulty that can occur fortunately only in a small minority of cases is in those who fail to respond to treatment; the attacks get worse and more frequent, so that one just has to struggle on without success. When in due course paediatric neurologists appeared on the scene, it was with great alacrity that such children were referred to them, and it is something devoutly to be wished that one could say that there was a dramatic improvement in the results. Somehow it was not obvious.

There were one or two other aspects in the treatment of epilepsy which had a vogue for a time, and though not by any means ineffective, did not endure for long. The first of these, the epileptic colony, was based on the fact that people who suffer from fits may be at a serious disadvantage where employment is concerned, and this is due to several factors. In the first place most people, and that includes employers, have an innate fear and a dislike of any form of nervous disease, and consequently are disinclined to employ such people in their workforce if they can avoid it; but a much more important factor is the ever present possibility of them having a fit at work and damaging themselves or other people, especially if they happen to be driving a vehicle, working high above ground level or with machinery. It complicates the whole problem of compensation. Finally, whilst it is true to say that most epileptics are mentally quite normal, there are some who are not, and they are at an even greater disadvantage when it comes to finding work. To counteract all these things the concept of the epileptic colony was born, where protected employment and constant supervision could be provided. It was also possible to provide an environment in which patients were least likely to have fits, and that, somewhat strangely, was to work them hard both physically and mentally, and to keep the environment cold and the diet sparse! Unfortunately such circumstances had an appearance rather too much like those encountered in an extreme and brutal form in the Nazi concentration camps, and in general the lay population took rather a poor view of them. However this brings to mind an explanation of why in earlier times so many epileptics suffered from burns, not infrequently fatal, by falling into an open fireplace, an occurrence incidentally that is directly referred to in the Old Testament of the Bible. The classical example here is of a man who goes to work in an office, which in those days were rarely centrally heated, has a few sandwiches for lunch and then returns home tired out after long working hours, struggling in the rush hour traffic and hungry on account of his very light midday diet. Thus far he remained free from fits because all the conditions of the epileptic colony applied. However his good wife now provided him with an excellent and more than adequate meal, after which he rose from the table leaving her to clear away and do the washing up whilst he stood with his back to the open fire, filled his pipe, looked at the ceiling and allowed his mind to go blank. There he stood, warm, fully fed, mentally and physically unoccupied, and in just the conditions to have a fit which landed him unconscious tail first into the glowing embers. How awful.

There is another not altogether dissimilar hazard that these people run, and that is that after a major fit they can end up face downwards and unconscious for long periods. It is not unknown for the head to lie in a shallow pool of water, and they drown in only a few inches depth of it.

Another regime which was not without effect was the ketogenic diet, which in its way tended to produce a somewhat similar blood chemistry to that of the epileptic colony. Unfortunately it wasn't easy to stomach such a diet because a person who is ketosed feels very unwell, irritable and nauseated, and in order to produce and maintain that state of ketosis they would be faced with a breakfast that consisted of the yolks of two fried eggs on fried bread with a couple of rashers of fat bacon, all washed down with coffee and cream, mainly the latter, and the rest of the day's meals were much the same. An exaggeration perhaps, but not all that far from the truth. The use of this treatment went out of favour many years ago, as have many others once much in vogue, and if the universally perfect treatment has not yet been achieved one can rest assured that great efforts are being made to find it.

In view of the fact that epilepsy affects so many people, many of whom are very eminent in their different spheres, it seems odd that the general public is still so very ignorant of its nature, and has such a great fear of being involved in its manifestations. I used to tell students of the dangers that an epileptic ran if they were unlucky enough to have an attack in a public place. What should be done in such circumstances is to leave the person strictly alone, merely making sure that they run no risk from traffic or other hazards of their environment. What usually happens is that somebody rushes to be helpful; and on regaining consciousness the unfortunate epileptic finds that his shirt has been ripped open, and his necktie is lying in the muddy gutter. His chest is sore because when he stopped breathing and went blue he was given artificial respiration, possibly even external cardiac massage. His trousers are undone, and his mouth feels painful because somebody tried to open his clenched jaws, and in addition there is something in it. Further investigation on his part reveals the remarkable finding that there are two of his front teeth lying loose, and in addition he is harbouring a piece of a finger. In a panic he inspects his hands only to find that all ten digits are in place. Inexperienced overenthusiatic busybodies beware!

TONSILS AND ADENOIDS

If in the course of my life I have had any influence on any aspect of the practice of medicine, it would be as one of the small band who campaigned, and to some extent succeeded in reducing the numbers of children who were annually led to the slaughter of their innocent tonsils and adenoids. This is a subject that has always been very difficult to deal with on a rational basis because it so often raises strong passions; yet in spite of this it has to be said that it is neither a minor nor an unimportant matter considering the number of operations done each year, which are measured in thousands, and not so long ago in tens of thousands. There is no other surgical procedure, except ritual circumcision, which even approaches such proportions, and both operations are alike in that they are not carried out on the sick, the lame or the halt, but on the most robust section of the population, namely children. How has it come about? The answer lies in the fact that the tonsils, which are nothing more than two small pieces of the body's very ample supply of lymph gland tissue, happen to be sited in a place where they are easily accessible to the surgeon, and if only they had been positioned just a few centimetres further down the gullet, none of this problem would have arisen. It is germane to note that everywhere else in the body similar lymphoid tissue is left strictly alone, except for the purpose of taking a small piece out for diagnostic purposes, or when it happens to be invaded by cancer. There was a time when tuberculous glands in the neck were removed en masse in an operation called 'block dissection', but that operation has now been abandoned as a bad one, yet removal of the tonsils continues. Nobody would suggest that tonsils are removed just for the benefit of surgeons, though the operation to remove them must indeed have profited them greatly in the past hundred years. Personally I recall that as a child I was singularly free from illness, though my brother suffered from bilousness, and our Hanseatic family doctor, one Klotz by name, decided that it warranted him losing his tonsils. Although I was innocent of any such illness, it was decided that I too should be thrown to the wolves, with the result that one morning both of us were invited to take a few deep breaths, and relieved of our tonsils and adenoids, only to awake with ghastly sore throats. The operation did my brother no good at all, and I am sure I gained no benefit, for in my case the indication for surgery had nothing to do with illness. The surgeon surveyed the family, and decided that my father was good for an extra £50 if he mutilated both of us at the same time, though it must be made clear that such is not the reason why most of these operations are done.

It would be a reasonable assumption that the function of the tonsils is to act as the first line of defence in any infection of the throat, something that affects practically everyone in northern climates, and usually several times a year. The condition is no more romantic than the common cold or a sore throat, but if one wishes to be more esoteric then it is called tonsillitis in those lucky enough to boast such organs, and naso-pharyngitis if they haven't. In medical circles nowadays all these infections are lumped together as an upper respiratory tract infection (URTI), and this is probably the commonest diagnosis ever made. It so happens that nearly all children get these infections repeatedly when they first go to school, or much earlier if there is an older sibling already there to bring them home, and the consequent loss of schooling worries the parents, who not unnaturally want something done about it. Unfortunately there is not, nor is there likely to be a satisfactory answer to the problem until the common cold has been conquered, but some people came to the conclusion that perhaps it was the tonsils themselves that had become the source of, rather than the victim of infection. If one believes that sort of thing then the simple deduction must be 'If thine eye offend thee, pluck it out', and so removing the tonsils became the accepted procedure, because it all seemed so rational. If there were no tonsils then there could be no tonsillitis, which is just about as rational as saying that if there were no prisons there would be no criminals. What seems to have been completely overlooked is that removing the tonsils does absolutely nothing to get rid of the ubiquitous environmental infections, though it certainly abolishes the first line of defence against them, and consequently instead of having tonsillitis the children now suffer from a generalised infection of the nose and throat, which in many ways is rather less desirable, and even the most radical of surgeons have not so far suggested removing both those parts of the body as a cure!

But to return to the original postulate on which the whole rationale of removing the tonsils is based, namely that the tonsils have themselves become the source of infection and are no longer a barrier against it; is it possible that such a thing can be diagnosed with any accuracy? A lot of people believe that it can be done, but the means available are decidedly limited. Almost all that a doctor can do is to get the child to open its mouth so that he can have a look at the supposedly offending organs, and then feel in the neck to see if the local glands are enlarged. The latter procedure has almost no diagnostic value nowadays, because they are nearly always somewhat enlarged in most children at all times. With regard to the appearance of the tonsils, they may be large or small or craggy or have whitish material in them. If they are enlarged, so argue the tonsil removers, they must have got that way because of chronic or repeated infection and so ought to be removed; if they are small, so people say, they have been scarred and contracted by chronic infection and ought to be removed; if they are craggy, they have been deformed by chronic infection and out they must come, and if they have spots on them there can be no doubt of their villainy because there it is staring one in the eye, and definitely they must be ablated. This sort of reasoning makes it possible to incriminate any and every tonsil, and in such an Alice in Wonderland existence it is just a matter of 'Off with their heads', and not so very long ago this state of affairs was almost universal.

Once it is believed that the tonsils are in themselves a source of infection, the next stage is to delude oneself into believing what other ill effects they can produce, and with a *backward* step of about a hundred years, the concept of focal sepsis is reborn. This is an idea that has probably been responsible for more iatrogenic mayhem than all the rest of the medical misdemeanours put together. What then is or was focal sepsis? Presumably the idea originated through a series of deductions, unfortunately false, from the undoubted fact that if there is an undoubted focus of infection such as an abscess somewhere in the body, not only does it produce swelling, pain, tenderness etc locally but if not adequately dealt with produces ill-effects elsewhere in the body generally. The patient looks ill, feels ill and is ill. Anaemia develops, the body weight falls and in extreme cases death may ensue. Nobody would gainsay all that. What the focal sepsis theorists propounded was the idea that instead of an obvious causative abscess, there was a hidden small unobtrusive symptomless nidus of infection that like its more obvious brother was spreading its poisons all over the body in a quiet and sinister fashion. If one believes in such a theory, it is then possible to attribute to it the power to damage the body and make it responsible for any and every combination of symptoms imaginable. At one time or another these supposed, though usually unproven dens of iniquity have been indicted as the cause of such things as pallor, anaemia, stunted growth, failure to gain weight, poor scholastic ability, night terrors, bed wetting, anorexia, recurrent fever, constipation, diarrhoea, abdominal pain, headaches and migraine, to name but some, but above all the cause of recurrent coughs, colds and sore throats. A totally comprehensive list would include almost every disease in the book.

With such a catalogue of ill-happenings to be laid at its door, every tonsil in the land is under threat, because there is no bodily or nervous disability that cannot be attributed to it. However the situation is even worse than that, because everything mentioned so far has been originated by the medical profession, but unaided they surely could not have wrought the havoc they have done in the throats of innumerable victims. Their accomplices have been the children's parents who for some inexplicable reason are only too keen and determined to have their children operated on, and they encourage or even drive their doctors to carry out their wishes. It is more or less true to say that when somebody asks the doctor, 'Should my child's tonsils be removed'? what they are really implying is 'If you do not agree to take them out, I will find somebody else who will'. The result of all these irrational and illogical deductions was that between the wars there were, in the large cities, more children who had lost their tonsils than those who still retained them. Such a state of affairs caused even the lay members of the local authority to raise their eyebrows and feel that something must be wrong somewhere when presented with the annual report and statistics of their Medical Officers of Health.

In the course of my practice I encountered an enormous number of children who were referred to me suffering from exactly the same symptoms for which their tonsils and adenoids had previously been removed on the assumption that they were the cause of troubles elsewhere in the body, but those troubles remained uncured by the operation. In view of this fact and the number of cases involved, it seemed improbable one was dealing with the occasional error of diagnosis, but that the conception of disease of the tonsils being the cause of many and varied diseases elsewhere in the body was in fact a misconception. To prove this point a series of fifty cases was collected (it could easily have been many more), in whom it was possible to make an accurate diagnosis of what had really been the cause of their troubles, and which in fact were in no way whatsoever connected with the tonsils. The vast majority suffered from undiagnosed asthma, and several were, psychological upsets due to parental discord and broken homes, but the crowning error is almost impossible to believe. Nobody would suggest that a mistake of such proportions is at all common, but it is chronicled here to demonstrate that if one is prepared to consider the tonsils as the *fons et origo* of other diseases, then dreadful mistakes are possible. It was a child who had been quite well until he started to lose weight, became lethargic and generally failed to flourish. In view of the absence of any obvious cause he was referred to an Ear Nose and Throat surgeon, who decided that the tonsils were the cause of the boy's ill-being, and as a matter of some urgency he was admitted to hospital for their immediate removal. The operation, which was done under general anaesthesia, went without a hitch and all seemed to be well, except that unlike the rest of the batch of children whose tonsils had also been removed that day, he failed to regain consciousness. Towards evening when completing a clinic, and happening to be the only consultant in the hospital at the time, I was asked to see him, and it was a relatively easy thing to diagnose that he was in a deep diabetic coma, and of course everything now fell into place. Just how a child could go through so many medical hands without getting his urine tested was never discovered.

Of course this was a quite exceptional case, but the point I was trying to make, and did make in a profound way in this series, was that it is not a practical proposition to incriminate the tonsils as the cause of some other general disease. It would have been pleasant to have been able to report that such views and such an unwise practice have now been abandoned, but regretfully that is not the case.

When at long last there was a more general scepticism about the operation, many comprehensive studies, some of them involving thousands of cases, were undertaken, and statistically they almost always failed to show any real benefit from the operation. The surveys of any value have always compared groups who had not been so dealt with, and even that type of study failed to show any benefit. In reality they were not really genuine controlled trials, because what was on trial was the outcome of a specific operation which happened to be removal of the tonsils and comparing the results with an equivalent group of children who had had no operation. When trials are undertaken to test the value of a drug or medicine, there is always a third factor of administering a harmless placebo which of itself could not affect the disease, and assessing what effect it had. Had these surveys of tonsil operations been much more accurate, there would have been another comparable group who underwent a totally different operation, such as perhaps the removal of a normal appendix or circumcision, and then a survey of the results in all three groups, but of course on ethical grounds alone such a project is out of the question. However, had something of that nature been possible, it is quite likely that the unneccesary loss of the appendix, or any other small disposable part of the body for that matter, would show much the same effect as losing the tonsils.

Over the years many attempts have been made to try and find justifiable indications for tonsillectomy, and so far only two indisputable ones have emerged. The first is following the development of a quinsy or tonsillar abscess, and the second is malignant disease. In a career spanning forty-six years I only once encountered an example of the former, and none at all of the latter, though it must be said that one would not expect that disease in paediatrics, so that it seems to be a reasonable deduction that very few such operations are really necessary. If then it is difficult to discover a really convincing medical reason for the procedure, it might be illuminating to discover why the children themselves thought that they had been so dealt with, and most surprisingly such a survey has been done. One youth was quite unequivocal about it and told the interviewer that it was done as a form of castration to punish him for masturbating and having lewd thoughts! After its publication I used to teach students and anyone else within earshot, that the young man's deductions were quite as soundly based as those that the medical profession employed to justify the operation.

It would have been nice to have been able to say something comforting concerning this subject, but the best that can be done is to relate that there is one aspect that is less awful than it used to be fifty years ago. To the best of my knowledge, the practice of holding mass operating sessions using a tonsil guillotine, with the operation done as an out-patient procedure has been abandoned. In 1933, when the numbers to be dealt with were far too great for in-patient accommodation, the practice of the Ear Nose and Throat department was to hold a session once a week when about a dozen children were shepherded into a waiting area in the Casualty Department, and then each in turn was taken to the adjacent operating theatre where they were anaesthetised using ethyl chloride, which has a very rapid action and is a very unpleasant asphyxiating type of procedure. The tonsils were then removed by the students using a guillotine, which was an instrument in the shape of a handgun, where the barrel was a flattened steel plate ending in a ring-shaped orifice. When the trigger was retracted, a blunt ended plate descended and gripped whatever (in this case the tonsil) was in the ring, and then the whole instrument was forcibly rotated through 180 degrees thus avulsing the tonsil from its bed. The process was then repeated on the other tonsil. Blood flowed very freely but was much reduced by a douche of ice-cold water poured over the child's face. Provided that the haemorrhage ceased completely, the children were taken home in the afternoon suffering from a ghastly sore throat and medical maladministration, though it is doubtful if such thoughts entered the heads of the perpetrators. It is surely just as well that this bloody, useless operative procedure is no longer performed.

As far as can be judged there is no serious disability, just as there is no obvious benefit in removing the tonsils, so why make all the fuss? This is partly on economic grounds, because it wastes a great deal of money and resources, but much more importantly because it carries a risk, admittedly a small one, but nevertheless a danger to life, and it is small comfort to bereaved parents to know that thousands of other children survived the operation. There is no such thing as an absolutely safe operation, and tonsillectomy is no exception. Some years ago the annual mortality in the UK was about fifteen to twenty persons, though this was subsequently reduced to about ten, but there is reason to believe that this figure is a considerable underestimate, because there is always the possibility, nay probability that the death certificates in these cases indicate the disease for which the operation was done as being the cause of death, and that is what appears in the Registrar's statistics. However, if only one fatality occurred, it is too high a price to pay for an unnecessary procedure, and one can but hope that one day it will be a subject of medical history rather than a current medical practice.

OUT OF EVIL MAY YET COME GOOD

COELIAC DISEASE

This disease, which was once thought to be confined to children, is now known to affect people of all ages, though there may be differences in the cause from one case to another. It is neither particularly common nor especially rare, but it is a condition of great importance because at whatever age it appears it remains for the duration of one's lifetime. The other remarkable feature of the disease is the manner in which a most satisfactory treatment was discovered, born out of an event that in every other respect was a period of unmitigated evil.

Prior to the discovery of the treatment, every paediatric department had its quota of cases who attended out-patients regularly for what seemed to be years on end, and periodically when their condition deteriorated they were admitted to the wards. Everyone knew that the treatment did very little good, and the children were a pathetic sight, anaemic, pot-bellied, wasted, possibly with rickets and very stunted in growth, so much so that in the USA the disease was known as Herter's intestinal infantilism. In spite of all this they seemed to survive, and one hoped and even expected that in the end they would recover. What is so surprising is that although the condition was so well known, everyone laboured under a misapprehension as to what the future outlook was for the patient. Had any paediatricians been asked what happened to these cases, they would have said that in the end practically all of them got better. We were all quite wrong, because when a national survey was undertaken it revealed the fact that the actual course was progressively downhill, and although some children did have remissions they were not nearly as many as had been imagined, and the mortality rate was really very high. How then had this false impression arisen? The answer lay in the fact there was a sort of merry-go round behaviour with the children's parents, where treatment was concerned. As already stated, the various treatments that were in vogue were singularly ineffective, very difficult and laborious to carry out and dietetically awful for the children. Although it was the same in all hospitals, after a prolonged period of treatment that produced no very obviously satisfactory results, the parents became disillusioned with a particular clinic, and in desperation left that hospital and tried their luck at another, with the result that each paediatric department was always losing some cases to other hospitals, and at the same time receiving others from elsewhere. Thus when a case no longer attended at a clinic, the natural presumption was that it had moved to some other hospital and of course this was correct, but with the exception that it was not always to another clinic but to another hospital's mortuary. Naturally there were occasions when one's own cases died, but not surprisingly it turned out that they had been treated elsewhere at some time or another, and with characteristic charity it was assumed that was the cause! When the true state of affairs was revealed in about 1936 it came as a great shock to all concerned.

The only treatment that was used concentrated on trying to control what was universally accepted as the cause of the disease, quite incorrectly as it turned out. Everybody imagined that these cases suffered from an inability to digest fat, and therefore they removed as much fat as possible from the diet, which in the circumstances prevailing at the time seemed a perfectly reasonable thing to do. Now with the benefit of hindsight it is easy to see why the measure did not help, because it turned out that all the fat in the stool was only a symptom and not a cause of the disease and therefore its removal from the diet would do no good. It was exactly comparable to the way in which rickets had been treated before the discovery that it was due to a lack of vitamin D. In that disease the main symptoms were decalcification and deformity of the bones, so it seemed logical to administer massive doses of calcium. In both diseases the treatment was of no avail. As far as coeliac disease was concerned, nobody in their wildest dreams imagined that a substance called gluten that occurs in wheat and certain other flours was the root cause of all the trouble. As nobody was aware of this fact, and though the substance gluten was known to exist, its name never even entered into any discussion on the subject, which explains why none of the treatments did any good. In fact rather than withholding wheat flour from the diet, the amount was actually increased in order to supplement the calorie requirements after the dietary fat had been so drastically reduced. Of course the measure proved an unmitigated disaster, though it was not recognised as such and it was thought to be just an ordinary relapse of the disease.

In view of the awful results of the treatment, it was quite natural that several different types of fat free diets were tried, and one of these, the so-called banana regime showed more promise than any of the others, and might have led to the discovery of the true cause of the disease some years earlier, had it been carried out with greater determination. What happened was that as bananas had quite a large food value in themselves, the children were given a diet consisting solely of overripe bananas, which improved their health enormously, but because by itself this was not an adequate diet, fat-free additions had to be made, and as they inevitably included gluten containing flour they immediately led to a relapse. Everyone was convinced that it was the bananas themselves that were beneficial, because they had never heard of such a thing as anybody being sensitive to gluten, and of course did not realise that this was the only diet in which the offending substance had been totally removed, but of course only temporarily. Therefore no attempts were made to study the effects of the various additions as they were made; had this been done and the effects observed, gluten might have been incriminated much sooner. The supposed magic effect of the bananas was so enormous that, when war broke out in 1939 and fresh bananas disappeared for the next five years, the government's paediatric advisers persuaded them to import the fruit in dried form exclusively for the treatment of coeliac disease. In the event it was left to the Netherlands to unravel the mystery, when through force of circumstances, their wartime privations included not only bananas but almost everything else, and it is said that when no bread was available they resorted to eating concoctions of tulip bulbs. An inspired paediatrician observed that whilst the severe privations did no good whatever to the nation as a whole, his cases of coeliac disease benefited as never before, and further study revealed that it was the absence of wheat flour from their diets that had cured the disease, and that it was the gluten content and not the starch itself that was the actual cause of the trouble. It was a terrible burden that the Dutch nation as a whole had to endure, but out of evil sometimes good emerges, and in this case it was definitely so. Subsequent advances in diagnosis and management removed once and for all the terrible prognosis that had previously obtained.

There is one further observation to be made which had nothing whatever to do with the practice of medicine, but is germane to commercial operations and the laws of supply and demand. Modern treatment of coeliac disease, which incidentally is much commoner than had previously been thought, now allows a very acceptable diet which is not all that different from the normal. This has been achieved by devising special recipes using gluten-free flour, so that bread, cakes, biscuits, pastry and other things can be produced. Naturally this led to an enormous increase in the demand for this basic material now classified as a therapeutic agent and subject to the economics of the pharmaceutical industry. Prior to the discovery of gluten intolerance, gluten-free flour was just a much unwanted by-product in the process of manufacturing slimming breads, which consisted mainly of gluten and air, and tasted like it! Unfortunately there was no demand for the by-product and as a consequence it was sold to animal feed manufacturers who, not even claiming to be a society of philanthropists, no doubt brought it at a giveaway price. When the considerable demand for it created by the new diets arrived, it was noticeable that the price rose dramatically and is now well above that of ordinary flour, and a gluten-free diet is extremely costly to provide. Alas it was always thus.

BURNS

Excluding that pyro-resistant trio Shadrach, Mesach and Abednego, and also the odd fire walker and fakir, burns have always posed a major hazard with a very high risk to life, grave disfigurement and disablement. Fire has also been a favoured method of execution for heretics and witches, and this has now returned as necklace killing, but as far as doctors are involved, their interest has been in attempts at saving life and minimising subsequent damage. Modern warfare, especially in the air, civil aircraft accidents, industrial disasters and domestic oil heater accidents have all tended to increase the incidence, and have led to the establishment of special Burns Units where nowadays most cases are treated. Before the Second World War things were otherwise, and burns came within the province of general surgeons as part of their emergency duties; and as a consequence, student dressers took part in the treatment of both in-patients and out-patients, an experience that gave them a wonderful opportunity to observe the terrible mortality rate, and in those who survived, the horrific disfigurement and disablement caused by the contracting scar tissue.

In the early 1930s a new and revolutionary treatment had been introduced which held out high hopes of a greatly improved prognosis in both survival and cosmetic results. Prior to this the standard treatment had been washing the affected areas with Eusol and the application of vaseline gauze. The new treatment was the use of tannic acid, which was accompanied by a propaganda campaign to try and stop the application of greasy dressings before admission to hospital. First-aiders were advised to do nothing more than cover the affected area with a clean dry towel. In-patient treatment started with a deep general anaesthetic, and then the Dresser's job was quite literally to scrub the whole area with a nailbrush using an ether soap solution. The edges of the wound were

171

rubbed with dry gauze to remove any loose skin tags, and the whole area was thus cleared of all debris. When this had been completed, a tannic acid solution was sprayed all over and allowed to dry, after which the patient returned to the ward and was placed under a heated cradle, and the burns were repeatedly sprayed with the same tannic acid solution at half hourly intervals, until a thick rugose crust, jet-black in colour covered the entire area of the burn. The theory was that beneath this protective crust the whole area would re-epithelialise with a minimum of scarring, and in fact this did sometimes happen, especially when only small areas were involved, but this outcome so devoutly to be wished was anything but universal. Unfortunately the area beneath the crust was an ideal medium in which infection could flourish, and only too often the protective covering concealed not healthy epithelialising skin, but a massive collection of thick pus. This was a major disaster and led to even worse scarring and deformity providing the patient survived. The tannic acid treatment didn't long survive, but it makes one wonder what the results might have been had penicillin been discovered contemporaneously. Clearly it would never have replaced skin grafting and the reconstructive skill of modern surgery.

With the outbreak of war and the very high incidence of extensive burns in the pilots who took part in the Battle of Britain, special units were created under the care of plastic surgeons, and from then on all cases of burns were transferred to their care. In all probability general surgeons were not unhappy to see them go.

CARCINOMA OF THE BREAST

During the three year course of their clinical training, students were obliged to attend some 150 clinical lectures which were given by the Consultant staff twice weekly between the hours of 1 and 2 p.m. The standard of the orations varied between the poor and the very poor, with just a minimal number of exceptions. It is more than dubious whether any self respecting student could have withstood such a battering with mediocrity, and consequently in order to satisfy the Dean on the one hand and save one's soul on the other, they banded together in small groups for the nefarious purpose of forging each others' signatures. This was necessary since the only official recognition of one's attendance was a signature on the record sheet, which was in the charge of the conniving epidiascope technician. I belonged to a group of four or five, which meant that we only needed to attend about once a fortnight, and with reasonable skill one hoped to get all the signatures on the list before the lecturer arrived, and then disappear without trace. If one was unlucky in one's timing then one had to sit through an hour of purgatory, and on one such occasion when the lecturer was quite one of the worst, his audience consisted of three people, myself and two others from the Far East, whereas the attendance list must have had over a hundred names on it. Presumably there was a fee payable to what was an entirely honorary staff, and as these lectures were one of their perquisites, nobody wanted to rock the boat or upset the apple cart, and consequently there was a great deal of connivance on all sides. However the story doesn't quite end there, because some years later two of our group of forgers were themselves appointed consultants at Guy's and thus became obliged to deliver these very same lectures. Of the ability of one of them I know nothing, but the other, S H Wass became a legend, and perhaps bearing in mind the suffering inflicted on us in the past, he delivered orations of scintillating brilliance, and when the title of the lecture was 'Swellings of the Testicle', it was a matter of standing-room only for the late-comers.

Be that as it may, in 1933 Charles Hilton Fagg, who was the senior surgeon at the time chose as the subject for his last clinical lecture 'Halstead's radical mastectomy', which he delivered just before he retired. The gist of his discourse was neither to describe the operation nor to consider its pros and cons, but to tell us about his appointment to the staff many years before, and as a young man, of his hopes and fears about the future of surgery. Amongst the former was the devout hope that Halstead's operation would no longer be performed by the time he retired, and of his disappointment and dejection at the failure to see his wish fulfilled. In fact the operation continued as the main line of treatment for at least a further thirtyfive years, and even now there are some of the amputees still surviving, no doubt a medical curiosity to the modern student.

During a total period of nine months as either a Surgical Ward Clerk or Dresser one must have seen about two of these mutilations performed each week, but regretfully it would appear that nobody was much struck by the awfulness, and in all probability never even gave a moment's thought to the trauma, both physical and mental, that it must have caused to the afflicted women. They had to suffer their illness, the disfiguration and the unpromising future, without either the kindly support of the associations since formed to help such people, or the interest of the media to comfort them in their misery.

Halstead's operation entailed not only the amputation of the entire breast tissue, the underlying fascia and parts of the pectoral muscles, but also most of the contents of the axilla, which could and sometimes did lead to permanent lymphatic obstruction and swelling of the homolateral arm. In order to achieve the removal of so much tissue, a vast incision was required, which even if it healed by primary intention—and it often did not—left a terrible scar. The students, being all male, very rarely dressed these wounds, which for the sake of propriety were cared for by the nursing staff, and we were taught absolutely nothing about the subsequent management and prosthesis, which was all arranged privately between the patient, the Ward Sister, the Fitter, and the Lady Almoner.

Guy's at that time would have tolerated nothing so mundane as a social worker. I do not remember, either as a student or when a House Surgeon, ever discussing her disease with any of the patients, and one wonders how one's colleagues who went into general practice coped with the situation.

Looking back, it now seems incredible that we students showed so little concern for the psyche and the suffering of those we were helping to treat, and it all seemed just a part of the normal process of a disease that was our concern, and at no time did our mentors attempt to teach us otherwise. Our business, and their's related to the origins, pathology, clinical picture and management of disease, not with the feelings of those who suffered from them, so that the care and concern shown by modern House Officers and students is an enormous improvement on a state of affairs that still fills me with shame.

In those days there was no thought of prophylaxis for malignant disease, nor was there any such thing as screening or any propaganda to encourage early diagnosis, and this, combined with a natural reluctance of many women to consult their doctor, who were nearly all men, led to some remarkably advanced cases appearing in out-patients. Huge tumours, not infrequently fungating and ulcerating, associated with massive axillary glands; and even the occasional patient exhibiting the condition of 'peau d'orange' caused some interest but no surprise.

A few years before this time there was only one treatment for the condition, where all the operable cases were subjected to Halstead's mastectomy, and one must assume that all the others were left to rot, anywhere but in a teaching hospital. By the time I had entered the wards, radium and deep x-ray therapy had become available and the latter was widely used postoperatively in all cases, and exclusively in the inoperable. Radium had a variable position in which there were some surgeons who used it exclusively in all their cases, thus avoiding the mutilation, though it was thought to carry a worse prognosis, but mostly its use was combined with surgery and deep therapy. Whatever treatment was used, the results were to say the least disappointing; recurrences were extremely common and the mortality rate high. As one who went into a speciality where cancer of the breast played no part, the memory of those times is singularly unhappy.

None of the cases originally dealt with in the wards were re-admitted there unless further surgical treatment was deemed to be possible, and all the other cases were dealt with in the Deep Therapy Department which was situated at the very top of the medical block, where none of us went anyway because it had no students attached to it. Consequently we remained totally ignorant of what went on there, and one imagines that the majority of the women deteriorated slowly or rapidly, and met their fate with the stoicism that people in general showed in those days.

Students were given no instruction in, and gained no experience of the management of terminal malignant disease, or for that matter any of the other myriad ills which allowed the patient to die at home. I feel sure that this contributed to the very long and totally unjustifiable time that it took before the idea of hospice treatment came into existence to relieve the intractable pain and improve the quality of what lifespan remained to the dying. Purely by chance, when I was an HS it fell to my lot to have the care of a man with widespread malignant secondary deposits, who was in Guy's because of his connection with a member of the consultant staff. His pain and misery left me in no doubt that the former at least had to be continuously rather than intermittently controlled, but how to do it? Morphine and heroine injections were effective, but they had to be written up and therefore couldn't be given as and when required without summoning the HS or HP. This often led to long periods when no effective analgesia was available, but I discovered that drugs even opiates given by mouth could be prescribed *pro re nata* (as required). By a lucky chance I tried a mixture of powdered opium and Pyramidon, which was a proprietary analgesic preparation, greatly superior to aspirin or phenacetin, and in Germany where it had originated was widely used in place of those drugs, as it could be bought over the counter without a prescription. In the UK there was a much more cautious approach, on account of its known tendency to diminish the white cell count in a few people, and the very occasional fatal case had been reported. In later years its use was prohibited and it was removed from the British Pharmacopoea. However it seemed to me that in the terminal agonies of malignant disease, such considerations were totally irrelevant, and as this combination of drugs turned out to be very effective in the continuous control of pain, it became a routine treatment at Guy's and was prescribed under the title of 'Pulv. Jacoby'. It remained in common use until the outbreak of war when much of Guy's was dispersed into the county of Kent. What happened to it after that I don't know, but such is fame. Sic transit gloria mundi.

After such a dark and dismal description of the position as I encountered it, how much pleasanter to think that if 'Chubby Fagg', as he was always known, had been able to give his lecture now, he would have found that Halstead's operation had gone, and the present position though still showing room for improvement, was so very much better than in 1933.

SULPHONAMIDES AND ANTIBIOTICS

'Behold, I will show you a mystery. . . We shall all be changed in a moment in the twinkling of an eye'.

It is absolutely impossible that anybody who was not present at the time can possibly comprehend just what it meant to the practice of medicine when these drugs were introduced. They completely changed the entire face of medicine, they cured diseases that had previously been some of the most awful scourges, and they opened up vistas of new treatments in medicine and surgery undreamed of before their advent.

Throughout this journey through medicine, frequent reference is made to the unpalatable fact of how little could be done to influence the course of medical, as opposed to surgical illnesses, though I do not think that anybody had this fact uppermost in their minds at the time, and in all probability it was rarely if so much as given a thought. We simply thought how much better we were at things than before the turn of the century, without being too meticulous in our calculations, and things had to be that way or a doctor's life would have been insupportable. Even in modern times when so many illnesses that were once fatal are now curable, there are still situations, most notably in malignant disease, where a somewhat similar attitude has to hold. It is post hoc, not propter hoc that brings things to mind, with the result that one simply accepts the facts as they are, and to make life tolerable one takes refuge in a mass of verbiage and platitudes that help to camouflage one's inability to do anything really useful. And then quite suddenly everything is changed, and the new drugs make treatment the master in what previously had been a hopeless situation, almost at the touch of a button. But it is only after the cure has been found and 'The old order changeth, yielding place to new', that one becomes conscious of one's previous

178

therapeutic impotence. Unfortunately these sudden and dramatic conversions are few and far between, because most of the great therapeutic advances have been gradual affairs, maybe over years, but the sulphas and antibiotics were not of that genre.

In order to make the point more clearly I have taken a liberty with the chronological sequence of events, and describe my first encounter with penicillin, even though it took place almost a decade after sulphonamides had become commonplace. It was so dramatic that its details have remained fresh in my mind ever since. I had read Florey, Chain et al.'s original papers, and knew that a substance they called penicillin appeared to have almost magical powers against certain germs, especially staphylococcal infections which were but little affected by the sulpha drugs; but that its production was a difficult and expensive business, so that none was available for general use. However it was reported that some had been supplied to the forces for experimental trials on wounds sustained in the war then raging, but that the prospects of any being made available for civilian use were gloomy. At that time I had under my care a young girl about five years old, the most beautiful child I think that I have ever seen. She was of part-Scandinavian parentage, with the blondest hair and the whitest, most delicate skin imaginable, not at all the ideal protection against Stevens–Johnson's disease which she had developed. In a matter of days she was covered in huge blisters, which rapidly became secondarily infected with staphylococci, transforming her into a dripping mass of pus. Her condition was desperate, and though she might have been treated with sulphonamides in the lack of anything else, they would not have been of any benefit, but anyway their use was absolutely excluded because they were generally considered to be one, if not the main causes of the disease. It was clear that she was going to die and her father was summoned from the War Office, when it fell to my lot to warn him of the impending tragedy. I noted that at our meeting he wore the red tabs and shoulder insignia of a full colonel, so I mentioned that there was a substance called penicillin that might help in the treatment of his daughter but none was available for civilians, though a limited amount had been supplied to the Army. That same evening, no questions asked or answered, a few ampoules appeared in the ward as we hastily read the instructions on how to use it. Within twentyfour hours what had been a hopeless situation was transformed to one where the child was no longer in any danger, and the miracle had happened. It is a lovely thing to record that her skin recovered without scarring and 'My Lady' was restored to her pristine beauty. When she grew up she married and had her own family, and is totally unaware of the landmark she represented in my professional career, even though I never set eyes on her again after her discharge. Surely it was more like a fairy story than a medical anecdote where they all lived happily ever after.

But to return to the correct sequence of events, sulphonamides antedated antibiotics by about a decade, and as students we were shown ampoules of the new remarkable blood red dye called prontosil rubrum, which was used in the treatment of pneumonia. The use of various dyes was no novelty in medicine, but before long it was discovered that the colour had nothing to do with its therapeutic powers, and the preparations changed to white tablets that could be taken by mouth, and unlike penicillin there were no difficulties with supplies. The whole picture of pneumococcal pneumonia was changed for all time, and in a common disease that previously had a mortality rate of 10%, it was now reduced to near zero, and likewise almost all its awful complications were also abolished. It seemed unbelievable. Of much less frequent occurrence, but much more fatal in its outcome, streptococcal septicaemia, blood poisoning in common parlance, lost its terrifying reputation and was brought under control, whereas previously it had been untreatable, and the only good thing that could be said about it was that it killed painlessly in less than a week. Now with sulphonamides it caused neither alarm nor despondency, though its sister disease, staphyloccal blood poisoning, remained a menace until the advent of antibiotics. The conquest of meningococcal meningitis was another of the great triumphs of the discovery, and it also replaced mandelic acid in the treatment of the kidney infection, pyelitis, so that a large number of previously dangerous diseases were now eminently treatable, and lost their menacing profiles.

It is quite remarkable how transient is the sense of appreciation of something miraculous, because within a year or so of the introduction of these two therapeutic marvels, they became nothing more than routine treatments, and the history of their origins showed none of the durability similar to that of the young Saint Bernadette at Lourdes. Florey and Chain were both knighted, but up till now there has been no suggestion of their sanctification. Every now and then penicillin gets a passing mention from the media, but those who have even heard of M&B 693 or prontosil rubrum, the names under which the sulphonamide drugs first appeared, must be very few and far between. The advances made by the discovery of the two drugs has been stupendous, but gaps remained in the therapeutic scene, most notably with TB, typhoid and a bacterium, not the virus called h. influenzae. However, in the end these problems too were conquered by the discovery of other antibiotics. As might have been expected, the conquest of TB which is a chronic disease took a very long time, and proved a very hard struggle even after streptomycin had been discovered, and though perhaps from the cosmic point of view it was the greatest of them all, it had none of the sudden impact of the others.

The modern physician will probably never know the joy of a common and dangerous disease suddenly transformed into a common and curable one, though malignant disease and schizophrenia remain the great hurdles still to be surmounted. That they will be seems certain, but it looks as though it will be a gradual process over many years, with research workers beavering away in laboratories all over the world looking for a cure. With the sulphas and penicillin it was quite different, because in those cases nobody was looking for a specific remedy for a definite disease, and they were almost chance happenings. The sulphonamide drugs resulted from the fact that every new chemical, and especially every new dyestuff produced by Bayer was passed to their pharmaceutical department to see if it had any therapeutic value, and many thousands of such substances must have passed through their hands and proved inert, toxic, valueless or a combination of all three, and had to be discarded. Just the one, a new industrial dyestuff, prontosil rubrum proved different. The story of penicillin is not all that dissimilar, since its outcome was the result of an academic investigation into a group of known antibiotics of various sorts and origins, one of which just happened to be a mould discovered many years earlier by a chance happening at St Mary's Hospital. I think that there were some half dozen or more such substances investigated, and they proved to be excellent inhibitors of bacterial activity, but unfortunately they were just as efficient in killing the host animal. All those other substances and their discoverers have remained in obscurity, and are likely to do so until eternity, whereas just one of them, penicillin, was brought from exactly the same obscurity to fame and fortune, not by somebody looking for a specific cure, but simply in the course of a pure scientific experiment.

Money rightly pours into cancer research, but let us hope that some of it reaches the pure academic workers because one never knows what might come out of their work. Atom bombs or penicillin.

PREMATURE INFANTS

The concept of special units which should undertake the care of premature infants is a relatively recent introduction. In England, paediatrics itself as a specialty of its own was a late development compared with several other foreign countries, and until 1939 such departments were almost exclusively confined to teaching hospitals, and this remained the situation until after the war. The idea of paediatricians having the care of the neonates in maternity departments had not yet dawned, or if it had elsewhere, most certainly not at Guy's Hospital, where there was an unfortunate rift between the consultant staffs of the obstetric and paediatric departments. As a result, the only liaison between the two was an unofficial arrangement whereby the Paediatric Registrar was invited to advise when requested by members of the Junior Staff of the maternity unit. The position in general was not very satisfactory, because obstetricians considered that the newborn infant was part of their sphere of practice and they did not want to accept a situation where there was one consultant looking after the mother, and another responsible for the care of her infant. This attitude of mind was reflected in the standard text books of obstetrics, all of which included a section on the care of neonates, written by a paediatrician, yet inferring that the care of the infants was the responsibility of obstetricians. What one found in practice was that once a paediatrician had been invited to advise, the Nursing Staff and the Junior Staff were very pleased to be relieved of the responsibility they had previously shouldered, and it would be found that these advisory visits became more and more frequent, yet in spite of this they remained unofficial for a very long time, until it was recognised that perhaps it might be a good thing to separate the responsibilities of looking after mother and her newborn baby.

It is a fortunate thing that the vast proportion of newborn infants are both physically normal and healthy, so that until relatively recently, certainly up to 1939, there were no such ideas in the minds of most obstetricians or paediatricians that every neonate should be given a routine comprehensive medical examination. This resulted in a situation where, for example, conditions such as congenital dislocation of the hips frequently remained undiagnosed until after the child had started to walk, and it was then too late for it to be corrected. It was relatively common to encounter adults with the characteristic awkward gait and a shoe built up several inches on the affected side, something that very fortunately disappeared from the scene many years ago. Such things as harelips and cleft palates were so obvious that there was no difficulty in diagnosis and referring them to surgical clinics. Jaundice of the newborn was then as now much in evidence, but naturally most cases were of the so-called physiological type with spontaneous recovery, and what is now known as haemolytic disease of the newborn, which was then called icterus gravis neonatorum, and it certainly was most grave, as there was no treatment for it, with the result that it not infrequently led the infant to the other meaning of the word. It may seem strange to modern concepts that the various things described here were just accepted as inevitable, and there was no great agitation to hand them over to paediatricians as of right.

In all probability it was due to this attitude of mind that low birth weight infants received so little attention. They were all called prems, short for premature delivery, even in the few cases where gestation had been normal, and as it was the case that any infant with a birth weight of 5 ½ lbs (2 ½ kg) or over stood a fair chance of survival, the definition of a premature infant was fixed at a birth weight below that figure. As a rough and ready calculation it served its purpose, even though the use of the term prem continued.

The management of these infants was recognised as a special problem, and the teaching was that there were three cardinal factors that had to be provided. They were:-

1. TO PROVIDE SUFFICIENT EXTRA WARMTH TO MAINTAIN BODY TEMPERATURE.

The smaller the infant, the more its body temperature was regulated by that of the environment (poikilothermia), and this was well-known, but it also has to be remembered that at

that time it was not known that these infants frequently
suffered from very low body temperatures in a clinical condition
now known as infantile hypothermia. The reason for this was
that their temperatures were taken with an ordinary clinical
thermometer, which at its lowest point gave a reading far
above that which actually pertained in the infant. It was not
until special low-registering thermometers became available
that the condition was identified, and found to be very common
not only in low birth weight infants, but surprisingly in heavier
ones as well. The usual method of providing the necessary
warmth was to keep the infant well swaddled and place its cot
next to the ward radiator in the ordinary nursery, as there
was nowhere else for it to go. Sometimes small electric cradles
were employed and hot water bottles had their uses. At about
the turn of the century and for some years later, incubators
had been in vogue, but regretfully they bore almost no
relationship to the modern piece of apparatus bearing the same
name that is now ubiquitous in special care units. They were
wooden frame boxes with walls made of blanket or similar
materials, but they were extremely liable to harbour infection
and thus became instruments of execution rather than life
preservation, so that none were in use in the 1930s. As there
was no separate accomodation in which to place them nor a
special nursing staff to look after them, it is almost a certainty
that the smaller the infant, the less these measures succeeded
in their objective. To add to the difficulties, the heavy swaddling
clothes used with the object of keeping the infants warm almost
certainly had a negative effect by acting as an insulator, and
thus preventing the external heat from getting to them, as well
as making breathing and movement much more difficult. With
hindsight it is clear that the efforts to maintain body temperature were a dismal failure.

2. TO PROVIDE A DIETARY INTAKE OF 60 CALORIES PER LB OF BODY WEIGHT PER DAY.

This of course was 20% more than a normal infant required,
and even that amount would have been difficult enough to get
into a tiny child, let alone the extra volume suggested and to
add to the difficulties there was a remarkable lack of suitable
apparatus with which to achieve the objective. The special
feeders that had been invented were very ill designed, and

most of the cases had to be fed via a tube passed into the stomach, though there was quite a vogue for the administration of a small amount of sherry wine before feeds, as it was thought to stimulate appetite! Much more often, dried extract of thyroid was prescribed routinely in the hope, rather than the expectation, that it would stimulate muscular activity including the sucking reflex. When it was possible to provide breast milk (but so often it was not), the question of what feed to use was settled, but when an artificial formula was necessary, disaster loomed on the horizon. The trouble was that nobody really recognised what the real differences between human milk and cow's milk were. Everybody's minds were concentrated on the different proportions of protein, fat and carbohydrate in the two milks, and yet the steps taken to make them similar, so called humanised milks, did not in any way compare with the genuine article. The actual discovery of these factors was many years into the future. Quite apart from all these problems, the actual management as to choice of feed, method of feeding, frequency of feeding and the actual amount of food that the infant might tolerate in practice, instead of in theory, was left in the hands of the nursing staff, who had a wealth of experience but very little scientific training to go with it. It is only fair to add that the medical staff were equally ignorant, and that is in all probability the reason why they were happy to leave things to the ward Sisters. With the benefit of hindsight it is easy to recognise that only the most doughty of this group of infants would manage to survive, and it was a phenomenon indeed if any one of them weighing 3½lbs (1½kg) or less did.

3. TO KEEP THE INFANT FREE FROM INFECTION.

This was perhaps the most satisfactorily managed of the three criteria. The reason was not that there were many things that could be done, but that in general and for most of the time, obstetric departments are relatively free from infection. On the other hand, in those days, if any bacteria did raise their ugly heads in such places there were no sulphonamides or antibiotics available to combat them. The streptococcus was the one most greatly feared, for it was the cause of puerperal septicaemia which could be fatal to mother as well as infant until the advent of sulphonamides. When that organism had been largely mastered, the staphylococcus took its place, and both of them in their time took an awful toll of premature infants, but it must be stressed that most of the time maternity departments were relatively free from infection.

It must be obvious that the outlook for low birthweight babies was gloomy, and it got even worse as the birthweight descended, though as in all things there are exceptions, and sometimes remarkable examples of survival were recorded. During my tenure as RMO at the Infants' Hospital in London a very small child was admitted which was reputed to have weighed eighteen ounces (0.6 kg) at birth. It survived without difficulty and made the national press, but it is more than dubious whether the stated history would have stood close scrutiny. Apart from such events, almost nobody in the obstetric world seemed to have much interest in this problem and complacency apparently reigned supreme, but there were two very notable exceptions. The maternity departments at Birmingham and at Bristol had Special Care Units, known at the time as Premature Infant Departments, which had been established with their own separate nursing staff, in their own separate accommodation, under the care of consultant paediatricians. They must have been founded some considerable time before 1939, and yet no more came into being until the third was set up at Pembury Hospital, Kent, in early 1940, after the Guy's Paediatric Department had been evacuated there at the outbreak of war. With the co-operation of the Medical Superintendant of that hospital, (Mr. E D Y Grasby M.D., F.R.C.O.G.) who incidentally was also the consultant obstetrician, a very small side ward was handed over for the purpose, and in due course it had its own nurses seconded from the maternity nursing staff. In the face of a world war going on, and incidentally none too well for Britain at the time, it would have been insane to have expected an allocation of funds to supply special equipment for the unit, but in fact the only absolutely basic essential apparatus that was required and was not available was oxygen tents. There were things called oxygen boxes which had been in extensive use but they were anything but efficient as so much of the supply leaked away, but it was discovered that with very little modification, the gas masks that the government had provided for newborn infants in the event of chemical warfare could very easily be converted into a most efficient substitute. In addition it was quite simple to maintain an ambient temperature as the internal volume was quite small, and the infants coud be stripped of the usual woolly coats and vests that added to their respiratory difficulties. Fortunately these masks were never required for the original purpose for which they had been designed, and if they hadn't been used as oxygen tents they would probably have been consigned to the destructor at the end of hostilities, without ever having been brought into use for any purpose whatsoever. Of course it might be that other people had discovered other uses for them in other spheres. The other helpful factor was the co-operation of nursing mothers, hospitals nursing staff and district midwives in setting up a breast milk bank, and thus providing a basis for dealing with the most urgent feeding problems.

At this point it has to be said that the one real tragedy of the care of these cases occurred. It had always been one of the major problems that these infants suffered varying degrees of respiratory difficulty, and at the time nothing was known about a special substance called surfactant which is essential for proper function of the lungs, and is lacking in premature infants. In the lack of such knowledge it was assumed that higher and higher concentrations of oxygen would be the correct treatment, and this was quite easy to achieve as more efficient incubators were manufactured. This form of treatment was carried out until it was discovered that some of the cases had become permanently blind from a condition called retrolental fibroplasia which was due to the high oxygen concentrations. In those days the monitoring of all the factors which in modern times are just routine was unheard of, and anyway almost no apparatus existed that could have been used in makeshift departments.

It would be a gross exaggeration to suggest that there was a sudden and dramatic improvement in the statistics of infant survival, but in a relatively short period the outlook for any infant whose birthweight had been 4 lbs (2.1 kg) or more was good, and as time progressed there was a slow improvement of survival rate for those of lower weights. At Pembury Hospital anyway, it was recognised that a special unit for low birthweight babies was a good thing, and as time passed it underwent several changes of location so as to provide more and better accommodation, until finally it moved into its first purpose built unit in what had been the shell of the old TB annexe of which I had been in charge in 1939, and have described elsewhere. It was indeed a happy occasion when a building that had once housed cases of a dreadful killer disease, which for practical purposes no longer existed, was given over to helping those infants who might otherwise succumb to survive.

After the war ended and the National Health Service altered the entire aspect of hospital practice in the United Kingdom, more and more Special Care Baby Units came into existence, but they could not have been all that ubiquitous, as suggested by the following incident. Pembury Hospital was honoured by a visit from a royal Duchess, who had almost certainly performed similar rituals on innumerable previous occasions, but this time she visited the Special Care Baby Unit. Due to the nature of its work the only people who were allowed to accompany her were the unit Sister and the paediatrician. She was entranced by everything that she saw, and wanted to know exactly what was what and how everything was done, to such an extent that the rest of the hospital and royal entourage who had been left waiting outside became restless, and an emissary was sent to winkle her out.

The whole attitude to the care of these infants has altered enormously, and a great deal of scientific research has gone into what had previously been done by rule of thumb, with the result that in the end the old attitude of disinterestedness of obstetricians has been replaced by the creation of professorial chairs in neonatology. To add to all this there has also been the introduction of intravenous feeding and assisted respiration so that the mortality rate is now extremely low and is almost entirely confined to those of very low birthweights and those with gross congenital defects, some of whom are also subject to genetic abnormalities imcompatible with survival. This is a happy story, not yet completed, and whilst the remaining problems are relatively small ones, their final solution will require the expenditure of an inordinate amount of money and effort.

At this point in time, April 1990, it seems imperative to add to what has been written above on this subject. The United Kingdom parliament, the press, the media, the churches and many societies such as those with the specific interests of either the rights of the unborn child, or of women to choose what happens to their bodies, have been engaged in a hotly contested debate to fix the new maximum foetal age at which a legally permissible abortion may be performed. It would appear that 24 weeks is likely to be approved. All this activity has simply come about due to the work done in special care baby units over a period of some forty-five years as described in the chapter above. It is certain that none of the participants in the debate gave much thought as to how this phenomenon had come about, but who would begrudge those units at Birmingham, Bristol and Pembury Hospitals a warm internal sensation that the work began so long ago had born such fruit, with surely yet another crop to come. Churchmen, politicians and activists gird up your loins for battles yet to come.

CHILD ABUSE

There is probably no medical subject more in the public eye and more misunderstood than child abuse. To judge from what is written and spoken by the media, almost everyone is an expert in the condition, and the legal profession who enter the picture in almost all cases appear to be just as, if not more ill informed than everyone else. Everybody, and one must repeat everybody seems to think that it is simply a matter of man's hostility to man, and a manifestation of human bestiality. Of course it is all those things but the misplaced word is *simply*, because there is absolutely nothing simple where child abuse is concerned.

It ought to be obvious to everybody that the situation has a very long history, dating back perhaps to the neo- or even the palaeolithic age, and yet the incredible feature is that in spite of that length of time it took thousands of years before the condition was first identified and described by Henry Kempe in 1969. For goodness sake, what was happening in all that long period? Were the media too ill informed or too lazy, were the ubiquitous legal profession too somnolent, the medical profession too unobservant or was everyone, as seems most probable, unaware that such a condition existed? Some might be tempted to say that it was just a phenomenon that had always been present and that was that, but they would all be wrong because the obvious cases that make the headlines are only the tip of the iceberg. It is only now becoming recognised that myriads of children are killed each year unknown to the authorities, and are recorded as deaths from natural causes. It is hoped here that some of the reasons for this sad state of affairs may be made a little plainer.

To comprehend the condition, one must disabuse oneself of the notion that we are faced simply with a matter of aberrant social behaviour, and realise that, as Henry Kempe made clear, *we are dealing with a DISEASE*, and a very serious one at that. It is because it is a disease that it took thousands of years before anyone recognised the fact. The reason that it took so long is that child abuse is an unique disease unlike all the others in the medical calendar, in which the causation, be it malignant, infective, chemical or anything else occurs in the one same body that shows the symptoms and physical evidence. In child abuse the abnormality that is the cause of the trouble is found in one person, the abuser, and the physical evidence of the disease in quite another, the child. When one is confronted with a straightforward case of assault it is perfectly obvious that the victim has been beaten up, and the guilty party has to be sought, arrested and brought to justice. In child abuse everything is so very different, yet most people do not recognise the fact and continue to deal with the cases as though they were simply matters of assault and grievous bodily harm.

What happens in this disease is that in the vast majority of cases the child is taken not to the police but to a doctor, and it is taken by either the abuser or more often by a close relative who gives a fictitious history of the events leading up to the injuries, or to put it more plainly, just lies. The damage that has been inflicted will appear to be quite ordinary, and could have been sustained by the various accidents that are supposed to have happened, and as they appear to be superficial, confined to the skin and underlying bruises, local remedies are applied and the case sent home. To the cognoscenti however, the injuries tend to be of a special type and may form a typical pattern, especially where severe shaking has been one of the forms of assault with the bruises caused by the thumbs over the shoulder blades and the fingers on the front of the chest, or vice versa. The damage to the head and neck are manifestated by signs of brain damage, but all these things are accepted by the non-suspicious as being in accordance with the history. What has to be remembered is that child abuse is not a one-off situation with just a solitary attack, but is an ongoing condition with chronic injuries dating from time past. This is where an x-ray of the whole skeleton is of value, because old fractures reveal their presence long after the patient's symptoms and signs have disappeared.

The explanation that one is given as to how the injuries were sustained is often perfectly credible, and unless there is some special reason for being suspicious, most people are reluctant to attribute the worst of motives to other people, and as a result the falsehoods are accepted. It requires someone who is familiar with this disease and of course other conditions, especially blood diseases which may have a similar clinical picture, to recognise the special types of damage associated with child abuse and thus be able to differentiate between the two. Just to complicate matters, both conditions may be present in the same child, and consequently it is a combination of all these factors that has led to the inordinate delay in recognising the disease as a definite entity. Just to make life more difficult, even when one is convinced that one is being lied to, it is possible to be mistaken. Long before 1969 I was asked to see a child who showed several large swollen and bruised areas, and the family doctor was very suspicious of their origin on account of the bad home background, and the social worker, in those days called the District Nurse, was convinced that the trauma was non-accidental in origin. All the mother would say was that if the child bumped herself these swellings suddenly appeared, and as I was as incredulous as everybody else, the child was admitted to hospital for observation and investigation, all of which proved negative. We became more and more convinced that we were being lied to, until one morning a nurse rushed up to say that the child had knocked her head on the cot side and now had a large lump there. This was no exaggeration because the little girl's head showed a swelling that not even the artists who drew such incidents in the *Beano* or *Tiger Tim's Weekly* would have thought reasonable to portray. The experience always stood me in good stead, and subsequently it was only after much cogitation that I was prepared to make a diagnosis of undoubted child abuse.

The overall picture of the disease in the United Kingdom has become clouded by a nationally publicised diversion into one aspect of it, namely the Cleveland affair. Here the situation concerned some hundred or more children who were diagnosed as suffering from sexual abuse, all occurring in the same area in a relatively short period of time. The method of diagnosis was based on the finding of, amongst other things, a somewhat relaxed anal sphincter, and although there is no doubt that such a thing may be a manifestation of sexual abuse, there is also the possibility that such an assumption is not infallible. However the basic nature of the disease did not differ from the principles described above. All the children would appear to have been taken to a doctor not the police in the first case, and presumably whoever took them probably did not even mention sexual abuse, but grounds of a different nature caused the doctors who were consulted to be suspicious that the history and the true situation did not tally. It was simply a matter of force of numbers and certain other facts that made other people suspicious that the doctors might not be correct in every case, and the matter then got out of control and into the hands of the police and the law. When it comes to a matter of diagnosis, no reputable doctor would argue the verdict in a case that they had never seen or examined, and certainly how many children in the Cleveland affair were correctly diagnosed and which were not, seems to remain in doubt and is no concern of this chapter. The point that must be made, because it remains one of the bugbears of the whole disease, is that when it gets into the hands of the police and the legal profession, they appear to be less reluctant than most doctors in deciding a matter in which by training they are not exactly well qualified to judge. Of course the sheer force of numbers in Cleveland distorted the overall picture, and made it appear that sexual child abuse was the commonest manifestation of the disease, and the position was not really clarified when the media took a hand and opened a hot line to all and sundry to confide their woes to television. One suspects that no matter what the subject, from sex abuse to seeing ghosts or flying saucers, a hot line to TV would attract a very large clientele. With the passage of time the matter will settle down as a source of news, and once again the whole picture will return to a balanced situation where a great deal remains to be done before anybody can feel satisfied.

This is not the place for a comprehensive description of the whole clinical picture of child abuse which has filled several volumes other than Kempe's monumental work, but one hopes that it has been made clear that the diagnosis and subsquent assessment of these cases can be a very difficult and even a dangerous occupation for the expert, who in this matter happens to be the paediatrician. Once again it has to be borne in mind that even the experts can be wrong. Therefore one may ask, can it be right, is it rational and above all is it fair to leave the assessment and the management of these cases in the hands of social workers? Whatever divers attributes they may have, and however diligent they may be, paediatric dignosis is not one of the things for which they have been trained, and consequently can they really be expected to have the expertise to diagnose what is going on? The answer is an emphatic NO, and the stream of fatal cases coming to court and reported in the press proves the point, and it is generally accepted that the total number of fatal cases which were neither identified nor investigated is very large. In those cases that are reported, one discovers that the social workers who have been given overall management responsibility are often debarred by law from demanding a sight of the child, or are put off by explanations that sound unreasonable and yet seem to be accepted, so that the cases drag on until a fatal outcome ensues. After each of these episodes it is usual for the unfortunate social worker to be pilloried and made to carry the can because of lapses of behaviour in a situation for which they have not been trained. Their employers, the local authority, promise to do better in the future, somebody gets dismissed, somebody else gets moved to another job, and shortly afterwards everything has returned to the point from whence it had started. Many people would turn to the established societies for the prevention of cruelty to children, but here until recently their record was not encouraging as press reports showed. It was not surprising, since their agents were once again non-medical people with even less qualifications for the job than the social workers. My personal experience of their activities was that they did not seem to me to be qualified experts in the disease, but what was equally lamentable or even worse was that they seemed to be unaware of their limitations. I found most of their agents to be both ignorant and arrogant, and I never managed to establish a happy relationship with them, though there is reason to believe that the situation has changed for the better recently. It could have been of course that I was just unlucky in my contacts or, perish the thought, maybe the arrogance was mine.

The ideal procedure by which to manage these cases still awaits a satisfactory answer, but one of the least desirable is that which was recommended by the 'Tunbridge Wells Study

Group on Non-accidental Injury to Children'. I have always been intrigued by that august body of opinion, because I happened to be the only paediatrician in Tunbridge Wells at the time it was originally convened, and in addition I was known to have had considerable experience of the subject, and incidentally was chief reviewer of the literature on child abuse for one of the leading medical journals. Maybe I was also reputed to be a tough and rather awkward customer where these cases were concerned. A number of people were under the impression that I must have been responsible for setting up the group, but I had to disabuse their minds by pointing out that although they had met in our renowned watering place, by which fact it got its title, I was never invited to attend. However be that as it may, the outcome of their deliberations was to spawn the 'Case Conference for Each Individual Child', and the members of the committee were to be:-

The Senior Paediatrician and his staff.
A psychiatrist.
The Ward Sister.
The Senior member of the Social Services Department.
The Health Visitor.
The representatives of voluntary agencies such as the National
     Society for the Prevention of Cruelty to Children.

Other people who should be invited to attend were the family doctor and a representative of the police force. The great defect of these recommendations was that there was no indication of who should take the chair or who was to be responsible for putting the results of their deliberations into practice. By implication it simply reverted to the old bad system of the unfortunate social worker back in the position of responsibility for recommendations coming from a bevy of people rather than just one. A committee of any sort is widely recognised as a euphemism for a group of people who will take no action, pass the buck and hope for the best, and by what one can determine from press reports this is exactly what is happening in spite of the 'Case Conference in Child Abuse.'

In theory there should be no difficulty in managing these cases, because all that needs to be done is to remove the child to a place of safety, which in practice usually means the children's ward of a hospital, until the abuser has been identified and the nature of his psychological abnormality has been treated and cured. Unfortunately it is the second part of the proposition that proves so difficult or impossible to achieve. In the first place the actual person who is responsible for the injuries may not always be that easy to identify, and this can be made more difficult on account of the widely held belief that it must be a brutal type of man from the lower classes, and this is something that is not necessarily correct. In one case in my experience the child's family were from the middle class, well educated and in comfortable circumstances, with the result that some people could not bring themselves to believe that a parent who was so personable and well behaved could perpetrate such a deed. Of course we ended up by calling the statutory 'Case Conference' where the overwhelming opinion was that the parents' story should be accepted. I felt obliged to say that if the child were returned to its home its next admission would in all probability be as a corpse, and I later took no pleasure in being proved correct. The subsequent events show how bizarre matters can be when powerful influences are brought to bear in cases of child abuse. The autopsy was performed by a highly skilled forensic pathologist whose findings seemed to me to be a little difficult to swallow, but of course were accepted without question by the court. It is understandable that the legal fraternity much prefer to have their chosen and familiar experts in forensic pathology, and nobody could deny their great expertise in these matters, but it may have a leavening effect to say that they also are not infallible, and some doubt is now being cast on the behaviour of Sir Bernard Spilsbury, who of course had nothing to do with this case, having died many years earlier. The outcome of the case was that with the aid of the forensic expertise and some extremely able legal gentry, the court was persuaded that this was not a matter of child abuse, and how could it be in such a nice family? Personally I retired from the fray with my tail between my legs, totally unconvinced by the verdict, but even worse befell the family doctor who sided with me, because he suffered such local vilification that he had to move to another practice in another area. Justification for our opinion and what seemed to most people our bloody-minded attitude came when a year or two later a second child in the same family succumbed, and this time the father was found guilty of murder and sentenced accordingly. Taking this case as just one example, it has always seemed to me that two dead children and their father in gaol did not do anybody very much good, or reflect very well on the system as at present administered. It would have been nice to be able to report that since I have retired from the active scene matters have improved out of all recognition, but from what one can gather from the press and secondhand reports, this is not so. One constantly reads of children being returned to their own homes time and time again, without any real guarantee of their security other than the natural inclination of the social workers who feel that it is the best place for a child. Then having done so, they fail to gain access to the children they are supposed to be protecting, being fobbed off with patently false explanations until finally the infants succumb, and once again the fat is in the fire. The sad example that has been described is most unfortuntely by no means unique.

In another case that fortunately never came to court, the circumstances were almost the complete opposite of what most people imagine to be the only pattern. The family were in the very high income bracket, and though I felt certain that the child's mother was the abuser, nobody other than the maternal grandmother would entertain such a preposterous idea. How could one imagine a well brought up ex-debutante who could have anything in the world that she desired, behave in a manner known only to the lower classes? Suspicion therefore fell upon the young au-pair nanny who was promptly sent packing, though I felt certain that she had nothing to do with the business. In this case the problem was solved by local mutual agreement where the child was taken into the grand-mother's care whilst the parents took themselves abroad and were later divorced. As far as one could say, this was an example of child abuse perpetrated by a mother in more than comfortable circumstances. I should doubt whether such a case is unique.

However to return to the basic problem of management, it is easy to see that with reasonable judgement there should be no difficulty in protecting the infant, but the overwhelming problem is how to deal with the abuser. Such is the revulsion felt by the general public, and probably the legal profession, that their gut reaction is one of hanging and flogging, and in lesser degree, that is what is generally handed out in the cases where the verdict is one of guilty. The real difficulty that has to be faced is that so far no reliable means has been found of identifying what disease process child abusers suffer from, and far too often it is just assumed that they are primitive beasts and should be dealt with accordingly. It might be more helpful if they were looked upon as having sick minds and dealt with as patients rather than criminals. In theory the people who ought to know and should be dealing with the abusers are the psychiatrists, but in practice they seem to find it difficult or impossible to give the sort of opinion that would settle the whole matter of how to proceed, and many of them are none too keen to be associated with the condition if they can avoid it, and who can blame them? In the end when most people have turned tail and fled it is left to the social workers to carry the burden. This is a responsibility that should never have been placed upon their shoulders because, as already stated but very justifiably to be repeated, they are not trained to deal with the cunning and the dissembling with which they will be faced, much less are they able to conduct a medical examination. In such circumstances it is unlikely that they would be able to detect the more esoteric signs and symptoms of damage to the nervous system, the skeleton and the nutrition, possibly even the psyche. Goodness knows it is difficult enough for paediatricians, and recently their situation has been made more difficult by the Cleveland affair where there was public debate about the accuracy of the diagnoses.

Thus the question arises that if the present state of affairs is unsatisfactory it is obligatory to suggest a better solution, and that surely would be to appoint one person to be in charge of the case with powers to make sure that the child is protected. Elsewhere in this book it has been suggested that treatment of the sick by a committee is rarely of maximum benefit to the patient, and in child abuse this is patently so. With the medico-legal implications of the disease it is clear that the final authority has to be the jurisdiction of the courts, but the only person with the knowledge and really in a position to make the necessary decisions is the paediatrician. No doubt such a suggestion will be greeted with shouts of 'What about the Cleveland affair', but the reply is that none of us is perfect, and anyway nobody has suggested that all the diagnoses were wrong, and for all one knows they may have all been correct. Thus it is suggested that in the final count the ultimate care should be with the paediatrician in concert with the psychiatrist, though it is certain that neither of them will be rushing to bear the burden. This would reduce the committee to two persons, which is in all probability one too many, and as the psychiatrist is not trained to recognise the clinical manifestations of the disease which are exclusively in the child, it must surely be the paediatrician aided when required by the other people who previously constituted the case conference. This would lead to the position where everybody would know where the responsibility lay, and they could make the necessary enquiries and investigations before the unfortunate infant corpse reaches the mortuary and the courts. This of course is something that paediatricians are most unlikely to agree with or accept; but in my own case it was the procedure I adopted until I was overruled, whereupon I retired from the fray being unwilling to be just an observer of a child being led unwittingly into the valley of the shadow of death, because that is what it so frequently turns out to be.

Since 1976, when I ceased to have any responsibility for these matters, a good many changes have been made, mostly on account of the sort of criticisms that have been voiced above. Also to no mean degree after the publicity of each disastrous case where death has resulted, with a history that almost any paediatrician could have foretold what the outcome would be. Originally when the disease was first described, the cases were mainly concerned with physical violence to infants and the title of the disease was the battered baby syndrome, but is now extended to children of all ages and consequently the new title. There has been further subdivision into cases of sex abuse, emotional abuse and physical violence, and local authorities have compiled lists of children at risk, which apparently are growing at enormous speed. The aim is to allocate a social worker to each case, and courses are held to help them in their unenviable tasks. These are no doubt a great improvement on what the situation was before; but it still seems difficult to see it being successful in its entirety. When things go wrong, who steps in to put them right, and have they the clinical expertise to diagnose exactly what is awry? It seems to me that there is still a lack of an expert in overall control, and whilst that exists the deaths will continue, and nobody seems to have suggested that the known disasters are decreasing in numbers, or to have denied that the unrecorded cases probably outnumber them several times.

Most certainly child abuse is a difficult and unrewarding subject, but perhaps things might be somewhat improved if it was thought of as 'child abuse; a disease' rather than as 'child abuse; a social disorder'. There is no doubt it would do no harm.

INFANTILE GASTROENTERITIS, DIARRHOEA AND VOMITING

Diarrhoea and vomiting in infants, D & V as it has always been called, used to occur all the year round in fairly large numbers, but about the turn of the century, when the warm weather arrived it reached epidemic proportions which led to its being called 'summer diarrhoea'. It has traded under a number of different titles, but with all of them it remained an awful lethal condition. The number of infants affected in those epidemics must have been horrendous and the death rate apallingly high, because when I became RMO at the Infants' Hospital, I noticed that in one of the wards there was a bell push with the subscription MORTUARY. It was no longer in working order, but when I enquired into its origin I discovered that when an epidemic was at its height the ward tended to become crowded with infant corpses, whereupon the ward sister would ring this bell to let the mortuary attendant know that he was to come and clear them away to make room for further admissions. It is a ghastly story, but apparently true, and perhaps brings home to one what those epidemics were like. In 1934 such epidemics no longer occurred in SE England anyway, but there was a steady stream of sporadic cases all the year round, and it was still the most important problem that had to be dealt with by paediatricians. In 1937, when only very ineffective treatment was available, the mortality rate in infants under the age of three months was 90%, a figure that made cancer look like the teddy bears' picnic; and between the ages of three and six months it was 40%. Beyond that age the mortality rate declined very steeply to almost nil. Goodness knows that all this was terrible enough in those infants who had been admitted with the disease, but what was much worse and a paediatrician's nightmare, was the fact that many infants admitted for some quite unrelated and completely recoverable condition such a pyloric stenosis, feeding problems, pink disease, rickets and many other illnesses became cross-infected and died. Their deaths were due solely and exclusively to their having been admitted to hospital.

The practice in children's wards was to isolate the infected cases as and when they occurred, but to allow the mixing of all other so-called clean cases. It just did not work, and cross-infection continued unabated, though there were a few places, of which the Infant's Hospital was one, where there was a system by which a limited number of non-infected infants were given the highest priority of isolation, and were architecturally separated from the rest of the inmates. It worked extremely well, and was instituted at Pembury when I took control in 1939.

With regard to infantile D & V, very little was known about its cause though many theories were advanced. It was said that the great epidemics of summer diarrhoea were due to dysentery and this may well have been so, but except in a small number of cases it certainly was not the position in the 1930s, and only rarely was it possible to identify a known causative germ of any sort in the stools. This of course gave rise to the idea that the cases must be due to a virus, but virological studies, such as were possible, gave no confirmation. Another theory holding sway for a number of years was that the symptoms were secondary to an infection in the middle ear, and this was true in a small number of cases. This unfortunately led to an enormous number of operations on perfectly normal ears, which merely accelerated the death of the patient. At the slightest suspicion of any redness of the eardrum, it was pierced with an instrument like a minature assegai, and the procedure was done incidentally without an anaesthetic. Surely it did nothing but harm. As an example of the extremes to which people could go was one HP who did one of these operations on all the infants with D & V during his night round so that he could forestall the consultant's request the following day. The man was a bit of a card, who later achieved no little fame with the Resistance movement in the Balkans, an occupation more suited to his bravado than a children's ward. Fortunately for my patients I had been taught by an ENT surgeon, Mr T B Layton, that it was impossible to tell the state of an infant's middle ear by inspecting it with

an auriscope, and that no matter what was happening if it
became infected it would always discharge its pus externally.
I think I barely ever did such an operation, and then only
under orders. This was just another example where the ethics
of medicine were allowed to exceed far beyond anything that
would be tolerated to-day.

In the end the true cause of the disease was disovered, and
very surprising it turned out to be, because it was a germ that
had been found in the stools of literally hundreds of thousands
of infants with D & V, but was always considered to be just a
normal innocent oganism. In fact they were not in the least
bit innocent or innocous, but highly dangerous if not controlled,
and as such had caused death and destruction on a massive
scale.

It then became possible to treat D & V in a scientific
manner, because about the same time advances in the understanding of intravenous fluid therapy and electrolyte balance
made it possible to maintain the infants in a reasonable state
of health until they overcame the infection. It was the lack of
understanding of these things in the past that had really been
the cause of so much difficulty in so many infants, and it was
the treatment with ill-regulated intravenous drips as much as
the disease that caused the deaths. These advances by
themselves led to a reduction in the mortality rate from 90%
to 10%, which was a startling improvement, and later
antibiotics that were able to combat the primary infection
were discovered. This combination of treatment was so effective that the death rate became almost insignificant, and as
not infrequently happens in a disease, when the mortality rate
falls, so does the incidence with the result that special units for
the treatment of these cases became redundant, and nobody
mourned their passing.

This highly satisfactory advance had one other enormously
beneficial effect on paediatrics, where there was no longer the
constant menace of hospital cross infection killing so many
infants. It relieved the wards of many of the burdensome
measures that had been taken on purely empirical grounds in
the hope that they would prevent the disease from spreading.
The nursing staff were released to more productive duties and
to everybody's benefit.

INFANT FEEDING

It is surely just a little bizarre that so much time, energy and ingenuity has had to be devoted to feeding human infants when the rest of the mammalian world has had almost no similar need. There was a time when the subject was enormously important, and at the turn of the century it occupied a great deal of any paediatrician's time, and some such as Eric Pritchard and Truby King (who was not medically qualified) dealt almost exclusively in this field. In addition, Eric Pritchard was largely instrumental in setting up infant welfare clinics, most of whose energies were directed towards the care and supervision of infant feeding. The situation has undergone a profound change since then.

Throughout history nobody has doubted that human milk was the right food for human babies, and if for one reason or another the mother was unable to breast feed her infant, the services of a 'wet nurse' were obtained and there was no problem, at least as far as the privileged were concerned. Equally it was always perfectly obvious in such circumstances that it would be advantageous if an artificial feed could be used, as this would obviate the need of a wet nurse, and of course it was absolutely essential if no such help could be obtained. The first attempts at artificial feeding involved using raw cow's milk in a bottle fitted with a teat made from stitched chamoix leather. The bottles were unsterile, the milk was unsterile, often contaminated with lethal pathogens, and it was impossible to clean such teats properly let alone sterilise them, even supposing there had been anyone who knew what bacteria were, what the word meant, or how to carry it out. Any infant who managed to survive such feeding was indeed a champion, but it is improbable that many, or for that matter any actually did.

The turning point came towards the end of the nineteenth century when Finkelstein showed that if infants were fed on unmodified boiled cow's milk from a sterile bottle 75% of them survived and flourished. From then on artificial feeding became a reality, and the only difficulty was how to manage the remaining 25% who were put into an omnibus group called 'feeding problems', to be dealt with by whosoever felt themselves qualified to advise. At this point it is necessary to step onto dangerous ground, because the truth of the matter is that any infant who is not flourishing is a diagnostic problem for an expert paediatrician, and not for the enthusiastic rule of thumb, trial and error amateur. Yet in spite of this dictum it was almost the universal practice for the latter course to be followed, and no amount of propaganda ever made any difference. The reason for wanting expert management is quite simply explained by the fact that the proper treatment can only be prescribed when the diagnosis is correct. What happens in most cases is that whenever an infant has vomiting, constipation, diarrhoea, failure to gain weight, cries excessively or is lethargic, the first assumption is that it is due to a dietetic cause, and as a result somebody changes the quality or the quantity or the mechanics of the feed, often all three of them, purely by guesswork and without having any idea of what the true cause of the trouble really is. The following is a compendium of some of the diseases that are nearly always misdiagnosed in the first instances as feeding problems, whereas none of them could possibly benefit, and may even be harmed by such a procedure. Pyloric stenosis, Down's syndrome, cretinism, hiatus hernia and gastro-oesophageal reflux, renal acidosis, galactosaemia phenylketonaemia, fibrocystic disease and many others. In the early 1930s several of these conditions had not yet been identified and were therefore undiagnosable, and no matter who tried to deal with them achieved little success, and unless there was a spontaneous remission the outlook was grim. Fortunately most of these problems have now been solved and have no further significance here.

Fashions in infant feeding, just like those in any other matter, change from one era to another, and in 1936 many infants, for one reason or another, were not breast fed, so that a substitute had to be provided, and several choices were available. For practical purposes all of them were made from cow's milk, though rarely some people thought that goat's milk was preferable, and even more infrequently ass's milk was obtained.

In spite of Finkelstein's work it was generally considered necessary to modify cow's milk so as to bring its constituents nearer to the proportions found in human milk, but the extent to which this was done varied enormously. When making a decision as to which artifical feed to advise, several factors quite apart from the health of the infant had to be taken into account. In the first place, refrigerators were almost non-existent in the less affluent homes, and by no means universal in the others, so that the keeping quality of the milk had to be borne in mind. Secondly, fresh cow's milk was not always pasteurised or even hygienically delivered. Thirdly, tins of evaporated milk, especially the sweetened variety, were often left standing on the kitchen table for the general use of the rest of the family in addition to feeding the infant, and lastly, dried milk was more expensive than any of the other feeds. Until the local authorities and later the government subsidised dried milk powder the choice most commonly fell on fresh, boiled, modified cow's milk formulae, and where expense was not a factor, dried milk reigned supreme. Although the nursing and medical professions tried to discourage the use of full cream sweetened evaporated milk when cost was all important, their advice was largely ignored because a 95 gramme tin of this milk cost 5p and was sufficient to feed a 3.5kg infant for three days. There is no doubt that many infants survived on this type of feed, though it made them inordinately fat and unless special care was taken they were very liable to develop rickets.

These various types of artificial feed served their purpose and generally covered most needs, leaving only a small group of special problems where vomiting, constipation or diarrhoea were intractable. Though the modern paediatrician is quite familiar with the aetiology in such cases, in those days when so many of the causes had not yet been identified, it was simply a matter of guesswork which finally ended in the diagnosis of a nonexistent group of diseases known as the 'gastric neuroses'. These were imagined, as there were absolutely no other grounds for the supposition, to be due to a non organic malfunction of the central nervous system, even to the extent of believing that the babies were behaving with malice aforethought!

In the modification of cow's milk to suit human infants three things received special attention the size of the curd, the percentage of fat and the nature of the carbohydrate. Although the curd of cow's milk is so much larger than its equivalent in breast milk and consequently seemed such an obvious thing to modify, it is doubtful whether it really made much difference to its suitability as a feed. Fortunately the heat treatment required in the manufacture of dried and evaporated milks reduced the curd size to such a degree that no further action was required, and only fresh cow's milk had to be dealt with. This was done by the addition of sodium citrate or lactic acid. As the former increased the sodium content of a milk that was already rather high for infant use, it remained in fashion for only a short time. Lactic acid milk was made on site by the laborious process of adding lactic acid (BP) drachm 1 (5 ml) drop by drop to a pint of milk, stirring vigorously all the time. This was almost the routine feed in the Children's Ward at Guy's Hospital, and it is a reflection on administrative attitudes at that time that nobody ever gave a thought to the unfortunate nurses who must have spent hours in the milk kitchen stirring away for dear life. With regard to the fat content, it was thought to play an important part as a cause of vomiting, and the idea was by no means confined to infants, as I was wont to remind students by suggesting that when crossing the English Channel in a force nine gale, the sight of a plate of well buttered crumpets was hardly likely to settle the stomach. There was one occasion when elaborating on the point, a student who had probably been over indulging the previous night had to beat a hasty retreat, and the noises off convinced the rest of the firm that it was a valid point. As far as infant feeding was concerned, if one wanted a lower fat content, the simplest way to achieve it was by the use of dried milks which were available in full cream, half cream and skimmed varieties, thus enabling any percentage required to be obtained. Full cream and half cream dried milks came into their own during World War Two, when in the face of food rationing, bombing and other unpleasantness, people were disinclined to spend long periods preparing complicated feeds, and the Government arranged for the production of national dried milks which fed the nation's infants for more than four years, and it is doubtful whether there had ever before been a better crop of them than the one it produced.

Sugar intolerance in infants turned out to be a much more complex problem because its cause was unknown until the discovery of the carbohydrate enzyme deficiencies many years later, when the conditions of alactasia, asucrasia and several others could be accurately identified and treated by avoiding the offending type of sugar involved in each individual case. However before this happy discovery a number of people had noticed that in cases where there were persistent frothy loose stools, the condition could often be improved by the use of dextrinised starch. The first to introduce the method was once again Finkelstein, who apparently prepared it in the ward in a frying pan, cooking the starch in hot fat to make his butter flour mixture. Be that as it may, in Glasgow there was a Ward Sister, Laura by name, who was in charge of the Children's Ward of the Royal Infirmary at the time when Sir Hector Cameron was the Professor of Surgery, and she too had her own method of achieving the same end. Apparently all the wards at the hospital had scotch ovens that burned all night, and she used to put the wheat flour in the slow oven in the evening, and by morning it was well and truly dextrinised. This product was subsequently made commercially and marketed under the title of Sister Laura's Food which was certainly still available in the late 1940s, but the main production of this preparation was in the USA where 'Dextri-Maltose' cornered the market, and was also widely used in the UK until the outbreak of war when its importation ceased. There was a very similar British product known as 'Mellin's Food' which could be used in its stead. The ultima thule finally arrived when it was realised that if dextrinised flour and dried milk powder were combined in the same package, it required just the addition of hot water to make a palatable beverage, and so the various commercially competing brands of malted milk preparations were created, not for use in infant feeding, but born out of it.

There was yet another method of modifying starch where, instead of dextrinising it by heat, it was partially predigested by means of a pancreatic ferment, but this product never achieved the same popularity as the others, due to two cogent reasons. The first was the fact that when prepared for use it retained the unattractive odour and taste of recently returned stomach contents, and produced the classic remark of somebody who when offered a cupful, demanded 'Do I eat this or have I just done so?'. The second reason was the label, which in order to attract two quite different markets stated that it was suitable for both infants and invalids. When an infant's mother read this she became singularly reluctant to give her healthy infant what was apparently an invalid food, whilst at the other end of the scale was the dyspeptic, choleric, gouty, ex-Indian Army colonel whose reaction was perhaps a great deal more vociferous when he caught sight of the tin, shouting 'I won't be fed on any b****y baby food. It appeared that in trying to kill two birds with one stone the manufacturers only managed to wing both of them.

From all the foregoing it is clear that the human infant proved both versatile and accommodating to flourish on all the diverse modifications made to cow's milk, and a great deal of effort was directed towards producing what was termed humanised cow's milk, in which the proportions of protein, fat, carbohydrate, size of curd and to some extent electrolyte content were brought as near as possible to that found in breast milk. They were neither more nor less successful than any of the others because proportions had little effect when the nature of the fat and protein were quite different in their chemistry. In fact all the different types of infant feed had about the same rate of success and failure, which is not surprising as the basis of their introduction was essentially guesswork, and it was only when that element was replaced by scientific discovery that all the black art of infant feeding was abolished.

Finally there has been one other great change in the attitude to infant feeding which has not been entirely beneficial, and it concerns the age at which mixed feeding is introduced. In early Victorian times it was the habit to breast feed infants two hourly by day and three hourly by night, until mixed feeding was started at the age of six to twelve months. Some feeding. Some mothers! Subsequently, in order to make life more tolerable, the interval between feeds was increased, and in the early 1930s it was usually four hourly with five feeds in the day. Mixed feeding was not introduced until after the end of the fourth month at the earliest. However the avant-garde brigade, encouraged by the pabulum manufacturers, began giving starch additions earlier and earlier in life. If a commercial firm manufactures such products they will naturally wish to increase their sales, and for that to be achieved only two courses of action are open to them. Either there have to be more infant consumers or else they must be got to start ingesting it younger and younger. Whilst there is no doubt that company chairmen are most admirable people even their best combined efforts are unlikely to make much difference to the birth rate, and therefore they have to encourage very early mixed feeding. In this they have been quite exceptionally successful, and now even neonates in maternity departments are often given additional farinas. There is no proof that this practice has any benefits, but coeliac disease due to gluten intolerence appears to be a much commoner disease than it used to be. Could there be any connection between the two?

PSYCHIATRIC MEDICINE

A glance at the Guy's List for 1986 shows that the Department of Psychological Medicine boasts no less than two Professors, nine Consultant Psychiatrists, with an additional five in the Department of Child Psychiatry. How many Senior Registrars, Registrars and House Officers attend their needs is not stated, but the total number of medical personnel engaged must be formidable, to which has to be added all the paramedical staff of psychotherapists, psychiatric social workers and others, so that the Department constitutes a small army in itself. By the nature of things psychiatry is a time consuming occupation, often slow and laborious in its progress, and when the teaching obligations are added on, it is probable that most of the people concerned are fully occupied. This set-up, as one might call it, has to be compared with the situation as it existed in 1931, where the total staff consisted of just one consultant psychiatrist, Dr R D Gillespie. To the best of my knowledge he had neither a Registrar of any sort nor a full time House Physician, and it must be presumed that any such help had to be borrowed from the Neurology Department. Not for one moment should it be thought that Guy's was dragging its feet in this respect, because in fact the Hospital rather prided itself in being in the forefront of progress, having previously appointed Dr Maurice Craig as the first psychiatric consultant appointment at any London teaching hospital. Dr R D Gillespie was his successor, not a contemporary.

From these facts it is almost superfluous to say any more about the quantity or the quality of student instruction in psychiatry, with the result that the average newly qualified practitioner must have lacked the ability to carry out meaningful practice in the subject even in the most minor degree. The pressure on Dr Gillespie must have been unbearable and the tragedy is that in the end he took his own life. Perhaps nothing better reflects the general attitude that a great many people held towards the subject, and it can be said only with sadness and contrition, that when the news of his death was announced, instead of expressions of regret, the reaction was more or less that it was just what might be expected in one of his calling. Instead of a recognition of what the burden of work must have done to him, the general attitude was that psychiatry as a subject, ranked very low and was considered just an also-ran.

Although lacking any personal experience in these matters, it is remarkable to think that when newly qualified practitioners went into general practice, where no doubt mental illness formed an enormous part of their future work, they would have spent not less than nine months on surgical firms engaged in a speciality where they might never again see a scalpel raised in anger, whereas their training in psychiatry consisted in just a handful of lecture demonstrations. These were given in one of the huge and gloomy hospitals for mental diseases, 'loony bins' as they were generally thought of and described, that tucked themselves away on the outskirts of London. What on earth could such a regime have taught anybody about such a vast subject? The answer is of course, almost nothing, because in the first place patients with mental disease are not as a rule exactly rich in physical signs that one can demonstrate to students, and even those selected for demonstration rarely performed in the manner expected of them when they were brought into a lecture theatre for a short period. The consequence of all this was that it left us none the wiser about their diseases, or psychiatry in general. The psychoneuroses, that huge group of diseases in which there is no organic disease of the brain, as opposed to the psychoses where there are such changes, although they occurred in vast numbers were never mentioned because they had nothing to show, and of course there was neither the time nor the opportunity to talk to them about their troubles. The students felt that they attended the course for two reasons. In the first place it was compulsory, and in the second they hoped for some startling demonstrations of the more lurid side of the diseased mind, and when these failed to materialise, interest evaporated. Even to those people who retained an interest the subject seemed obtuse and largely incomprehensible, and they knew that they would never be able to understand it through the way they were being taught.

Psychiatry at the best of times is not one of the easiest of subjects to comprehend, and the effort required was not forthcoming when the entire subject was looked upon as nothing more than a sideline in a general training. The text books were almost equally obscure because so many psychiatrists at that time were very long on loquacity, verbosity and obscurity, and somewhat short on comprehensibility. The speciality was in fact really only just emergent and there were no landmarks such as the M.R.C. Psych. to separate the sheep from the goats. A lot of the practitioners had the gift of the gab, a box full of technical terms and the ability to delude people that they knew what they were talking about, when in reality they did not. That sort of thing did nothing to raise the respect for the subject in the main stream of the profession, most of whom anyway were sceptical. It was extremely difficult to equip oneself with the minimum knowledge required by the curriculum, and had it not been for a single easily comprehensible text book, I should never have aquired even the miniscule understanding that I did manage to achieve.

As far as the final examinations were concerned, there was no separate paper, nor even a section of one dealing with psychiatry, as there was in what would now be called community medicine, though it was theoretically possible to be faced with a question on mental illness. Fortunately the chances were not very great, and a glance at the list of examiners whose autograph names are appended to my certificate after passing the College examinations contains the name of no psychiatrist. Although the examiners who acted for the University of London remained innominate, there was most certainly not a single question, either written or at a viva voce, that dealt with the subject. It has to be remembered that at the time there was still a widespread belief that any form of mental illness cast a stigma which the patient had to bear in addition to their illness and in many cases the odium extended to their family as well. General Physicians as a group did not think highly of psychiatry, and many of them held it in contempt, and this type of attitude was heightened by their practice of referring their difficult and awkward cases to that department, not because it was thought that it would do the patients any good, but simply using it as a dumping ground in order to relieve themselves of the burden. Psychiatry was neither a popular nor a respected subject in those days.

There was however one exception to these observations in the remarkable example of the Seal Hayne Hospital, which specialised in the treatment of shell-shocked soldiers during the 1914–18 war. What the boundaries of this condition really were is not very clear, as to some it was an honourable 'war scar', and others considered it as a blot on the escutcheon. As a child I recall that one of my contemporaries had an older brother whom it was said had been discharged from the army on account of shell-shock, and was away in hospital for treatment. Not surprisingly, my friend bathed in a marvellous degree of reflected glory in having such an eminent relation. Many years later it was something of a surprise to discover that his absence had nothing to do with trench warfare, as the young man had been dishonourably discharged from the army on account of some criminal activity, and had then spent a number of subsequent years in prison. Thus, whilst the diagnosis remained in use it covered a very wide spectrum of conditions, and the term was not resurrected in the Second World War. However there is no doubt that a genuine trench neurosis did occur, and in due course as the true facts of life and death on the Western Front emerged, it is little short of miraculous that any soldier who survived there for any length of time did not develop it.

As an example of this, there was a professional infantry soldier who had gone into the trenches in 1914, and apart from being wounded several times, remained in them until the end of the war in 1918. Quite apart from anything else, to have survived that length of time was almost a miracle as the prognosis for officers was measured in a matter of months or less, and when asked how he had managed to withstand the ordeal, replied that he had been so frightened all the time that he never had the courage to desert, or the good fortune to develop shell-shock, so he just had to carry on with the job. What medals for gallantry he was awarded is not recorded, but it would seem that a Victoria Cross would not have been out of place for that fact alone.

There was another example of how this strange diagnosis could be used by the Army itself for its own purposes in the case of Siegfried Sassoon, one of the small group of poet soldiers of that war. He had joined the infantry on 3rd August 1914, and apart from wounds and diseases spent the next four years in that occupation where he watched the slaughter of his men and the deaths of his fellow poets. Following a wound of the right shoulder in 1917 he was invalided home for treatment, and when he had recovered he felt that he had to make some protest against the conduct of the war with its appalling holocaust, and though not himself a pacifist he made contact with some of the very eminent ones including Bertrand Russell. Subsequently when he came before a medical board and presumably expressed his views, he was promptly packed off to Craiglockhart War Hospital near Edinburgh for 'special treatment'. It would seem that the Army preferred him to be a case of shell-shock, which he certainly was not, rather than have an eminent though awkward customer on their hands! Unfortunately for the Army, the physician in charge felt unable to confirm their diagnosis, but the patient was for some time kept in the hospital where he could cause no trouble, and it is an unfortunate fact that the practice of putting dissidents into mental hospitals has not yet been universally abandoned.

However to return to the Seal Hayne Hospital, it was the creation of one of Guy's Hospital's general physicians, Dr (later Sir) Arthur Hurst, who introduced his own personal methods of dealing with the complaint. He was not, nor did he claim to be a psychiatrist, and for that matter was far more renowned for his work on gastro-enterology, and even when I was ward clerk on his firm he gave no impression of a great interest in mental illness. He must have been an exception amongst the general physicians of his time.

This review of the position in relation to mental illnesses as it was when we were students makes it clear that it would scarcely have been possible for us to have had less instruction than that which was provided. After qualification we all went our separate ways, ignorant and ill-equipped to deal with any aspect of this vast and ubiquitous disease, which must have at some time or another touched us all, no matter in which field we practised. Those who went into general practice must have felt the most deprived and no doubt had to learn their lessons the hard way. In retrospect it was not really a very pretty picture, but even before the war broke out things were rapidly improving, and at Guy's Hospital a new self-contained custom-built clinic with its own staff of gargantuan proportions came into being, and the entire specialty has flourished ever since. The days when the final examination candidates could be reasonably certain that no questions on psychiatric medicine would trouble them have long since gone, and some if not all will find themselves faced with one paper on that subject alone. Moreover there are now special examinations for higher qualifications, and the final emblem of respectability is the creation of The Royal College of Psychiatry.

SEXUALLY TRANSMITTED DISEASES PREVIOUSLY CALLED VENEREAL DISEASES

Hospitals as a general rule, unless they happen to specialise in this area of disease, rarely if ever advertise or parade their VD departments in the most prominent places. Even those hospitals that do so specialise, tend to trade under euphemistic titles such as the 'Lock Hospital', and no doubt the Seamen's Hospital' at Greenwich had more of its activity given over to venereal diseases than was the average practice in other hospitals. Guy's was no exception to the rule, and the department was almost cut off from the rest of the hospital buildings. It had its two (male and female) innominate entrances somewhere near Crosby Row, which was about as far away as one could get from St Thomas's St and the Maze Pond, from which all normal access to the hospital was obtained. It was possible for the medical staff to gain entry from the ordinary out-patient buildings, but it was so designed that nobody could wander into it by chance.

Women students did not appear in the medical school until after the war, so that the students' experience was more or less confined to the men's section, where they attended evening sessions. Ocasionally there were syphilitic cases exhibiting primary or secondary manifestations, but mostly they were without either signs or symptoms as these had been cleared by previous treatment with arsenical drugs, and were now just undergoing the prolonged course of treatment that was required. In fact the combined total of all those cases were greatly outnumbered by others suffering from active gonorrhoea, a condition that did little to attract our interest. The treatment of syphilis was by then almost exclusively by the intravenous injection of organic arsenical drugs which had replaced mercury, though not completely, because it still had a place in the treatment of the initial stages of an acute attack.

Previously it had been the basis of all treatment, and even as recently as 1920 had led Earle Moore to coin his aphorism, 'Two minutes with Venus, two years with Mercury'. In practice all the treatment was carried out, not by students as elsewhere in the hospital, but by orderlies who were not trained nurses, and who had incredible skill in getting drugs into, and blood out of veins.

The arsenical drugs were always referred to by their pharmacological serial numbers as 606 and 914, rather than their correct, if somewhat cumbersome chemical titles, arsphenamine and neo-arsphenamine. This preference turned out to be more than justified when the Consultant Venereologist, who certainly had a down to earth outlook that well befitted his calling, and a sense of humour to match, related with great glee the following incident that had happened to him that day in his little kingdom. He had been visited by a Central European doctor, who in the course of a discussion about the current treatment of syphilis had said to him 'Doctor, in your practice you use much of the arse-feminine?'. From that moment onwards I never felt at all certain that I would manage to get the name right, and for ever after confined myself to their numerical titles.

As far as gonorrhoea was concerned, the treatment just consisted of urethral and bladder washouts using a solution of potassium permanganate, but that was carried out by the orderlies, whose skill with the catheter was reputed to be the equal of that which they possessed in performing venepunctures. The female side, as far as we were concerned, was forbidden territory, but we were a very privileged group to be invited there to see a case of infected Bartholin's cysts. The demonstration was conducted with enormous tact and propriety by Mrs Rawlins, who was in charge of the ladies' section. She was a remarkable person, and one of the original founders of the Monte Carlo Rally in which she drove her Riley 9. In those days it was a contest, so she said, where amateurs got into their cars in the bleak midwinter of Northern Europe, and tried to drive through frost, fog and snow to the sunshine of the Principality. There were no sponsors, no travelling mechanics and no team managers en route. From what has been said it is clear that the knowledge to be aquired in the VD department on the clinical aspects of syphilis and gonorrhoea was very limited, and was mainly confined to therapy, because the primary and secondary lesions healed very rapidly with treatment. In any case the diseases were becoming less common than they had been, and one imagines that with the advent of antibiotics there was even less to see.

However in spite of what went on in the VD department, the two diseases, especially syphilis, loomed very large in everybody's considerations in the rest of the hospital, on account of the natural history of the disease with its long course of primary, secondary and tertiary stages, and its extraordinary protean manifestations. Girolamo Frascatoro had recognised as early as the 16th century that 'the moon had often four times circled the Earth before clear symptoms of the disease appeared', but by far the most important statement was that of Sir William Osler, 'know syphilis in all its manifestations and relations, and all things clinical will be added to you', but much more commonly quoted as 'know syphilis and you know medicine'. What all this meant was that even in 1930 it was still quite possible that the initial infection might never have been treated, and though Paul Erlich's 'magic bullets' had improved the therapy far beyond the powers of mercury, the consideration of syphilis loomed large as a possible diagnosis in almost every case in almost every department of the hospital. To the neurologist, tabes dorsalis, general paralysis of the insane (GPI), and other nerve and blood vessel manifestations were reasonably common conditions, and in the general wards there was nearly always an aortic aneurysm and a number of other types of cardio-vascular disease. To one very small selected group this fact was a godsend, and they were the House Physicians of those consultants who were examiners in qualifying and higher examinations in Medicine. Their unfortunate House Physicians had, every three months, the unenviable and unpaid task of finding sufficient suitable cases for the candidates to examine, and then be quizzed about. On the surgical side, syphilis of the bones, 'the boring pains of the Psalmist' and arthritis such as Clutton's joints were by no means unknown. A great deal of nonsense was talked about syphilitic disease of the kidneys, which if it occurred at all must have been a great rarity. Because of all these possibilities, it meant that amost every case admitted to the hospital had a routine Wasserman syphilis test, and even more certainly in the ante-natal clinic, where they needs had to bear in mind the ancient biblical warning, 'He visits the iniquity of the fathers upon the children to the third and fourth generation'. In those times people clearly were not mealy-mouthed about apportioning the blame, both physical and moral, where the origin of congenital syphilis was concerned. Fortunately, arsenical treatment during pregnancy almost guaranteed the prevention of infected neonates to such a degree that the condition had almost disappeared, except in those cases where a mother had slipped through the prophylactic net. In the delivery suites gonorrhoea was much more of a problem when infection of the newborn baby's eyes could cause blindness, and so as a prophylactic measure every newborn infant had silver nitrate drops instilled into its eyes immediately after delivery. The drops themselves frequently caused a mild inflammation which was very transient, but this procedure was so very effective that in my whole career I only ever saw one case of a full blown gonococcal eye infection. It was in the genito-urinary department that gonorrhoea really made itself felt as the chief cause of urethral strictures, which had to be treated by passing dilators at frequent intervals. This was a procedure that really required considerable skill, something that most medical men did not possess, much to the detriment of the patients. The Surgeon in charge of the genito-urinary department at that time was a very unusual type of man, rude, aggressive, large and frightening, though said to be very different when you really got to know him. This may well have been true, but as the appointment came right at the end of one's clinical course and anyway was purely optional, very few students elected to do it. The result was that most people qualified with a remarkably inadequate knowledge of the subject, but that was something that applied equally well to so many other aspects of student training.

With the passage of time and the use of antibiotics, the incidence of both syphilis and gonorrhoea decreased, to such a degree that routine Wasserman tests went out of fashion as did the use of silver-nitrate drops in neonatal eyes, and it seemed that the utopia of no venereal disease was nigh. However there were always distant rumblings that this complacency was unjustified, since it was said that the incidence was actually starting to increase again, especially in the face of the ever extending permissive society that had emerged. Then came the bombshell: the discovery that AIDS had suddenly become a terrifying menace, something that has given the subject a worldwide publicity never previously dreamed of. Perhaps if the sufferers had been confined to the innominate masses it might have taken much longer to make its presence felt; but with the death of a film star and an ex-royal valet from the disease, added to the now openly-acknowledged fact that considerable numbers of the people whom the media refer to as personalities are or were homosexuals, has added a completely new dimension to the whole sorry story. Perhaps the greatest change that has been brought about is that sexually transmitted diseases are no longer consigned to a hospital's back parlour, but the victims may even find themselves visited in hospital by royalty and Cabinet Ministers, and children who for so many generations were shielded from knowledge of these things may witness usually rather ill directed publicity in the media. One can but wonder where it will all end.

SURGICAL INTERLUDE

Had circumstances been but very slightly different, it is probable that I should have been a surgeon and not a paediatrician. The fact that it did not come about dates back to the period immediately after passing the 2nd M.B. B.S. examination, when it was the practice for those students intending to become surgeons, to spend a further six months in the Medical School, doing an advanced course in anatomy and physiology which was specially designed for the Primary F.R.C.S. examination. This arrangement was probably due to financial considerations because most medical students were in receipt of a grant from their local authority or some other body, but either way it terminated after qualification. As there were very few or no subsidies for post-graduate study, it meant that done in this sequence the extra six months taken up by the course was subsidised, but if done after qualification it was not. In order to join the course, one had to get the permission of the Dean of the Medical School, who not only ruled our academic lives, but as Professor of Anatomy, arranged, controlled and ran the course, and decided just who should or should not be allowed to enrol, and without such tuition it would have been impossible to pass the exam.

Consequently after passing the 2nd M.B. B.S., I went to see the Dean to request permission to join the Primary Fellowship class, and his reply still rings in my ears: 'Certainly not Boy! Good morning,' and that was that because I should never have dared to argue the point with him. Maybe, in his judgement I was quite unable to manage anything on such an elevated plane, but even with the passage of so many years it still seems an odd decision. Although I hadn't been an outstanding anatomist, I certainly wasn't a duffer at it, and a few weeks earlier had won the Physiology prize, the subject that constituted the other half of the Primary F.R.C.S. examination, as well as the Junior Proficiency prize which took into

223

account all the pre-clinical subjects, and by inference I must have had some ability in anatomy. I suppose that he just didn't like me, and I am sorry to say that throughout my career at Guy's my relationship with him brings back no happy memories, and I shed no tears when I went into other spheres that ensured that our paths should never cross again. In the modern world it may seem incredible that students should be so cowed by such a man, but in those days it was the accepted way of life for the young to obey their superiors, and I never questioned his decision. Perhaps, had I been a bit older, or my parents had been in the UK they might have taken up the matter and no doubt had their way, but to me the decision was final. Without an F.R.C.S., a future in surgery seemed just impossible, for it was an essential requirement in a teaching hospital even before one got one's foot on the first rung of the ladder towards consultantship. Such was the rarified atmosphere in which we lived at Guy's, that I had no idea until years later that there were a great many surgeons on the staffs of non-teaching provincial hospitals who had no higher qualifications of any sort, and had received only minimal training, yet conducted large and lucrative practices. They achieved such positions by joining a partnership of good General Practitioners who held the keys to these doors, and in due course when a vacancy arose they were appointed to the staff of the local hospital. It would be quite wrong to suggest that all these surgeons were of the same ilk, and there were many others who were properly qualified and trained, but it was by no means the absolute rule. After the war and with the introduction of the National Health Service, such methods of appointment became impossible, and with the passage of time there can be very few, if any left who still practise the art of surgery.

But to return to my own experience in the surgical field, it all began when I was appointed a House Surgeon (HS) to Mr Robert Davies Colley. This position is the lowest rung on the ladder of surgical training, but even so an HS was allowed to perform occasional operations such as removing an appendix under the supervision of his Chief or the Registrar, but much more important than that was the experience gained in the emergency work. At that time the Guy's system arranged that each of the four surgical firms went on emergency take-in for a full seven days on end, and although it was exhausting it was a marvellous experience. The stress of a week's emergency duty was obviously far more than anybody should have been asked to bear, because there was no compensatory relief from the firm's normal activity, and an HS was fortunate to get as much as five hours sleep in twentyfour hours, and very often even that was interrupted. On the final day of one of these take-in weeks I had retired to bed utterly exhausted at about 3 a.m., only to be awoken by the night porter an hour later, when he apparently told me that Night Sister had phoned to say that there was a male patient in some pain, and would I please come and see him. I am reputed to have replied: 'Tell Sister to take ½ grain of morphia, give half of it to the patient and take the rest herself' and then fell back into a deep sleep. Next day I was summoned before the Superintendant, Sir Herbert Eason, to explain my behaviour, and all I could say was that I had absolutely no recollection of the incident. I suppose that in his youth, Sir Herbert had been through the same mill, and beyond a routine reprimand nothing more was heard of the matter, and it is highly improbable that seven days continuous emergency duty exists anywhere nowadays. Fortunately neither the patient nor the night sister came to any harm.

During a take-in week the official arrangement was that the senior surgeon had overall responsibility, and all the cases were admitted under his care; but in fact he never had any knowledge of or contact with them until some days later when he conducted his routine teaching round. At no time, nor in any circumstances would he be called out to deal with emergencies, and it was the more junior consultant, the Assistant Surgeon, who had to be contacted. However in most cases the Registrar was almost or equally as experienced as his superior, who could therefore quite safely delegate his responsibility down the line. The result was that the appearance of an assistant surgeon in the hospital in the small hours of the morning was about as common as an iceberg in a Saharan oasis. In practice it worked out that all the emergency work was done by the Registrar, who in his turn could delegate as much of it as he wished further down the line to the HS. In my case the Registrar, Alec Simpson Smith was a brilliant surgeon, very experienced, and quite a character whose career was tragically cut short in the North African campaign at Tobruk. At the time of our association he was very much engaged in obtaining consultant appointments, and it involved him in a great deal of social activity, so that when he discovered that I had a modicum of surgical skill, he was quite prepared to delegate much of the work to me. As a result, when cases of acute appendicitis were admitted, all I had to do was to inform him and then get on with the job. It so happened that these were the commonest cases admitted, and during the six months that I held the post something like thirty or more cases must have passed through my hands. In addition to this experience where I was in full charge, there were also the other more major operations such as perforations, strangulated hernias, complicated fractures and road accidents, where one worked in close co-operation with the Registrar, so that at the end of six months one had acquired a modest ability in the surgical field, and most important of all the confidence to perform on one's own in the operating theatre.

Following this experience I had a period of three months waiting for the paediatric House Physician (HP) post to become vacant, and I filled in the time doing locum Resident Surgical Officer appointments, a grade between an HS and a Registrar, in various non-teaching hospitals in SE England. Here I discovered that I was expected to do all the emergency work, including perforated peptic ulcers and strangulated hernias. I suppose that youthful enthusiasm and confidence carried me through without disaster, but I must have had more than a fair proportion of luck: and here I ought to pay tribute to my alma mater. It was generally acknowledged at that time that a Guy's training was not aimed at the academic heights, such as those that ruled at University College Hospital, but it did claim to turn out doctors who could face any situation calmly and practically, and in my case I must have absorbed some of that ability. On one occasion I opened an abdomen as a suspected perforated gastric ulcer, only to find the tell tale fat necrosis of acute inflammation of the pancreas (no connection with diabetes). It came to mind that Sir Heneage Ogilvie had taught us in a similar case that there was nothing to do in such circumstances other than thorough drainage of the abdominal cavity, and so well did I follow his advice, and so many tubes did I insert, that at the end of the operation the patient's abdomen resembled nothing so much as the skyline of a northern industrial city prior to Britain's disastrous manufacturing decline. By a stroke of good fortune the patient recovered, and as I was never again to be faced with a similar situation I used to claim that I was probably the only surgeon with a 100% recovery rate in what was a rather fatal disease!

After entering the realms of paediatrics my surgical career had apparently come to an end, and so it was for a number of years until fate decreed otherwise. The cause of the change was an infant with the condition known as congenital hypertrophic pyloric stenosis, a disease of early infancy which usually has to be dealt with by a Rammstedt-Fredet's operation, one of the most satisfactory surgical procedures ever devised, and which has not been altered or modified in any way since it was introduced in 1912. Whilst there is no such thing as an absolutely safe operation in surgery, because one never knows when something unexpected will rear its ugly head, the mortality rate of this operation is now insignificant, though this was not always the case, and in the 1930s it stood at about 5% in paediatric centres, but was as high as 20% in some other places. The cause of death when it did occur had little or nothing to do with the surgery, except in the rarest of occasions, but was related to the dehydration and the upset of the blood chemistry, or most common of all, the hazard of a cross infection by the germs of diarrhoea and vomiting in hospital. In order to reduce this risk and its high mortality rate, David Levi devised a somewhat different approach that I came to know when I worked under him at the Infant's Hospital, in London, and fell under his spell. In most centres the routine procedure was to admit these infants and correct the dehydration and the blood chemistry by means of intravenous fluids, or a procedure requiring less skill where fluids were injected in the tissues under the skin or into the abdominal cavity, and then several days later do the operation under a general anaesthetic. This entailed keeping the infant in hospital for ten to fourteen days even if no complications arose. The risk of developing diarrhoea and vomiting was very considerable, and if it did occur was very fatal. The Levi technique was based on two principles; firstly to have the infant in hospital for as short a period as possible, and secondly to keep it as far away as one could from any other source of infection. To achieve this the operation was done without any pre-operative replacement of fluids, no matter how wizened the infant appeared, and therefore was performed under a local anaesthetic using a technique that barely upset the infant at all. Subsequent fluid loss replacement was done by the simple and natural way of feeding by mouth, so that sometimes the infant was discharged home straight from the operation suite, or anyway a very few days later during which time it was accommodated in an area far removed from the general wards and their infected patients. By this method he was able to publish a series, probably the first ever of one hundred consecutive cases without a death.

In a totally different way, and for several different reasons Rammstedt's operation holds a unique position in surgery. The first of these is associated with its relative rarity, so that outside any large paediatric centre only about ten to fifteen cases are admitted each year, and all these infants are diagnosed by, and then admitted under the care of a paediatrician who chooses the surgeon he wishes to do the operation, after which he then again takes over the management of the case. In fact this arrangement turns the surgeon into nothing more than an incidental performer, a classical hewer of wood and a drawer of water, a role to which as a general rule surgeons are not partial. Obviously the whole business requires a co-operative effort, and by the nature of things it is nearly always the same surgeon who is invited to do the operation to the exclusion of all the others, with the result that there must be many excellent general surgeons who have performed almost every operation in the surgical calendar many times over, and never done a Rammstedt's operation. This was certainly the position at Pembury hospital, to which the main part of Guy's paediatric department was evacuated at the beginning of the war in 1939. In the early days we were able to call on the services of Mr E. C. Hughes, a retired Guy's surgeon who lived locally, and by a fortunate coincidence had previously always done the operations there; but the time came when I had an infant needing surgery, but Mr Hughes had died and none of the other surgeons had ever done such an operation, so it meant sending the case to a paediatric hospital in London, a procedure that had never appealed to me at all on account of the fact that once one starts on the practice of sending one's patients to other hospitals it spreads like a cancer, and ends by turning the department into little more than a reception and distribution centre.

When that happens it becomes unattractive to junior staff, which in turn leads to a reduction of standards until finally it becomes a vicious circle. Naturally there are some things such as cardiac, thoracic and neuro-surgery where the facilities are available only in special centres and one's cases have to be transferred there, but Pembury Hospital always tried to keep such practices to a minimum.

The urge to do Rammstedt's operations myself was overwhelming, especially as it had the added advantage that for the first time it would bring the total management of these cases under one consultant, instead of having to share it with a surgeon who, as was pointed out earlier, fills a role that such forceful people do not really enjoy. Although I felt perfectly confident that I could do the operation, I had to consider the ethics of a paediatrician taking up the knife as a Principal, because all my previous experience had been in a junior position working, at least in theory, under the aegis of a full consultant surgeon who carried the final responsibility, even though not present in the theatre at the time. In addition to those considerations, one had to take into account that there is no such thing as an absolutely safe operation, and there is always the possibility of the unexpected happening, and especially in this disease of opening the abdomen and discovering that the expected tumour just isn't there. Although this has been known to occur, it should be an extremely rare occurrence because pyloric stenosis is unique in that every case has the unique finding that before operation one can feel the tumour in the upper abdomen, that comes and goes as you feel it. This is something that occurs in no other disease, and without such a finding there should be no operation. However if this particular mistake has been made, it is immaterial whether the surgeon is the President of the Royal College or a first time paediatrician surgeon, because there is nothing that either of them can do except close the abdomen. When I had considered all these matters I felt perfectly certain that I could manage the surgery, but still felt it necessary to have some professional surgical cover for safety purposes. I therefore approached one of the Pembury surgeons, Mr J J Bell, and as far as I am concerned, to his eternal credit and my eternal gratitude, he agreed to assist me. That evening, after all the routine operating lists had been done, we set about our task, which as expected caused no difficulty, but I can't say that I spent a very restful night because it was interrupted by nightmares in which I played a principle part in the proceedings in the mortuary, the Coroner's Court and before the Disciplinary Committee of the General Medical Council, so that the following morning I could hardly wait to find out what had happened. At this point it is necessary to explain that in all infants after a Rammstedt's operation some further vomiting may occur, but mostly this is of a minor character and can be ignored. However, sometimes it can be quite persistent for as much as three days, and this led one American surgeon to put all his cases on an intravenous infusion for that length of time before starting feeding by mouth again, but this seemed an extreme view and I never knew anybody else who followed his example. What worried me was the possibility that the operation had not completely relieved the obstruction and would have to be done again, something that was admittedly rare, but by no means unknown even in the hands of professional surgeons. This would be shown up by the vomiting continuing for more than three post-operative days, and so if my case had any post-operative vomiting one would not be able to tell what was causing it for at least that length of time, and the agony of uncertainty would be prolonged, because I knew who would be blamed. As against all those possibilities, some of the cases never vomit again and go straight ahead to a full recovery, and it must have been beginner's luck because my case did just that, and henceforward I knew that what I had thought I could do in theory was now a fact. From then on I operated on all my own cases, and even a few of other people's, so that in the end the total exceeded 250, with an acceptable mortality rate of under 0.4%, though naturally I wished that it could have been nought. I never developed a fashionable practice in these matters, though somewhere there is a man who directs an eponymous firm of brewers, and another who is head of a small island state who passed through my hands, and on another occasion I received an enquiry from the Royal Navy who could not make out what a high midline scar, inflicted by a paediatrician on the abdomen of a would-be recruit indicated. Now it is one of the nicer aspects of this disease that most of the infants who suffer from it grow up to be both physically and mentally above average, and Dr Cameron used to tell us that Paavo Nurmi and many other Scandinavian Olympic champions carried Rammstedt's scars on their abdomens. It was on one such occasion that I noted how one of the students on the firm was developing a broader and broader smile until he opened his shirt and revealed the evidence that he too belonged to the select band. When I answered the Royal Navy's enquiry, I added that I felt sure my ex-patient would make a most excellent addition to Her Majesty's Navy.

It would be a gross exaggeration of the truth to suggest that one's surgical colleagues approve of or encourage paediatrician surgeons (not to be confused with Paediatric Surgeons who are a new breed of highly-skilled specialists) though I was lucky in being accorded their benign tolerance and acceptance of the fact. Although it was known to my immediate colleagues that I indulged in this practice it was not noised abroad, and this led to an interesting and even rather amusing result. The Paediatric Section of The Royal Society of Medicine arranged a meeting on 'The Treatment of Congenital Pyloric Stenosis' and invited Mr (later Sir) Dennis Browne, who was an extremely eminent Paediatric Surgeon at the Hospital for Sick Children in London to lead on the surgery, and Mr David Levi to describe his personal technique. As it was well known that I treated some of my cases without an operation, by a much derided medical regime, I was invited to speak third as a sort of comic turn. Dennis Browne gave as was his wont, a learned, clear and forceful discourse, in which he chose to stress the importance of the skill of the surgeon, and especially the use of an instrument he had devised which was a special 'spreader' that he felt was essential to the success of the operation. I am sure he didn't mean to, but he did rather give the impression that if you wanted your cases of pyloric stenosis to survive you had better send them to the Hospital for Sick Children. David Levi, in a less flamboyant style described his method, the results of which it would have been impossible to have bettered in practice, or to have been better received by the meeting. Lastly it was my turn to talk on the medical treatment with a drug called atropine methyl nitrate, a drug that avoided operation altogether. I doubt very much whether I influenced anybody to try the method, because sometimes it failed to cure the condition and an operation became necessary after all, and anyway even when it was successful it took a much longer time than an operation to complete the cure. On the whole British people are wedded to the idea that 'the operation was a great success but unfortunately the patient died', and consequently the surgical method has always held the field. However some devilish imp had got into me, probably because Dennis Browne had laid such emphasis on the skill of the surgeon, and I decided that this was the time and the place to make public that I was the person who operated on my own cases, and in fact my results were significantly better than Dennis Browne's. This had nothing to do with surgical skill, but was due solely to the fact that I drew my cases from a rather more affluent area of the country, and consequently they tended to be in a better physical state when diagnosed, and secondly the isolation facilities at Pembury Hospital were superb, which meant that the chances of contracting hospital gastro-enteritis were negligible. As can be imagined, the news rather stunned the meeting and led to a mixture of hilarious laughter, good natured chaff and some vitriolic comment on the ethics of it all. However it did show that it was possible for a paediatrician to have some surgical skill, and I believe one or two others followed my example, though I doubt whether anyone is doing it nowadays. I am afraid that my revelation rather took the wind out of the great man's sails, and I don't imagine that it did anything to endear me to him; but many years later I was fortunate enough in a cross country dash, and with the aid of my Registrar Dr Pauline Cole, to save the life of one of his young relatives, so perhaps he forgave me. I do hope so.

All the foregoing raises a point that I feel should be made, and that is that surgery is not at all what popular imagination thinks it is. All my life I have had a sympathetic leaning toward the subject, and with very few exceptions had more affinity with surgeons than paediatricians, so that I would never wish to denigrate them or their art, especially as in recent years I have personally benefited greatly from their services. However in my opinion the delicate, tapering, long-

fingered, dexterous hands required for the job are a myth, and
those of my greatly revered ex-master, the late Robert Davies
Colley, were much more reminiscent of a couple of York hams,
and yet were just as dexterous as those of anybody else. The
actual amount of manual skill required is greatly overstressed,
and compared with that of an old-fashioned plumber before
the advent of self-joining pipes, is minimal. Anyone who ever
saw a wiped joint being made would know how extremely
difficult it is, and as a DIY I never got anywhere near success.

Great surgeons, just like any other medical greats need a
high intelligence, a wide knowledge, and that indefinable
thing, clinical acumen as well as massive humanity. The
manual dexterity is relatively unimportant, and in fact some
of the greatest surgeons have not always had a great deal of it,
though to name names would be invidious indeed. I recall a
discussion on some specialised surgery where one of the
comments was: 'If I had that sort of disease I would get Lord
X to decide what should be done, and Sir YZ to do it'. Both
of those very eminent persons were surgeons.

This surgical interlude certainly added a zest to my practice,
and I was fortunate in the benign tolerance shown me by the
real surgeons, and perhaps by accident I was able to make a
small repayment to one of them. On various occasions interested people used to come to the theatre to watch the
performance of the strange paediatrician gone surgeon, and
they included a very able Australian Surgical Registrar who
was within a few days of taking his final viva for the F.R.C.S.
By a strange coincidence he was asked about Rammstedt's
operation, and replied that he had only once ever seen one
done, and that was by a paediatrician. The rest of the time
was spent discussing the ethics of physicians masquerading as
surgeons, and no time was left to ask him any other questions.
Of course he passed with flying colours, which I am sure he
would have done anyway, but he was one surgeon who had
cause for gratitude at my efforts, or at least so he said!

Perhaps as a bit of tail corn, it might be added that as a
result of our surgical ventures in pyloric stenosis, and the more
legitimate activities of substitution transfusions (described
elsewhere), the Matron of Pembury, the late Miss Jane Jacobs,
who later became Senior Nursing Officer to the Ministry of
Health, headed an appeal that collected sufficient funds to

provide the Children's Ward with its own completely-equipped operating theatre which was a great convenience to us, and removed the irritant to the real surgeons of finding their facilities being used by outsiders. It cost a lot of money but I fear it did not long outlive my retirement.

ANAESTHETIC INTERLUDE

It is surely true that everybody bar perhaps a few masochists has no wish to suffer pain, and thank goodness from the medical aspect the point has now been reached where almost every situation can be controlled. It was not always thus, and one wonders just how anyone managed to face the terrors of surgery before proper anaesthesia was available. I found it a spine-chilling experience when visiting the historic Guy's operating theatre in St Thomas's St, to try and imagine what it must have been like to endure operations there, and in much the same way in the surgeon's cabin on HMS Victory, and the even much earlier warship Mary Rose. Can one really visualise the amputations and cutting for stone on people who had nothing to rely on, other than alcohol and biting on the bullet to relieve the agony. I suppose that *si opus sit*, a large dose of opium afforded some relief.

If all this sounds quite horrifying, it is salutary to remember that, until quite recently, an enormous amount of dentistry was done without any anaesthesia, local or otherwise, even in places that should have known better. It was doubtless this prospect of dental surgical pain added to ordinary dental pain, that left a legacy, not yet completely eradicated, of an inordinate and unnecessary fear of dentistry. This has been the cause of so many people refusing routine inspections, as a result of which it not infrequently resulted in a full set of dentures before the age of thirty. Fortunately this attitude is now disappearing, but I remember that when I had just qualified, there was a general practice in the Borough High Street where we did occasional evening locums to supplement our incomes, and there was a notice in the waiting room that announced 'Teeth Extracted, One shilling each; Painless method, one shilling and sixpence'. The latter method consisted of injecting a saline solution into the gums as tightly as possible, but it contained no local anaesthetic and no analgesia was produced.

My own involvement in this sort of thing was one occasion on a Sunday morning when I was doing an RSO appointment at Gravesend, and a merchant seaman with toothache appeared in Casualty demanding that I remove two of his teeth, and vociferously informing me that he would have nothing whatever to do with a local anaesthetic. I pointed out that I was not a dentist, and that if I gave him a painkiller to control his symptoms he could attend a proper dental clinic the following morning. He would have none of it, and as he was rather a burly fellow I felt obliged to co-operate with his wishes, and therefore I removed the offending teeth. The episode nearly killed me, and he did show some signs of pain, but at the end of the operation he was a great deal less shattered than I was. I think that these various episodes indicate that though anaesthesia must have been considered a very desirable entity it was accorded a very low priority in the medical profession, and the system as it existed at Guy's in the 1930s tended to confirm it.

Thus, for example, when the surgeons did their operating lists they had a consultant anaesthetist allocated to the session, but he had no junior staff attached to him, so that when the surgeon decided, as he usually did after one or two major operations, that he had done enough for the day, he left the hospital and the anaesthetist followed suit shortly afterwards. The rest of the list could not be dealt with by an anaesthetic Registrar, for no such person existed, nor so far as we knew was such an appointment contemplated, so that the rest of the anaesthetics were given by the House Officers, and this was considered the natural thing. They certainly gained a good deal of experience, because it fell to their lot to anaesthetise all the emergencies and everybody else who happened to need one. If the modern person should consider this a rather primitive practice, it is as well to remember that in many other countries it was the nurse's rather than the doctor's job to 'do the dopes'. It is obvious that the status of a full time anaesthetist didn't carry a lot of kudos, and consequently not a lot of people specialised in it. Of those who did, some were decidedly odd characters such as the consultant to whom I was attached as a student. He was a very jolly and charming man, much liked by everybody, and he let us do a great deal of the work almost unsupervised, whilst he sat in the anaesthetic cupboard sniffing ether. The anaesthetist attached to one of the consultant surgeons was a Knight of the Realm, who had been honoured for his part in various operations on Royalty. He was a firm believer in keeping the patient as light as possible, and this resulted in the abdominal muscles remaining very tight, which made the surgery a good deal more difficult, and the constant song in the theatre was 'F*****s, I can't shut the abdomen, you'll just have to get the patient deeper', and to the students he was known as 'Sir Rigid as a Board'. We were quite unaware, and probably so was he, that he was decades ahead of his time, when all anaesthetics would be kept very light, and the disadvantages, from the surgeon's point of view, controlled with curare like muscle relaxants. At that time if one wanted to be the surgeon's friend, one sank the patient as deeply as was compatible with safety, when the surgeon could twang the abdominal muscles rather like guitar strings, even though the after effects were rather nasty.

Under this system where the consultant anaesthetists did such a small proportion of the work, and the House Officers such a lot, it was almost impossible not to become moderately competent at the job, with the result that for a number of reasons I continued to give occasional anaesthetics throughout my career. This practice must have become much less common later on, because just at the time I joined the ranks of the established Registrars, a Resident Anaesthetist was appointed at Guy's and this heralded a complete change of attitude.

For a brief period as a House Officer I gave anaesthetics to the presumably less affluent private patients of consultants and surgical registrars, for which the fee was three guineas, and it was paid direct to one by the surgeon. What they charged the patient one never knew, because one had no pre- or post-operative contact with them other than the very brief period before they were rendered unconscious in the anaesthetic room. As one was completely hidden by cap, mask and gown, the patient could have had very little idea of who was anaesthetising them, and they must have remained sublimely unconscious of the fact that he was a very junior doctor, or they would never have accepted the position. These sessions took place in small nursing homes that all seemed to be located in the less salubrious parts of SW London, and the facilities that they provided in the operating theatre consisted of an oxygen cylinder and nothing else. As House Officers owned no equipment of their own, it was a matter of borrowing what one could from the kindly Theatre Sister at Guy's, who had been accustomed to the practice for many years, but even so, the apparatus that one took to these sessions consisted of little more than the basic 'rag and bottle', and a gag to force the jaws apart and an airway to insert when that had been done. Even at this distance I still shudder to think that one had absolutely nothing with which to deal with an emergency, and what one would have done in a crisis is impossible to say. Fortunately I was never faced with one, and I do not think I ever contemplated the possibility, such was the confidence of youth. There was one celebrated occasion when I gave an anaesthetic to a patient in one of London's very posh West End nursing homes, where I discovered to my surprise that they too provided the same lack of everything as did the grotty nursing homes, and to match it the fee was the same.

The chemical agents in use in those days were just emerging from the chloroform era, and although it had such a sinister reputation as a liver destroyer, it took an awful long time going out of use. The reason for this was its excellent practical advantages, especially from the patient's point of view, because it was non-irritant, easy to inhale and very rapid in action when compared with ether. From the anaesthetist's angle, it was extremely simple to use and the apparatus required was minimal, and in an emergency as for example controlling continuous fits in a patient's own home, one could manage by using nothing more than a part of the bedsheet and a bottle of chloroform even without a special dropper. However in the South of England it was no longer in hospital use except as a mixture with ether for the induction stage, after which the anaesthetic was maintained on ether alone, everything being administered on a gauze mask. As the patients started to lose consciousness they struggled and bellowed like tethered bulls as they were pinioned to the trolley by nurses and students, but fortunately they remembered little or nothing of it when they regained consciousness. At that stage they were more troubled by vomiting, headache and a monster hangover added to the post-operative pain and discomfort. It was clear to all that there was room for enormous improvement, and fortunately it wasn't long in arriving. By 1938 there had been two major developments, the first was the widespread use of the Boyle's machine which allowed the anaesthetist to combine the use of gas, oxygen and ether as required, and later the introduction of the anaesthetic Trilene. This enormously increased the types of anaesthetics that could be administered, which was greatly to the patients' benefit especially in reducing the post-operative toxic effects. However there was still the unpleasantness of having a mask put over one's face and inhaling the various gases before oblivion ensued, and the second advance was the arrival of the so called basal anaesthetic which produced unconsciousness whilst the patients were still in their beds in the ward, and it lasted until after they returned there from the operating theatre. This was Avertin (Bromethol) which was a godsend to the patients, but rather less to the ward sisters. In the first place it had to be administered rectally, with great care to make sure that it was retained, and then a nurse had to keep watch over the unconscious patient until taken to the theatre, and again after their return from thence until consciousness returned. The other difficulty was that the dose for each patient had to be calculated on body weight, and then had to be freshly prepared for each individual patient in the dispensary. It then had to be delivered in a vacuum flask at the correct temperature and at the correct time ready to be administered. Kept for any length of time it was unstable, so that the ward arrangements became extremely complicated on operating days, which anyway had been a ward sister's nightmare even before the introduction of Avertin. However from the patients' point of view it set a standard that had to be equalled or excelled by any new development, and this appeared fairly soon afterwards in the extremely rapid acting, short duration drugs such as Evipan and Pentothal, which could be given in the anaesthetic room of the theatre suite. Nothing ever advances without some snag appearing, and here it was related to the fact that disposable syringes and needles had not yet arrived. As an economy measure, needles were re-sterilised again and again until they were so blunt as to make it difficult to get them to penetrate the skin and enter a vein, and in addition to this, as in all things, some people are more adept than others when it comes to getting needles into veins. A classical example of this occurred after the evacuation of the Allied Forces from Dunkerque in 1940, when a flood of casualties arrived at Pembury Hospital and every-body was pressed into service to deal with them. I found myself once again as an anaesthetist and on one occasion there was an almighty rumpus going on in an adjacent anaesthetic room, so I thought I ought to go and see if I could help. What I found was a House Physician unsuccessfuly endeavouring to get a needle into the vein of a wounded Able Seaman who greeted me with the following tirade: 'I have b****y well been twice to Dunkerque in a destroyer under fire from the Huns, and in the last voyage had half my b****y buttocks shot away, but all that was nothing compared to this b****r trying to get into my vein'. One assumes that he must have left us with a poor view of civilian hospitals, but there is no doubt that seamen are a tough lot, and I hope forgiving.

It must be obvious that at the time this sort of thing happened anaesthetists did not rank very high in the medical hierarchy, and quite frankly they were thought of as technical dogsbodies, because they didn't have to indulge in what are the true heights of medicine, diagnosis. In the case of one forceful specialist surgeon, he unashamedly instructed the anaesthetist as to what drugs he was to use, exactly when he was to start and equally exactly when he was to cease. As said previously in this chapter, in some countries it was not even considered the function of doctors, and was done by the nurses. Consequently when the National Health Service was estab-lished and it was proposed to rank anaesthetists and surgeons as equal consultants, it came as something of a shock, and gave rise to no small alarm and despondency as to what would happen when there were two 'captains of equal rank' on the same ship. I must admit that as an interested observer I feared the worst, but I am only too happy to admit that I was wrong because in most cases a modus vivendi was found and the old spirit of co-operation still exists. However, there was one case where one of the 'captains' was an extremely awkward customer, possibly mentally disturbed, and the association became a nightmare to all the other people concerned, and in the end it took no less than two official enquiries, and tens of thousands of taxpayers' money before the problem was solved. To counterbalance such episodes, there have been other inestimable advantages from the new arrangement in that expert anaesthetic services have now been made available to everybody, and a large body of highly skilled people have been trained, many of whom have extended their activities into the realms of intensive care, respiratory problems and the treatment of tetanus, so that only elderly practitioners can recall the period when the equality of status between surgeon and anaesthetist would not even have been considered a possibility.

ETHICS AND ADVERTISING

If this chapter had been written at the time I entered the wards and for some years afterwards, it would have required very few words indeed. If a doctor advertised, his name was removed from the Medical Register: it was just as simple as that, and very few medical men tried it on. Of course there are always subtle ways by which a few can manage to sidestep the regulations, and for one very fashionable West End practitioner the essay proved a singularly double-edged weapon in a most unexpected way. There was nothing whatever to stop one having one's photograph published in a fashionable journal, so long as it had nothing whatever to do with one's professional activities, and a picture in the *Tatler* showing Doctor X and family on holiday on the beach at Frinton would be unexceptionable. So much better if it could be next to one of Lord and Lady Y at the same resort. The venue might just as well have been at a charity ball, a Hunt ball, a race meeting (definitely not a greyhound track) or a wedding. The question was how to get one's visage selected, because the competition from the aristocracy, the rich, the nouveau riche and personalities from the entertainment and sporting world was intense. That indeed was the question, and a fashionable practitioner decided that some unusual activity would be the answer, when his choice fell on flying a light aeroplane, which was very uncommon in those days. All seemed to be going well until the occasion when a peer of the realm urgently required his services, and the physician was summoned to his bedside. Unfortunately he was aloft in his plane which was without telephonic communication, and it proved impossible to contact him. Unfortunately his Lordship's condition could not brook the delay, and so another physician was summoned in his stead. For him it was a very fortunate choice because from thenceforward he made uninterrupted progress up the medico-political pathway to fame and fortune. The only heights achieved by the aeronaut was the altitude at which his aeroplane was flying.

In the present climate, things have not quite reached the stage where a medical man can publicise his virtues in a full page spread in *The Times*, but the possibility of such a happening may not be all that far away, because solicitors and some other professional people are now permitted to advertise, and the general trend in these matters is such that it can't be long before the medical profession follows suit. Publicity-seeking in some parts is now florid, and the competition to get on TV and the press is so intense, that at times it becomes undignified. Of course it all depends on whether one feels that medical men should endeavour to maintain a status or join the ever enlarging 'unacceptable face of capitalism' and let the rest go hang. It is entirely a personal matter, since there is no evidence that either way it affects the end product to any degree or disadvantages the patients in any way. A very good case could be made for the view that when doctors were dignified and aloof, they had very little to offer suffering humanity, but now that they have the wherewithal to treat and cure so many previously resistant illnesses, they might just as well sell them in the market place like any other commodity.

The change began with the advent of the Radio Doctor on the BBC before the war, when his charm, his common sense and his fruity voice captivated the nation. His advice was sound, he confined himself to the common things that people could understand, and he never strayed into the realms of speculation of sensationalism. He broadcast, as did all other doctors, under a cloak of anonymity, though many people knew that he was Dr Charles Hill, the Secretary of the BMA. As time went on the anonymity gradually slipped away, until his political involvement revealed his identity to all and sundry. Now that all restraints have been removed, what is less acceptable is the failure to comply with the Trades Descriptions Act, and for everything to be described as a breakthrough or a first, and to be published in the national rather than the medical media. In the past such things originated as papers in the reputable medical journals accompanied by a bibliography of all the relevent references, so that it was possible for the profession to assess the validity of the work, yet even under that system the vast proportion of the material that filled the pages of the journals could happily be forgotten a few weeks later. Unfortunately when these things appear in the press, TV, and radio, the public are apt to think that what they see or hear are facts, whereas so often it is nothing but fiction. Goodness knows it is difficult enough to give students a balanced view to help them to separate the real from the imaginary, the possible from the probable, and to take into account all the variants that complicate the picture, and in those circumstances one is dealing with people who have already had several years of scientific and medical training. In order to make such things comprehensible to the lay public, all the ifs and buts have to be removed, with only the central core presented as though it were established fact, which most often it is not, and consequently they get a totally false impression. Even when teaching students the orthodox views of the current state of medical practice, I always told them that practically everything that I had been taught when I was a student was now known to be untrue, and I feared that much the same fate awaited the pearls that I was dropping before them. I regret to report that I have *NOT* been proved a false prophet. Apparently the public has an insatiable appetite for matters medical, and so it behoves those who feed them to recognise that they have a responsibility to measure what they say. No doubt the primary objective of doctors is to inform, but they should always bear in mind that the target at which the media aim is to entertain, and enlightening the audience is only an incidental fact in achieving their goal. Very often the final product turns out to be so very different from what one imagined it was going to be, and to some extent it makes one wonder whether the modern system is really an improvement on the old. There is of course no possibility, and in all probability no desire to turn the clock back, it is only a reflection on the alteration of views since 1934.

The other and not unrelated change in medical ethics concerns the matter of money. Once upon a time such a subject would not have been discussed in public, and medical fees were very much a private matter between physician and patient. Things have changed very much since then, not only in the astronomical rise in what is charged, but also how it is collected. The National Health Service provides a comprehensive non-fee-paying service for everyone, but even the State is not a bottomless pocket, and thus there are certain disadvantages which can be avoided by resorting to private practice. A very large part of this is now financed by specialist private insurance bodies, which, admirable though they are, can only lead to a situation where those drawing on their benefactions work not on the basis of what a service is worth but on what the market will bear. Consequently, before a patient attends a medical consultation, their instructions are as likely as not to be essentially about coming armed with a cheque book and the necessary insurance forms. Well and good, for that is how commercial transactions are conducted, and here is the crux of the matter. A great deal of medical practice is now in fact commercial, and as such those who conduct it have forfeited their privileged professional status, and must trade in the market place like other business men, rather than expect the government to grant them those special considerations which they might have expected before it all happened. It is very reminiscent of women campaigning for sex equality and then demanding male gallantry as before.

At this stage it has to be admitted that a new ethic has arrived in the practice of medicine, which will undoubtedly be satisfying for economists, doubly satisfying for entrepreneurs, and trebly satisfying for those doctors whose first priority is money, and only secondarily the supposed calling of the profession. What one is referring to is the encouragement of a private health service, where everyone stands on their own feet, and be damned to spoon-feeding by the state. The modern government aims at efficiency and value for money so as to extract the maximum benefit for the least expenditure. On paper and in Parliament a highly commendable objective, but in the practice of medicine despicable. Caring for and treating the sick is not an economic process, and it is a pity those who govern these matters do not get themselves some experience of these facts. No matter from which political persuasion they come, Members of Parliament see to it that when they need medical care they get it either privately or with special privileges on the State service. It would do a member of the Cabinet a power of good to have to sit for four or five hours on a hard bench in an out-patient waiting hall till their turn came, having spent the intervening time pondering on what the ordinary life of the people they are supposed to represent is really like. Not a hope of that in hell.

I have not seen it elsewhere, and no claim for originality is made for the statement that the National Health Service was created to care for the sick and ailing, and the private health service was created *to make money*, and no matter how much it may be stressed that the care in private hospitals is just as good as it is in the State-run institutions, it still remains that their basic raison d'etre is financial, and in a very big way when one observes that various health organisations are up for sale at a price running into billions of dollars or pounds sterling. There is yet another matter which seems so far to have received scant attention, and that is the fact that the eminent physicians and surgeons who work in the world of private medicine were trained wholly, fully and exclusively in the National Health Service at enormous cost to the State, but as far as I am aware not one penny is contributed to these costs by a service which could not begin to function without the skilled personel to whose training they have not contributed a brass farthing.

By all means let there by private medicine for those who can afford it, either directly or through insurance, but only after the recognition that it is ancillary to, perhaps even a parasite of the National Health Service, and for goodness sake do not try to make it too efficient or too inexpensive, because caring for the sick is a matter of that well known cliche 'tender loving care'. Long may it be so, and let private practice look after itself.

CONTRIBUTIONS

It is given to few, in fact extremely few, to make profound contributions to medical science, especially those of the kind so beloved by the media and always referred to as breakthroughs. Events such as smallpox vaccination, the discovery of x-rays, insulin, antibiotics and the like are not everyday occurrences, but there is no shortage of lesser attempts, as the medical literature so clearly portrays. In the United Kingdom alone, the two leading weekly journals, the *Lancet* and the *British Medical Journal* print millions of words, to which must be added all the other periodicals, often very learned, that are published at less frequent intervals, all of which combined adds up to an enormous quantity of material. Multiply that figure by the number of other nations producing a similar or even greater quantity of work, and it all ends up with the staggering sight that greets one in the journal section of the library at the Royal Society of Medicine in London. But here comes the rub. Practically all those words prove to be largely irrelevant, and are consigned to limbo almost as soon as they are printed. The *Index Medicus* documents, indexes and catalogues them, after which they are filed away, in the main never to be seen again, except perhaps as a reference extracted in order to make an impressive bibliography for yet another unmemorable contribution to the literature. The facts are unflattering but few would contest their validity.

Prior to 1939, medical men wrote papers only if they thought they had something to say, and only too frequently even they were mistaken in their ideas, with the result that most of it was of very little or no consequence. However after the War it became a sine qua non that any aspirant to consultant status had to be able to produce a list of their published works as the tail piece to their curricula vitae, and the longer the list, the better their chance of success. Under the old regime, a demand such as that would have reduced the field of applicants to a

247

mere handful, so that with the new system it is essential for every member of the junior staff who aspires to consultant status to spend a period doing research or working on a project, the main and often the sole object of which is to enable them to produce some written work at the end of the time. It is of course a perfectly laudable activity, which gives people a better comphrension of the nature of research, but for which, let us face it, most of them have neither the bent nor the inclination to make it their life's work. Unfortunately the trouble is that it simply adds enormously to the bulk of the literature material which has been produced for just that purpose, so that most of it makes no worthwhile contribution at all. However apart from the potboiling forced on aspirants by the system, a good deal of other quite important though not world-shattering work is done, and that is the zenith to which most people aspire.

The Children's Department at Pembury came in that group, and by its very nature had to be restrained within such bounds. It was a small unit with a small staff, all heavily engaged in the everyday work of caring for the patients, but in spite of this several small additions were made to the sum total of paediatric knowledge and practice, and as in practically all such cases, it is the combined efforts of a number of people that contribute to the end result. One of these minor achievements lay in the fact that we recognised and described a completely new disease, idiopathic haemosiderosis of the lung, which has been detailed elsewhere in the book. Of course it was not a very important disease, except to the afflicted, and it was not a very common disease, because if it had been either of those things, somebody else would have described it years earlier, but as a corollary, when knowledge is as great as it is to-day, finding a new disease is not all that easy.

A further addition in the same field was our discovery that the disease toxoplasmosis did occur in the United Kingdom, whereas previously it had been thought not to do so. Once again, this was a joint effort that began with the admission of a mentally handicapped infant with a much-swollen head due to water on the brain, which when examined by the House Physician, Dr Bruce Symonds, himself now an eminent paediatrician, discovered some remarkable changes in the inner lining of both eyes. In a combined effort with the Registrar, Dr

Leonard Sagorin, now a consultant paediatrician in Durban, we eventually came to the conclusion that we might be dealing with a case of toxoplasmosis. This was supposed to be a somewhat exotic and esoteric tropical disease, not expected to occur in a child whose foreign wanderings had not extended beyond the confines of Tonbridge in Kent. Although the child had all the clinical features that were required for a diagnosis, it was still necessary to prove it. Our first line of enquiry was directed to the Royal Veterinary College in London, because animals were known to be possible vectors, and from them we received the rather curt reply that the disease did not occur in Great Britain. A dead end to that road. The next avenue of exploration was the Wellcome Foundation Laboratories in Beckenham, Kent, especially as I passed their gates each Wednesday on my way to the local maternity hospital nearby. When I presented myself at the reception desk I asked if they could tell me whether there was anybody who was knowledge-able about toxoplasma infections in animals. Greatly to my surprise, instead of a long wait I was shown almost immediately into a room where a small committee was in session, and I was invited to take a seat. Everyone had a broad grin on their faces, and there was some laughter as I was subjected to some cynical quizzing, which I totally failed to comprehend until I discovered that some of the research staff had become inter-ested in the veterinary aspect of the disease, and they were holding their very first meeting to discuss their future plan of action. By an extraordinary coincidence I had happened to arrive at the same time, and they thought that I was a plant organised by a joker elsewhere in the establishment, sent there to take the mickey out of them. When it became clear that I was no such thing, I was accorded the full and overwhelming co-operation normally provided by all the branches of the Wellcome Foundation that I ever encountered. Of course they knew all there was to know about animal infestation, which it turned out was quite widespread in the UK. Our first point had been scored.

The next and final requirement was a series of blood tests which unfortunately could not be done in Britain, and there-fore the specimens had to be frozen and sent by air to Scandinavia, something not very easy or inexpensive at that time. The arrangements were made and the costs defrayed by

Pembury Hospital which was owned, managed and financed by the Kent County Council. How pleasant after all these years to be able to pay tribute to that body in whose service I was employed for a number of years. I think that during that time I must have broken every rule in their book at one time or another, and all these misdeeds were met with good-humoured tolerance of what must have seemed to them my nefarious activities. In my experience they were most certainly NOT the penny-pinching, ghoulish, heartless, parsimonious body that local authorities are so frequently portrayed as being, and I shall for ever be grateful to them for their benevolent tolerance of my acitivites.

The serological tests proved positive and the diagnosis was established, and the subsequent publication of our paper led to one of the biggest hunts through the inmates of the hospitals for blind and handicapped children, which revealed that toxoplasmosis was, and for that matter still is a disease found in Britain, possibly more often affecting adults than children, which is a good thing in view of the fact that it seems to do the former but little harm, whereas it can be disastrous for the latter. One assumes that if we at Pembury had not identified the condition when we did, somebody else would have done so later, but surely the feather in the cap is inscribed Pembury Hospital.

Unquestionably the main contribution that we made to paediatrics was concerned with visiting hours and facilities in children's wards. As a background to understanding this situa-tion it is necessary to revert to the many previous occasions where it has been stressed what a fearful risk there was of a possibly, nay probably, fatal cross-infection whenever an infant was admitted to a paediatric department. There was no clear knowledge about what caused the trouble or how it spread, and in addition it seemed quite impossible to prevent it, because the generally recognised practice of isolating the infected cases after they occurred had little or no effect. When Guy's Hospital Children's Department moved to Pembury Hospital in 1938, the building that had been erected there for the accomodation of abandoned, homeless and orphaned healthy children seemed to offer a possible answer to the problem. As the inmates had all been moved to safer situations in the western counties, it lay empty, and its architecture made it obvious that with relatively minor alterations it would allow us to isolate the 'clean' (uninfected) infants from every other patient in the ward, and in addition all the cases of gastroenteritis, which constituted a large percentage of the admissions, could also be isolated in a different separated area. The nursing staff were rigidly divided into groups according to which area they served, face masks were worn by everybody all the time, (quite unnecessarily as we now know) and all the children, no matter what ailed them, were nursed on a modified barrier regime. Finally absolutely no visiting of any sort was allowed. It was a blunderbuss arrangement and draconian in its severity, but it *worked*, and we were able to publish our results in *The Practitioner* that showed a safety record that was probably unique. That the regime was unpopular with the parents would be a gross understatement, and in all probability some children suffered a temporary psychological trauma that would have been less or totally absent had visiting been allowed, but it *was* temporary, and they all recovered from it. On the other side of the balance sheet was the fact that all those infants were all still alive, and to one who had taught students ad nauseam that 'Death is so permanent', it seemed that the end justified the means.

When in due time the cause of the terrifying and lethal infantile diarrhoea and vomiting became clear, and the intricacies of controlling the dehydration associated with it by intravenous drips were fully understood, and effective antibiotics were available, infantile diarrhoea and vomiting lost its terrors and there was no longer any need for such severe measures as had previously been in force. Visiting the children again became possible, and the question arose of how much and how often. We knew from previous experience that some children never settle in the strange and rather terrifying hospital environment, and that all of them were extremely upset when they had to be dragged from their parents at the end of visiting time, and as this affected all the children at the same time it left the ward in temporary chaos. After a careful assessment of all the factors and long discussions with the Ward Sister Mrs Anne Bowley, it was decided to try an experiment of 'unrestricted visiting', and by that it meant exactly what it said. Parents, visitors and siblings could visit when they liked, as often as they liked and could stay as long as they liked. In theory it should have produced a shambles, but we based our expectations on the fact that the vast proportion of people are reasonable human beings who do not abuse a system and make it unworkable, and this assumption proved correct. In some cases parents wanted to remain in the hospital with their children for the entire period that they were in-patients, and consequently this meant that they too had to be provided with beds and food. This was not something catered for in the hospital rules, and therefore subterfuges of various kinds had to be invoked, but even when these were discovered, the Matron and the administrative staff turned a benevolent blind eye on such activities, and they in their turn made a significant contribution by controlling the various committees that were supposed to be controlling them.

The real point was that the arrangement worked admirably, everybody could see that it worked, and the longer it went on the less unusual it seemed, until in the end it was looked upon as the normal routine, and there was no longer any need to keep it secret, with the result that the facts became public property. We even received requests for the admission of children from people in other parts of the country, but as these were mainly for them to have their tonsils and adenoids removed, it had to be pointed out that there was no Ear Nose and Throat department at Pembury Hospital; but much more pertinent was the fact that any child in hospital under my care only had its tonsils removed over my dead body. When the requests were for other medical reasons we tried to oblige. In the practice of unrestricted visiting we were some two or three years aheads of other hospitals.

As the news of our practice became noised abroad, other paediatric departments followed suit, though not always to the same degree, and there is a story of one ward where pressure was being exerted on a reluctant nursing staff to liberalise their arrangements, with the result that they posted a notice outside the doors announcing 'Unrestricted visiting is allowed between the hours of 2 and 4 p.m. on Wednesdays, Saturdays and Sundays'. If most of one's colleagues were sympathetic to our views, some paediatricians, led by Dr S R Meadow were openly opposed to the whole concept, and it is only fair to say that on some grounds they had a point, mainly that it was too severe an imposition to expect a parent to be boxed up with their offspring for twentyfour hours a day, and in this they had my sympathy; but as nobody was forced to do it I think they were on a losing wicket.

It is in the natural course of things that when some new idea or practice is introduced, especially if it faces difficulties or resistance, somebody will form a society or association to further the cause, and in this respect hospital visiting of children proved no exception. The National Association for the Welfare of Children in Hospital, NAWCH, came into being, but personally I could never think of the ladies who directed their activities other than as 'nautch girls', gently gyrating as they attended their annual gatherings. Of course they did a lot of good in furthering these practices, but the laws of physics state that 'To every action there is an equal and opposite reaction', and in some places their efforts stiffened resistance nearly as much as they broke it down in others. At Pembury we knew it was a good thing and was bound to spread, no matter what happened.

We made one further essay into trying to get our department to look as little like a hospital as possible, but in which we achieved only limited success. After the publication of our article on the prevention of cross infection, the future Lord Llewelyn Davis took an interest in our architecture and we managed to get the building redecorated in a colour scheme devised by him, in which the standard white, bottle green and 'shit-brindle', at that time de rigueur for hospital ceilings and walls, was replaced by a combination of pastel shades totalling several dozen in number. A generous donation allowed us to convert the entrance hall into a bright and welcoming reception area, and though nobody would have thought of it as home, it was good deal less ominous than such places used to be. Where we failed was in our attempts to get the nursing staff out of their uniforms and into civilian dress. Even our enlightened nursing controllers wouldn't stand for that, because apparently it contravened the rules and regulations of the General Nursing Council. To a degree we managed a partial camouflage of those uniforms with pretty flower patterned overalls, and if by any chance a Nurse was seen *not* wearing her cap nobody reprimanded her. Perhaps after all, our old professor of Physiology, Dr Marcus Pembrey was right, and that all things really did work together for good. At least, those who took part in this episode hoped that they had managed, to some extent, to make a child's admission to hospital a less unpleasant experience than it had been before.

Nobody could possibly claim that all the contributions which we made to paediatrics amounted to any world-shaking total, and as time passes it will be forgotten where these things originated, but is pleasant to recall that when we retired from the scene we hoped we had left it just a little better than it had been before. Of course there is nothing unique in that.

JOURNEY'S END

By repute it is better to travel hopefully than to arrive, which is something that must have been written with the medical profession in mind because doctors, unlike the clergy, are not renowned for longevity, and many of them stumble, trip, fall and topple over the edge of the precipice before the final destination is reached. Thus in a group photograph of some twenty-two of us taken at the time we entered the wards as clinical students in April 1931, only ten of us were alive in 1988, and that number is now probably considerably smaller. How many of them reached the consultant's retiring age of sixty-five before their demise it is impossible to say, but the three people with whom I was closely associated as a student during our clinical training are all dead, two of them well before sixty-five, and the third only just made it. As can be seen, it is almost the rule for doctors to die in harness.

However for those who are destined to reach the terminus, the first warning sign appears on one's sixty-fourth birthday with the arrival by post of an official notification that one's contract with the National Health Service will end on the same day one year hence. In fact one requires no warning, and for that not inconsiderable number who view the prospect with trepidation the receipt of the document must come as a nasty shock. Fortunately I did not number myself amongst them. During the following 365 days one is an interested observer of the arrangements, in which one rightly has no say, to appoint one's successor, and as each day passes the time to sweep one from the scene draws nearer. There is nothing unusual about these things because they have all happened so often before to other people, and they left one totally unconcerned. Now it is a singularly personal matter, so how does one react? To an unfortunate few it is the realisation of a terrible nightmare come true, and some people never manage to come to terms with it. After the knife of the guillotine has

255

dropped they continue beheaded to locum sessions, to haunt the hospital, take their mid-day meals in the senior staff dining room, hunt down old colleagues and engage them in boring conversations, so that with the passage of time they become somewhat unwelcome ghosts of the past. I remember some time ago, when I was still an active member of the staff, walking in the hospital grounds and suddenly realising that an encounter with an 'old bore' approaching from the opposite direction was inevitable unless I took some action. I looked at my watch and made out as though I had suddenly remembered some important engagement. I turned tail and fled. I am still ashamed at what I did, but I determined that nothing similar should happen to me, and from the day I retired, my return to my old haunts has been almost nil. To the majority however, retirement comes as a most welcome relief from a bondage ruled over more than anything else by that implacable monster the telephone, especially the most villainous one by the bedside. It takes some little time to be able to look at it as one retires for the night and realise that it is not going to get you out in the small hours of the morning. The fact remains that no matter how one reacts to the situation, a new and different life is approaching.

At last the end arrives and the final session, be it an out-patients session or a ward round is at hand after all the years of service. Most hospitals mark the occasion with some sort of recognition in the form of a gathering of one's colleagues, junior staff past and present and any friends who may be around at the time, all of which softens the blow at parting, no matter how ready one is to go, because it marks the end of an era, and to the person about to retire, the opening of the final chapter. In my own case I served two quite separate hospitals and thus had the prospect of a double dose, and the experience at each could not have been more extreme. At one of them I arrived for my final out-patient session, but my House Physician and my Registrar who should both have been present failed to appear, so I had to do their work as well as my own. When all had been completed I walked out of the building unobserved by anybody else, nobody to say vale or good luck or thank you, and I never put foot in the place again. Some months later I was invited to a staff dinner, but it was an honour I declined.

My other experience was very different. Not only was the recognition of one's previous service accorded all the usual very pleasant celebrations, but as an added bonus some months later the Children's Ward at Pembury was renamed with an eponymous title. It is an unusual honour whilst one is yet alive, but all the more gratifying for that. The Department had been started in September 1939, which made it the second oldest non teaching provincial hospital paediatric unit in England. It is perhaps a matter of interest to record that the oldest, which is the department at Nottingham, was founded many years earlier by Dr Braithwaite, who had been Dr Charles Cameron's first Paediatric Registrar at Guy's Hospital, and I had the honour to be his last. Without undue modesty, I think it might be claimed that the Pembury unit had a reputation, some might say a notoriety well beyond its small size, and one way and another it nurtured at least a dozen people who became consultant paediatricians in Britain, Australia, New Zealand, Canada, S Africa, the West Indies and possibly elsewhere.

Some people find the change in status unhappy, intolerable or become excessively bored, and therefore continue to do locum tenens sessions for as long as possible, but as one of the more fortunate types I never had nor desired any further professional activity. I estimated that in the preceeding forty years I had conducted something in excess of 7000 out-patient clinics and done 12000 ward rounds, so that the novelty had tended to wear off and I felt that I could do without adding to the score. I play no golf, bridge or other games, and when anyone asks me what I do with my time I find it difficult to explain, except to say that my life seems busier than ever before, and that retirement is something much too hard to inflict on the old and should be kept exclusively for the young.

UNEXPECTED RETURN TO BASE

In February 1988, as described in the chapter on cardiology, I joined the coronary club, and spent a short time in the High Dependency Unit at Pembury Hospital. After an uneventful recovery I made unmistakable progress in the wrong direction, and early in December I found myself back in Guy's Hospital almost exactly sixty years after I had entered it as a student. It was not surprising that there had been some changes, the most profound of which to me was that the original and beautiful building known as Guy's House had been abandoned to the administrators, whereas it had originally accommodated all the surgical cases, who were now placed elsewhere. Another building known as Nuffield House which had been erected in the early 1930s with a benefaction from Lord Nuffield, and had been for the exclusive use of private paying patients, was just abandoned, apparently awaiting some other use. However the second oldest building known as Hunt's House, which as students and junior staff we had always thought of as the most ill-designed for its purpose was still very much in action, and apparently a great deal busier than the time when it housed the medical cases, and two ancillary departments. My admission was something of an emergency, and I was despatched to the cardiology department in Stephen Ward where the most striking change to me was that, whereas it used to be a strictly male preserve it now was a mixed ward of men and women, with a rough division of each sex to its own area. At the time of my admission the only vacant bed was amongst the ladies, and there I found myself to the surprise of neither I nor them. My next door neighbour was a good lady of advanced years with perhaps some cerebral changes because periodically she let forth a string of expletives that would have done credit to the stevedores who manned the Thames Wharf docks before the war. After a comparatively short sojourn on the distaff side I was moved to a bed amongst the men, and purely by coincidence it happened to be almost exactly opposite the one to which fifty-seven years previously I and three others had been sent by the Clinical Tutor to examine our first real patient during the three month preclinical course before we entered the wards as full clinical students. Probably the event would not have stuck in my memory had it not been for several factors. In the first place, we were all highly embarrassed in case we appeared as raw students, which is what we were, instead of 'doctors', as most of the undergraduates were thought to be by the patients. Of course with all the subsequent people we examined we had an air of confidence, lacking only in that first encounter. However there was another matter which concerned us. The patient we were sent to examine suffered from Hodgkin's disease, in those days a fatal illness, and his name was Mr d'Eath, which seemed so ominous, even though it was pronounced differently. Had things not been so, I should never have remembered either his name nor the disease from which he suffered. Of course the unfortunate man has long since been dead, but also, so I remembered, were three of four of us sent to examine him, and as my own situation was none too encouraging my nostalgia was somewhat mixed.

Apart from such profound changes as a mixed sex ward, and the fact that many of the nurses, House Officers and consultants had not trained at Guy's, the thing that struck me was the apparent absence of medical students. During my time of training they were an integral part of the system, with every patient allocated to one or other of us. We were responsible for writing and keeping their notes up to date, and in addition we did many of the investigations they required. In many ways we were closer to the patients than anyone else on the medical side, and the experience was invaluable. At one stage some eight students congregated in a group, obviously awaiting whoever it was who taught them. Though reluctant to respond to my beckoning, presumably they thought I was some elderly nuisance factor, I eventually managed to persuade them to talk, and they told me that their appointment was now reduced from the standard three months of yesteryear to only eight weeks, during which they had but little contact with the patients. On the whole they gave me the impression that they were not pleased, and certainly they will not be the same Guy's doctors as of yore, but my subsequent experience of the junior staff made it clear that the end product was just as good or possibly better than it had been previously.

The hours worked by junior doctors were very much in the public eye and so I studied them as far as I could. Certainly they were very busy in and out of the ward, one moment with syringes, sometimes with x-rays, sometimes examining patients or sitting at the ward desk usually on the telephone. I never saw anybody of any status doing a ward round accompanied by the Ward Sister, though I presume such things must take place. They appeared to be on duty for as much as three days and nights on end, which seemed to me at the pace they went was too long. In our day we did emergency duty for seven days and nights on end and then three weeks of ordinary work, which consisted of a morning round with the Ward Sister or Staff Nurse, another with the consultant on two or more afternoons a week, out-patient sessions, and long periods in the operating theatres. Clearly we worked hours that were much too long, and although the nature of the job has changed, so have the present incumbents. What the solution is I could not see, because the nature of hospital work can only be carried on by constant pressure on the junior staff, and unless their numbers are greatly increased there can be no let up. The latter solution is not as simple as it seems. We had to grin and bear it, but the modern generation is more voluble and publicity conscious, and unless legislation is introduced, which will complicate matters even further, I suspect they too will have to grin and bear it, or get out of the kitchen if they cannot stand the heat.

I was taken from Stephen Ward to the operating theatres of the cardio-thoracic unit, and when the anaesthetist emerged he told me that as a child I had looked after him, and of course our positions were now reversed. I don't know why, but it was a great comfort to me when I was in what seemed a none-too-promising situation. Of what happened after that I have no recollection until about three days later, when I could take note of my new situation on the post-operative ward. Not surprisingly, with the exception of one or two young men who had suffered spontaneous pneumothoraces, all my fellow patients were in the age range of fifty to nigh eighty, and we each had a large teddy bear in bed beside us. One's immediate reaction was that they indicated our return to a second childhood, but not at all. They had a very useful and practical purpose of being hugged tightly to one's chest when one needed to cough, a manoeuvre which reduced the pain in the chest incision to no mean degree.

It was here, more than in the previous ward that one observed the profound change that had overtaken the nursing profession. All that remained from the olden days was that they made the beds and dispensed the various medicines from a purpose-designed wheeled container. The latter bore much the same relation to the simple ward trolley of 1930, as the modern supermarket does to a small corner shop. They also served the meals from an enormous heated container delivered from the kitchens, but they did not clear the plates post-prandially. This was done by a non-member of the nursing staff, whose only obligation was to remove the plate and tip anything left on it into a bucket and pass on to the next bed. It so happened that I was smitten with almost complete anorexia, and for the nine days I was in the ward I ate practically nothing, but of this fact the nurses remained completely unaware. I dare say that this was an unusual occurrence, but it is a gap that needs attention. If a patient is confined to bed by need of a drip or other form of treatment, the nurses attend to the needs of nature, but nowadays one is shot out of bed very shortly after the operation, whereupon one takes oneself off to the bathroom and lavatory unattended. It is an excellent idea, and it relieves the nursing staff of having to wash and brush up the patients, a task that must have occupied them for many hours in times past. They still have to keep the temperature, pulse and respiration charts, but they now all carry stethoscopes because frequent blood pressure readings have been added. They are fully occupied with the many pieces of complex apparatus now in common use, and unheard of in the 1930s, but their duties are so very different. This was perhaps best demonstrated by the fact that what all the patients in a post-operative ward have in common after open heart surgery is a rather painful chest, and it was interesting to observe them at night trying to find some position which would allow a period of sleep. One minute we were in bed, the next out of it in an armchair, pillows this way, pillows that way, take a little walk, have a little drink. None of this concerned the nursing staff at all, and anyway there was nothing they could do about it, but in the olden days if anybody in a ward got out of bed at night the nursing staff would have been buzzing about like bees round a jam pot. Surely one of the changes for the better.

For most of my career as a consultant, hospital wards had strict visiting hours, occasionally liberal, usually restricted. It was noticeable that there was now unrestricted visiting, and as might be expected, not in any way abused by the visitors. I could not help wondering whether this great humanitarian advance had in any way been influenced directly or indirectly by our pioneering efforts at Pembury back in 1949. I hope so. Ten days after my operation I was discharged.

In 1928 I had entered Guy's Hospital as a raw untrained 'colonial', and in 1944 I had left, as I hope a not altogether incompetent paediatrician. In early December 1988 I re-entered their portals as a total physical wreck, and left them twelve days later incredibly restored to health. I owe much to my alma mater, and fortunetely it has not been an entirely one-way traffic, because from 1939 to 1944 I bore single-handed almost the entire burden of teaching Guy's students paediatrics. I do not think that those who ran the hospital were ever cognisant of what debt they owed to me, or of what I owed to them. So let it be.

It would have been nice to have been able to report that from thence forward progress was uninterrupted, but it was not to be. Medical and surgical consultants are greatly flattered when they are chosen to treat other doctors in their various and divers illnesses, but they are forever cognizant of the fact that if anything unusual, unexpected or unpleasant is going to occur, it will always be in these patients. In my case, everything went well for nearly three months until I was smitten with the very rare and very obscure condition known as Dressler's syndrome. The use of the latter word frequently indicates that nobody really knows the cause, and 'so let it be with Dressler's'. Whatever the origin, I found myself back in Guy's hospital for another fourteen days as a source of some interest, especially to those young doctors about to sit the examination for the Membership of the Royal College of

Physicians. Obviously they had dimly heard of the disease but had never seen a case, and it was quite amusing to see them approach my bed wondering whether the aged F.R.C.P. would submit to a physical examination by aspiring M.R.C.P.s. I must say I found it a pleasant experience. To me, the main feature of the disease was the attacks of excruciating pain, associated with collections of fluid on both sides of the chest and around the heart. It was assumed, not unnaturally, that these were the cause of the pain, but for personal reasons, as the sufferer and with a good deal of medical knowledge, I was not in entire agreement. The fact that the fluid collections disappeared many moons ago, but the pains have remained in their full vigour, makes me think I was correct. The standard treatment for Dressler's syndrome is a prolonged course of steroids, which is reputed to work dramatically. I dare say that it does in other people, but obviously not in doctors. It would be untrue to say that it had no effect at all, because it produced me a gastric ulcer which some weeks later perforated in the middle of the night, and once again I was in hospital to have the perforation repaired. Anybody who has had this sort of trouble will know that it is a rather painful condition.

The mere fact that the troubles still persist has rather lost sight of the fact that what started as a major heart disease is now forgotten in the face of the persistent gastric troubles. Perhaps all this makes it clear why one doctor always expects the worst when treating another, and in my case nobody was disappointed.